KRYAHGENETICS

THE SIMPLE SECRETS OF HUMAN ALCHEMY

(...are you ready?)

I0752161

This Unearthly Presentation By:

Laura Lee Mistycah & Hal ©

Updated Version

LIBRARY OF CONGRESS

CATALOGING-IN-PUBLICATION DATA

KRYAHGENETICS: The Simple Secrets of Human Alchemy

Second Edition, 2014 - Updated 2026

ISBN:978-0-9707117-5-5

SECOND EDITION OF KRYAHGENETICS
By Laura Lee Mistycah

Mistyc House Publishing
816 West Francis Ave. #244
Spokane, WA 99205-6512

Cover Art and Illustrations by: Laura Lee Mistycah

Editing by: Ronnie Rennae Foster, Estée Danielle Sabourin, Kathy Shogren, Theresa Ramdas, Jothibai, Kallenthra
2026 Editing by: Nancy Buss, Laura Lee Mistycah, Shumlorah,
Graphics by: Laura Lee Mistycah – Map clean-up by Laura Bold
Spiral clean-up and revision by: Marina Lukatela
Pirate Talk Consultant: Travis King
Final Layout by: Laura Lee Mistycah, Sirena Bernal and Russ at Grey Dog Press

Printed in the United States of America

Warning: ***The information in this book is intended to inform and entertain. Any enlightenment or healing that may occur as a result of reading this book becomes strictly and solely the responsibility of the reader.***

For the Love of Humanity, the Earth, the Animals, the Nature Spirits, & the Innocent...

It is time to WAKE THE HECK UP!
STOP WAITING FOR SOMEONE ELSE TO FIX THINGS, AND START TAKING ACTION YOURSELF!

This book was written for YOU, it is in YOUR hands, and it is up to YOU to start making waves.

The most loving thing we can do right now is fearlessly stand up to, take on, and take down the socio/psychopathic tyrants that are perverting, torturing, and destroying everything that is beautiful and authentic.

The Corruption/Virus has got to meet the Anti-Vir**us**….. US!

You are holding a book of Keys…..

What you do with these Keys could change history.
These Keys could make YOU a Hero and a Legend…

Are YOU Ready???

(See this decree as the "feature video" on top of my YouTube channel)
https://www.youtube.com/@RWSProductions55

TABLE OF CONTENTS

FOREWORD

By Vrahc' Kahnym

This is a very special book.

I first had the opportunity to read the original edition of *Kryahgenetics* in early 2007, almost a decade after Laura Lee wrote it.

Since then, almost another seven years have passed and *Kryahgenetics* has stayed by my side as a trusted and reliable companion on my sometimes turbulent and confusing Spiritual Journey and Mission here on Planet Earth, which Laura Lee's guide Hal humorously refers to as "Dysfunction Junction" *...more on that in the following chapters* :-)

Kryahgenetics is more than a simple book printed on paper to me.

It is a living and evolving Entity, and it custom-fits its own expansion to my spiritual growth and the pace of my evolutionary process.

There is always a good and comforting surprise and a new revelation to be found in its pages. It reveals as much to the Seeker as she or he can handle at the time, depending on their ability to listen to the whispers of the eternal Universal Wisdom that is speaking to them through the Cosmic Gateway that is *Kryahgenetics*.

It is a friend to me first of all, and then a teacher and guide. I can feel Love emanating from its pages. It inspires and motivates me to follow my Heart and Higher Calling and change the world around me for the better.

Kryahgenetics is like an ever flowing well-spring of Wisdom, Inspiration, and Encouragement. You, the Reader, can decide how deeply you would like to dive into its cleansing and rejuvenating waters to explore the hidden secrets of the Outer and your Inner Universes.

Like ocean water and ocean currents, *Kryahgenetics* can trigger powerful and unexpected cleansing waves, or fun-inducing surf in your life. Or it can simply become like still crystal clear lake water, a perfect mirror to reflect back to you your true own authentic Being and the Beauty that exists inside.

Kryahgenetics confirms what you have always known deep inside of your soul. To me, it is a Confirmer, Evolver, and Inspirer all merged into one.

Truth is powerful and timeless, and at the same time simple and subtle. It makes sense when you hear it, read it, and connect with it. This is what Kryahgenetics is, does, and how it can work in your Life.

Thank you to Laura Lee and Hal for making this essential and inspiring information and awareness available to us again.

As I am writing this short introduction in late 2013, my intuition tells me that the World is now finally ready and hungry for this Knowledge.

Enjoy the experience and discover the Magick that is Kryahgenetics in the following pages.

Much UV-Love, UV-Light, and Laughter to you all,

Vrahc' Kahnym

AUTHOR'S NOTE

As you stroll, skip, or dash through the pages of *Kryahgenetics,* you will find that it has a different *ring* to it, and a totally different style than most of the books you have read. This book was never intended for *everyone*, just those who are here for *a specific Cosmic Clean-Up Mission…and since you are reading this book now, that means YOU!* Each chapter is deliberate and purposeful, and if you are aware that it is *circular or spiral in its nature,* you will realize that it builds on itself. You have to go through the entire revolution and start the cycle over again before you can fully understand it and put all the pieces together. It is on the second read or revolutionary spiral that you really begin to comprehend its meaning and content. If you get in sync with this book's energy and intent, you will understand the purpose of each concept on each page, and that this information is very necessary. It will bring you a heightened awareness of the bigger picture, and thereby give power to the permanent healing of yourself and others … no matter what the illness or malfunction is…even if it is money-lackitis!

There are multitudes of cryptic messages, plays on words, and blatant, hard-to-miss truths that you may or may not want to look at. **There are even some coded or encrypted messages that are written to activate certain codes in specific people! Many times, I questioned the way something was written (and so did Ronnie, and Nancy, the main Final Editors)** …..I would then take it to Hal, and his reply most of the time was, "Keep it that way, someone somewhere will get it. It was written specifically for them, not you!" ***That is one reason why the literary style and grammar, plus the creative use of wordage and ellipses, are sure to break all the rules of accepted protocol…*** So if you have any structure issues, it may be a rough read. On the other hand, it might be refreshing and amusing… It's your call.

One of the reasons for this lawless, *unearthly* presentation is that I have these *Esoteric Friends* who sometimes re-route *my thoughts* into *their thought tracks,* as they try to put their 2-cents….. *I mean 5-cents worth* into what I'm doing. They tell me that they foolishly volunteered to do a service project here on Earth, and that they *cannot* leave until they get the job done, and get it done right! I guess I was part of this volunteer effort too, *or so they tell me*, and they've come to help me… so I can help them! (Sometimes their tactics are so goofy and outrageous that I think they must have gotten caught in some cosmic goon gas or something, and are missing a few brain cells!) But I listen to them anyway and take their advice, and somehow in the end, things always miraculously work out! It absolutely defies all logic to me, but I play along and sometimes even patronize them …and oddly enough, they have gotten me out of so many hopeless messes that by now, I think I'd be a foolish frog ***not to trust them!***

They tell me that the secret combination that unlocks every lock and exposes the truth has to do with *Love,* or has some kind of joke or humorous element intertwined in it. They say if we would just operate from our Hearts/CoreStar and lighten up a bit, we could get this life figured out quicker and laugh ourselves clear through the next dimensions!

That's what they tell me anyway, and you know …I'm starting to believe they are "RIGHT ON!"

They go by the code #555, carry a very strong male vibration, and are total Goddess worshipers …*I mean they really* ***love*** *women!* They have the highest regard, respect, admiration, and awe for the feminine ray that I have ever encountered. Having them around is quite an experience, and feels like days of old. They are the epitome of *valor* and *chivalry* returned! They seem to be on 24-hour guard, because when I go back and reflect on it, I have to admit they have always been there *in some form or another,* ready and willing to pitch in and give me a boost.

These 555 guys are a kick to have around, and totally entertaining. They say they like to eat popcorn, drink root beer, and watch "*The Human Drama.*" They tell the funniest *and sometimes corniest jokes* I have ever heard. They use a lot of puns, old clichés, and are especially fond of using lines from books, movies, and commercials to get their point across. The result is that they make me laugh while they teach and challenge me!

I have been consciously aware of these *wise guys* hanging out with me since 1993. Through the years I have grown to love and adore them in spite of their "off the wall tactics" and bizarre methodologies. I know they have my (and everyone else's) best interest in their heart, and they point things out to me that I may never have thought of or given any credence to, if it weren't explained to me *(as only they can do)* from their point of reference. They have truly expanded my awareness of this and other Universes.

When I first told my former husband, Robert about these friends/advisors, and explained to him that they go by the name *HOWELL* (which could be a play on words for "how well," or howl, or just plain Hal), he got the funniest look on his face. He was real quiet for a moment, and then he said, "Nah, it couldn't be... no ...I'm sure it couldn't be..... nah....."

Totally puzzled I asked, "What in the world are you talking about? What's going on?" He looked real uneasy... got quiet again for a few seconds... and then responded. "Well, there's this Master that has been working with me for a while who is a highly evolved Being, that I have a tremendous regard and respect for. His name is Haltone, or Haltonn or something like that, so nah, I'm sure it couldn't be the same one. You see Haltonn wears these robes and is so sophisticated and serious...so dignified... so stately..... I'm sure it's not the same guy."

He paused for a moment... and then looked over to the corner of the ceiling, and verbally responded to something. "What? ...What? ...Are you serious?"

By now I'm totally perplexed, he's obviously talking to something or someone I can't see, and I feel like I'm deliberately being left out of the conversation. He went on, "You're the same guy she talks to? Noooo... You what? ...You had to appear to me that way in long robes and say, *'Greetings, dear one,'* because sometimes I can be a pompous peacock, and you thought I wouldn't have given you any credibility or even the time of day if you would have come to me the way you really are?"

Then Robert looked at me with a goofy expression on his face, and I could see and feel all his paradigms shifting. He then said, "Honey, they're the same guy! ...I can't believe it, *it's the same Master*... They tricked me!"

It was totally a downhill ride from then on. After Robert got some of his composure back, Hal started telling us jokes and straightening out some misperceptions. We laughed so long and so hard I had tears streaming down my cheeks, *and fell out of bed twice*, literally rolling with laughter. (It felt so great to laugh with that much voltage... It was ***seriously*** healing!)

After that, Robert's "fallen Master" went into his HAL pun jokes like: "Go on, do it just for the Hal of it!" ..."Hey Robbie, why don't you write another shaman book and title it, *"The Howl-ing*?*"* I will help you write it and be your *ghost writer,* it will be *Hal-atious!*" ..."Of course I'm an angel, do you want to see my *Hal-o?* " ..."Come on now, how could you doubt whether or not I'm for real, did you think that I was just some lousy *Hal-ogram* or something?" ..."Yo, Robert, I think you should take me on your next expedition and we can go find the *Hal-y Grail!*".....and it went on and on and on.

It's been over 3 decades since that *Hal-arious* night of mega endorphin infusions. There were times when we got together and Hal started giving *unsolicited* advice and words of wisdom which Robert didn't particularly want to hear, so he'd say things like, "Go away popcorn breath, I didn't ask for your opinion!" .....And I laughed and thought to myself, "Go for it Hal... only you could be so bold and entertaining!"

As you read the rest of this book, may its Spirit and intent be felt in your heart; may the words and concepts trigger your own memories; and may the truth of your personal life's experience be revealed and recalled, while coming alive and making absolute sense. Above all, know that you are in command here. You are the one this book was written for, and you are the one who decides what to accept or reject. I would advise that you read through this book in its entirety, and then go back and study it, because as stated before, there are concepts and terms that you won't understand until after the book has been read from cover to cover, and maybe not even until the second time around!

With that in mind... *open your mind, let your Heart/CoreStar be the ushers to show you where, when, and how to move through the darkness and the fog. Then perhaps inner strength, laughter, and warm fuzzies can replace the dread, anxiety, fear, and anger of the past and continue into your forever.*

Do you have the courage and determination to step out of the terrors and nightmares that are so diseased and dysfunctional, yet so familiar and comfortable... and move into a new magickal, mystical, and enchanting but uncharted reality dream? I for one am going to give it my best shot!!!

I dedicate these encrypted messages, silent codes, triggering mechanisms, and words of encouragement that leap over faith and hope, and ascend into the land of trust... to all of us with the audacity to think that we can individually and collectively make a difference in the outcomes here and who wins this game.

YOUR FELLOW COMRADE... AND INSTIGATOR

Laura Lee Mistycah... *and of course,* **HAL**

WELCOME

Here you are at the threshold of the beginning of the rest of your life.

CONGRATULATIONS!!!!!

You are absolutely, without a doubt, an amazing phenomenon!

Who but you, could have created the life that you are living, with so many wild and crazy experiences that, "Been there, done that, but declined the tee-shirt 'cause the closet's too full," pretty much describes your past? And yet here you are, still alive to review and tell about it…and all this without ever having read or even seen the rules or instructions to this place!

(Yeah, I can hear some of your thoughts now, "But REAL MEN don't ask for directions or read instructions" …And I must mention here…nowhere in this Universe could that asinine, irrational, senseless code be accepted, upheld, and defended the way it is on Planet Earth… What a strange tribe!)

To you minority of **rebellious** ones who **DO** clarify instructions, who **DO** read rule-books and plans before starting a project or activity, (even if that plan is in your head and you get your data from your intuition), I now give you some private information that has never been in print. I now unveil to you the secrets and the unknown. I now, *for the first time in **your** life, reveal to you the rules that can make sense out of the insanity. I now disclose the blatant and bare truth about what's really going on!*

** The truth is that __U__ are now in the middle of a giant colossal, inter-dimensional role-playing game, and __U__ are a key player in this one.*

** The joke here is that hardly anyone knows it, and hardly anyone has read the rule book…(until now)…and if you're one of those wise guys and gals who reads ahead, you'll know that the secrets and rules are on the next pages. So now that __U__ have the rules, let's see what __U__ can do...Let's see how __U__ can change the outcome of this amazing game!*

Yours Truly,

HAL….. A.K.A. HOWELL *OR* ***The Spy in the Sky***

ADVENTURE GAME RULES

YOUR ASSETS:

- You are a **Beam/Being** of Light, an extension of the God/Goddess Force with infinite possibilities as to who and what you become and accomplish.
- You have qualified Guides, Guardians, Instructors, and Angels who give you constant 24-hour surveillance, assistance (and sometimes *intervention*).
- You came in-coded with incredible talents and powers that can alter your reality *and* the entire game outcome.
- You have the ability at any moment to transcend your state by going *neutral,* or into a place of *deep peace*, simply by contemplating *the things you* ***love.***
- You have the constant choice and freedom to *change your mind* or *your viewpoint...* (even if you thought you were right the first time).
- You carry the keys and codes to transform your reality, break the spell, and see through the holographic illusion.
- You possess the inherent ability to respond with laughter at any given moment (even if you feel angry or threatened), and alter your state and the state of any*one* or any*thing* around you.
- Your spirit is an eternal, indestructible extension of the God/Goddess force; therefore, you cannot *really* get permanently injured or hurt. From this point of perception/power, you have the option of becoming "fearless," which makes it nearly impossible to intimidate or control you.

YOUR LIABILITIES:

- You came into this game with a virus called "Altered Ego," which tricks you into thinking *it serves you*, when what it's really trying to do is *destroy you!*
- You have AMNESIA and you can't remember who you are, where you've been, or why you are here. (Whether or not you wake up in this lifetime depends on how **you** play the game.)
- You are in a giant hologram (Holographic Universe) that looks and feels so real... it's hard to believe that it isn't!

- You've been brainwashed by your genetic imprints and your environment into perpetuating the lies, deceptions, and illusions of tyrants.

- You have a variety of defects in your physical and emotional bodies.

- Time is speeding up, and "outsiders" are slipping holograms into The Hologram to confuse you and perpetuate their personal agendas.

- You can depend on other players ("well-meaning" friends, associates, and family) telling you, "You're crazy," and that you should play the game *their* way!

- You lost (or were never given) your hand/guide book and didn't know the rules…(*'till* ***now***.)

YOUR CHALLENGE:

- **TO** keep A Head….. *Your Head!* …in this game. This is accomplished by finding the clues and experiences that trigger and activate Memory Codes. *(Some are found in what could be considered the most* ***unlikely*** *places!)*
  HINTS: ~If you don't like being alone, maybe it's the company you don't like!?
  ~Make Love…not War!

- **TO** take responsibility for **ALL** your actions, and if you make a mess… *Clean it up for Heaven's sake!* **(Blaming other people just makes a bigger mess!)**

- **TO** surround yourself with people and things that inspire Love, Creativity, Truth, Honor, Expansion, and Passion. **HINT:** Love it or leave it – OR Leave IT alone.

- **TO** figure out that YOU make the rules to YOUR game of Earth Life. The other players are only hanging around because **YOU INVITED THEM! …**(*Even if you don't recall sending out invitations).*

- **TO** break the dream-spell by *getting the cosmic joke!* **HINT:** When you're the most stressed, irritated, or even terrified… **STOP** …Ask yourself, "What's funny about this?" When you *get the joke,* your laughter outburst can literally….. **SET YOU FREE!**

- **TO** understand that you are a key player in this giant role-playing game. Tell yourself, ***"It's Just A Game,"*** when feeling overwhelmed, depressed, and defeated, will help you to *get a grip and have the will to find creative solutions* sooner, which will make you a *Hero* or *Shero* in your game!

- **TO** remember that the strongest force, *or the strongest will* prevails and wins! **HINT:** Courage and fearlessness are Siamese Twins!

- **TO** realize that, ***"Cheaters Never Win"*** in this game, and are always brought back to the beginning to start the game over. **HINT:** Karma is alive and well now!

HINT: Your enlightenment (*believe it or not)* just might arrive through some serious love-making, and with a smile on your face! This combined with the ability to cultivate Love and compassion… wherever you may be or go…and to laugh and find humor in your life, are some of your secret codes to winning this game!!!

NOTICE: Some players in this game will find these hints and cryptic messages totally ridiculous, absurd, and even upsetting. To this you are reminded of the *IMMORTAL WORDS* of **The Moody Blues** in, "Nights in White Satin."

"Red is gray and yellow white
But we (You) decide which is right
…And which is an illusion."

Remember Your Sense Of Humor *…..Don't leave home without it!!!*

Good Luck & Good Journey… ***The Howell-Meister***

KRYAHGENETICS

The information in this book may seem interesting, amusing, and sort of random at times, if you're not aware that each chapter is purposeful and deliberate. Each page is filled with information that is imperative for anyone doing self-healing, or assisting someone else in their correction process. Without some of this background on "what makes a Being tick," there is no way you can completely figure out what and where all the pieces are, and also how to fix one of these Beings if it's broken. As you read along, and put it all together with your own studies and background, you'll realize that this information does serve an important purpose in understanding the big picture. Without this understanding, complete healing is difficult to accomplish, and as absurd as it may sound at times, the informational journey you are about to embark on actually is very scientific!

The word KRYAHGENETICS is what I call ***"simpplex..."*** It can be very **simp**ly explained, yet on the other hand, it has com**plex**ities that are beyond our comprehension.

There are two parts or elements to this science that are very powerful in and of themselves, and when coupled together, make a dynamic duo.

The 1st element, ***kryah,*** is the encompassment and direction of magnetic fields through:
TONE/SOUND - LIGHT/COLOR - GEOMETRY/MATH - LOVE/COMPASSION

The 2nd element, ***genetics,*** meaning:
The information and life-force encoded and imprinted in the blood.

There are five gifts or keys that we all have been given. Once understood and used deliberately and properly, these keys can lace and weave these two elements together to create alchemical change in the holographic fields. They can bring about total balance and trigger quantum evolution. They can also connect you to what might be termed "Super Human Powers!" The possibilities are literally limitless. When this is accomplished in wholeness, aliveness, and synergy, it will create the highest octaves in this reality! If we trust ourselves enough to learn, *or rather remember,* how to effortlessly and skillfully activate both of these elements, then we just earned our tickets into inter-dimensional consciousness!

If you are reading this book with pure intent and desire, you will surely figure out what those 5 magickal keys are!

The purpose or function of this spiritual science you are about to be presented with, is to use the *kryah* to correct and heal the fractures, distortions, and imbalances that are causing death, decay, and destruction in the *genetics*. This includes:

A- What we have created in this lifetime since conception, and are personally responsible for.
B- What we were given by our ancestors genetically.
C- What imprints and codes we accumulated and acquired during the many experiences we had in past lives/existences.

The sciences and information associated with *Kryahgenetics* are very vast and literally awesome. The creativity and engineering that is intertwined within these two elements are absolutely mind-boggling, so a lot of understanding has to be re-routed from the head, then through the Heart/CoreStar in order to more fully and accurately comprehend its purpose and function.

The dichotomy here is that many of us have been very skillfully trained to UN-plug from our hearts because of past experiences we perceived (or rather mis-perceived) about Love, and that using our Heart's/CoreStar as front-line receptors can cause the deepest, sharpest pain imaginable. Oddly enough, it is Heart/CoreStar energies and emotions that we need to tap into, in order to jump-start our own unplugged Heart/CoreStar generator.

This scenario goes around and around until somewhere, somehow, we find the intestinal fortitude and courage we need to open our eyes and take that giant leap of trust... *not faith,* and get a grip, so we can have a good look at our deepest, darkest, scariest pits of terror, agony, and despair. At this point, we must be ready and willing to jump right into the middle of the worst part...to shine the light, hear the tones of truth, and feel the geometry and emotions of how we perceived a holographic illusion of pain, suffering, death, destruction, and victimhood. Then, *and only then,* can we once and for all get a grasp on the plug extended to us from the God/Goddess Force of our Higher Selves- ***Soul Suemas*** , and plug back into, *or reunite with,* our **unpolluted Heart/Mind.** Once engaged into this power source, we automatically dismantle and dematerialize all the holographic lies and illusions of separation/betrayal from our *true* Source that we previously bought into.

This **alchemical** process can be done at any time, but usually doesn't happen until we are so sick and tired of the pain and suffering drama, that we will do anything to change the scene..... *even if it's the "T" word.....* ***TRUST!*** Sooner or later, there will come a time when the pain is so debilitating and caustic that we will figure we have absolutely nothing to lose, and be willing to do whatever it takes to make the necessary changes. In this state we are then able to open ourselves up wide enough, ***without resistance,*** to receive and embrace ***the change/alchemy!***

There are many options at this point, one being to handle it ourselves, in our own way...perhaps through help from our spirit guides, meditation, solitude, and sincere, passionate desire and resolve. This is a grand and stupendous way, but most people find it more reassuring to be with a warm soft body that takes their hand and guides them through it..... a facilitator...one who "knows the *entangled* ropes," so to speak.

Whatever option we choose, and once we get plugged back into and are operating from the wisdom and essence of our Higher Selves - ***Soul Suemas*** , there is one more step remaining. We must then keep re-enforcing and anchoring that connection until there is an absolute merger or marriage of our physical selves and the all-knowing, all-feeling spiritual God/Goddess Self. This my friends, is what the buzz-word ASCENSION actually, really, truly, honestly is: ***total operation from your Heart/CoreStar. In this superior position, inter-dimensionality is possible...****using your Heart/CoreStar to command the brain and the creative centers.*

I can hear many of you asking, ***"What exactly is a Heart/CoreStar?"*** *(Good Question!) The Heart/CoreStar is the control center where your spirit/soul resides. It sits in the middle of your chest and covers the area from the clavicle to the solar plexus. It is our original blueprint or operating system in which the Heart/CoreStar is the command center and tells the head/mind and loins/creative centers what to do and how to do it. Incidentally, this command center got totally corrupted and buggered up when the Chakra Systems and Kundalini Snake were introduced and imposed upon us. Calling BS on these systems and* *removing them is one of the 1st steps in getting back to your original, authentic blueprints and operating systems. This is a HUGE step for many who have been indoctrinated/schmoozed into aligning with and being subservient to the Chakras and kundalini. (For more information and illustrations, see article, "The Secret Behind the Chakras," Chapter 20.)*

So basically, Kryahgenetics is a methodology by which we can remove the blockages of pain, suffering, guilt, and fear that impair our ability to access or operate from the Heart/CoreStar… re-uniting SOUL-LY with our Higher Selves - ***Soul Suemas***!

Now, there may be a challenge here for some of your perceptions. Once the merger/activation is complete, the idea is to stick around and help clear the corruption down here instead of running off to take up residence in *The Land of Ascended Masters!!!* (I can see it now, all of the new Ascended Masters hanging out, exchanging Earth stories, enjoying their new status, basking in Love, Light, sound, magnetics, and color, soaking up some rays, and totally losing track of the *Earth-time illusion*! …So many of them never make it back in time to help and assist the rest of us tired and weary Earthlings in changing the outcome of this drama!)

Well, to ensure this scenario never plays itself out, I have some news for any of you considering such a dastardly thing. It's only *wimpy, namby-pamby* Masters that stay within the gates of Ascended Masterdom without coming back and earning their service stripes… and the way that is done is by assisting others in their evolutionary process and perhaps even bringing some of them back with you! Besides, the Ascended Masters' parties are much more fun and outrageous with more of us there. Wouldn't you agree?

In the alchemy of *Kryahgenetics,* learning how to identify corrupt holographic files/fields, and then having the information and capabilities to correct them, is what this process is all about, and the more we do it, the more creative and proficient we get. The speed and accuracy by which we accomplish this depends on two things; our *desire and our willingness to do it* …..**eternally kicking and screaming and digging our heels in…or…dancing, laughing, and zooming… IT'S OUR CHOICE!**

Through years of research, study, and personal experience, I have developed ways of detecting and deleting the scary monsters and phantoms, (even the ones that are sneaky and try to hide) from our cell memories (***NOT soul memory***). This process should not be mistaken for the "deny and bury" or cover-up techniques that we so often try in an effort to cope and make it *appear* that things are functioning properly. The *Kryahgenetics* methods I use, take the anxiety and fear-charge off, so you can evaluate the experience from neutral ground. In this state, it becomes very obvious how to figure out what the experience was all about, and how it actually served you. **(*Every experience*,** if looked at from certain viewpoints, has elements in it ***that serve you…*** **every single one!)** In this superior position, you're back in your power and in a state of command--being *at cause* instead of the brunt of *ill-effects*. At this point of ***neutrality,*** *which I think is a relative to deep peace,* you can take action on the re-connection process to your Higher Self or ***"Soul Suemah."*** The results are phenomenal, amazing, and magickal.

Apparently, I have been encoded with some of the activation keys that awaken and jump-start the alchemy of self-correction in DNA coding, in those I facilitate for. Intuitively, I find that I am not only capable of identifying the corrupt and distorted files, but also know how to catalyze their correction (even with intricate decoys and defense mechanisms). Now, this Alchemical Magick extends even farther. What has been occurring is that I am also able to relay or duplicate these keys, which can then be transferred to others through certain Kryahgenetics processes that I use.

What this means is that once I have had a few sessions with someone, they now have some of the same keys and codes I have accessed, sort of like downloading a program. If the receiver is capable, ready, and willing, they too can facilitate healing and correction with much the same "code" information I have. In a way, it's like duplicating a benevolent part of me. *I'm not quite sure how this works, or why..... it just happens!*

I think one reason this does happen is because I have this very radical belief system, which has convinced me that there is no such thing as incurable! I have been a party to, and a witness to, too many "incurable diseases" that were totally transformed and reversed when given a proper environment mentally, physically, spiritually, and emotionally. I have also seen some pretty bizarre symptoms that, when understood fully, were relatively easy to correct, (even though many "traditional" allopathic professionals were totally stumped) and so they responded with the old, "Here's some drugs. You'll just have to live with it, *(and then you'll probably die with it.)* Now have a nice day and I'll see you at your next check-up."

I believe we were all given the blueprints to correct anything, *even grow back body organs and parts that have been removed...* if we could just figure out how to access those blueprints, and know how to read and implement them! If we have the information and innate ability to grow an organ at the beginning of life, we must have the recipe to do it again! (We just need to remember where we filed it!) How many times have we heard of people's tonsils growing back? And what about tumors and warts, *those darned things are always re-creating themselves!* So why not ovaries, or a thyroid, or a kidney.....an organ is an organ.....tissue is tissue...*right?*

I think it is about time for an extensive overhaul of our consciousness grid, and I am ready and willing to be one of the rebels who instigates such a thing! Why don't we take the disease, degeneration, and painful suffering leading to premature death, and put them in the archives for future reference, (just in case someone decides they would like to experience those things once in a while for variety) and replace them with life, vitality, and regeneration?

Why *in this world* do we have to get senile, decrepit, and crotchety when we get a few years under our belts? Why are we constantly associating aging with pain, degeneration, fear, and suffering? And why is there so much money being dumped into the care of people who have lost all quality of life and ability to function... AND THEN COME UP EMPTY-HANDED FOR SOLUTIONS?!

What kind of a bass-ackwards system have we bought into here?

Why don't we buy into the other crazy consciousness design, which tells us that we should look forward to aging because the older we get, the wiser we get... and the wiser we get, the stronger and more vital and virile we become? Why don't we buy into the idea that we can create and maintain these high levels of activity, strength, mental clarity, and wisdom? Then, when our contracts are completed here on Planet Earth, we can throw a giant party and invite all our friends to come and celebrate our completion! When the party's over, we deliberately and gracefully lie down, go to sleep... and release our Spirits. (What a wild and crazy concept! What have we got to lose but our decrepit thought blueprints that say we are subject to every malaise under the star, and once we start to degenerate... "we're toast!" ...Basically, OLD = DETERIORATION, DECAY, SUFFERING, HUMILIATION, AND DEBILITATION!)

Why not trade that blueprint in, and try an opposite polarity on for size? What if we thought of our body's aging like we do wine, cheese, and antiques... the older, the better? I know, I can hear some of your thoughts right now, "but pain, suffering, disease...it is all a part of the program here, and we need it for strengthening our character. It's good to experience these things so we can develop compassion and understand the joy of service." Yes, this is all true, but how many lifetimes do we have to experience the same lessons over and over again? Could it be that maybe, just maybe, one of our lessons might be that of total correction? A lesson that teaches us how to turn inside to the creative God/Goddess force within all of us and ask, "If all things are possible, IF I AM A MASTER CREATOR WITH UNLIMITED INTELLIGENCE WITHIN ME, then I wonder, do I have the ability to alter the program here and do something different this time around for a change?"

I have done much contemplation on this subject and my conclusion is that for me, there is no doubt about it. In this lifetime I want to try something new and radical, like turn consciousness ***in my reality*** inside out and upside down! I want to do the health and regeneration thing this time, instead of sickness, pain, and disease. If there is anyone else out there who wants to join me, there's plenty of room in this thought system because there are so few that truly believe it is *possible* ***and*** *probable!*

Now this does not mean I have total command over my body and emotions at this time...because I'm not there... ***yet...*** but I can tell you that it has improved immensely over the years, and I am learning more about how to apply and integrate this command every day. I believe that these capabilities are activated by an *ab-soul-ute* red-hot desire to get this puzzle figured out in this lifetime, *and do it with humor, Love, and finesse!*

(Funny isn't it..... the previous statement seems to have some of the clues to the treasure hunt, *and the treasure itself.....* all in one convenient package!)

My experience and involvement with the Love/Life Science of Kryahgenetics, has taken me quantum leaps ahead in my understanding of our capabilities for regeneration in all areas of our lives. Through the years I have researched, studied, and gained proficiency in many healing modalities such as: Emotional Debris Sweeping, *which I developed to clear electro-magnetic and other debris from the body*, Foot Reflexology, Muscle-Skeletal-Cranial Balancing using Directional Non-Force (D.N.F.) Chiropractic techniques, Deep Tissue Compression/Stimulation to release physical and emotional blockages, Rapid Eye Therapy, Neuro-linguistic Programming (N.L.P.), Direct & Remote Body Scanning for physical and nutritional deficiencies, and Remote Correction Transmissions. I have even taken these skills to the realm of our pets! I have come to the conclusion that *Kryahgenetics* is a prime factor which is intimately intertwined in all of these modalities. It makes no difference if I am "tuning into" a person, an animal, or a "pet plant," the principles are still the same.

Just an interesting tidbit of information here: when I am involved with this Kryahgenetics Love/empowerment energy, one of my personal physical responses is a high demand for water. I know it takes water to conduct electricity; therefore, I must be moving mega amounts of energy, because every time I even contemplate assisting someone in one of these modalities, my mouth starts to get dry, and I get extremely thirsty. Even writing this book gives me cottonmouth! Perhaps another explanation is that water is associated with emotions… (draw your own conclusions.)

You are probably wondering at this point, what can be expected if you were to come to me for a Kryahgenetics session. Well, I could tell you what a typical session might be like, except…..*there isn't such a thing as a typical session!* I never know what is going to happen, nor can I guess where my client's Higher Self - ***Soul Suemah*** might take us, so I have to be prepared for just about anything and then totally let go and trust my Higher Self - ***Soul Suemah*** at all times.

In the beginning, I take a history of my client to get some background on where they are and where they have come from. I like to have them come in with a "wish list" of things they would like to address, delete, or get more clarity on. I like to be in a room with appropriate music, and a nice safe atmosphere. I use the elements of fire (candles), water (a fountain and water to drink), earth and stars (the Aurauralite/Aulmauracite Power Rocks), *(See Chapter 22)* and air (ventilation and plants). It's also important for me and my clients to be in a place where there will be no distractions: hold phone calls, have someone else handle children or pets needing attention, etc.

You may have noticed that I said, "I'd like to have these conditions." In this *practice what you preach business,* you have to be adaptable and be ready to assist at a moment's notice. I once did a session in the back seat of a car, on the freeways of Los Angeles, in the dark, in rush hour traffic!

After I have orchestrated a healing, loving, relaxing, safe environment, I get my client's verbal permission to work with them and for physical contact. Once that permission is given, I am free to start, knowing I have permission to access their internal information. (This step is important as some people have never had the luxury of granting someone else permission to touch them or to help them by accessing their energy fields. This interaction in itself can be very healing and empowering!) I then have my client hold an Aulmauracite Rock in each hand, and give them a few minutes to get to know these Rocks and feel their energies. Next, I ask them to take some deep breaths, in through their nose and out through their mouth, to give them some serenity and oxygen. This breathing also helps them adjust to the Rocks at a deeper level. Once we have achieved a state of trust, peace, and neutrality, I begin scanning their systems including their central nervous system with my hands. When I have gotten in sync with their energy field, things start to happen. I may hear a phrase or words that have to do with some sort of trauma this person has had either in this life, or some other life. I may get pictures of an incident that has played itself out. Now, sometimes these words or pictures seem meaningless, and the client gives no indication of any recollection or connection to what I am picking up. This is where total trust in the process comes into play. Invariably, as I patiently move the energy blockages and collect more data, all of a sudden a light will go on, and my client will start getting rapid recall of a situation they had either selectively forgotten, or militantly protected and guarded to keep them from consciously remembering.

NOTE: *Even if you have blocked a memory, (because at the time you didn't have the tools or resources, and/or there wasn't anything you could do to correct it, or because it was extremely terrifying, or there were threats involved making it unsafe to remember,) the anxiety and fear energy of that situation continues to run through your nervous system. As a result, there is a restricting or even a cutting off of nerve, blood, and energy supplies. In addition, it takes a tremendous amount of energy to keep these memories blocked and guarded. Once you create a safe environment to address and release these situations, and use the experience to empower you instead of victimizing or destroying you, that energy which was used to hold* *these memories out of your conscious mind can now be freed. The energy that comes rushing to the surface can now be utilized in other ways and put you in a position of feeling the freedom of having your life-force back to use as you consciously see fit!*

During these times of lovingly moving the blockages, it is vitally important for me to stay in my Core (*center*) and not get frustrated at what is.....or rather isn't happening. When you meet up with aggressive resistance, that force will tend to want to overpower the facilitator. I remember several times when the resistance was so strong that *I fell for the trap and started to get sucked into the black hole* of my client. My thoughts were, "Boy, you sure have a serious mess here, I wish I knew someone who could help you..... maybe your God/Goddess Higher Self - ***Soul Suemah*** can't even fix this one!"

Another trick the *"resistance"* pulls, is one of overpowering drowsiness for both the client and the facilitator, sort of like the field of poppies in "The Wizard of Oz." Your biggest desire is deep sleep... RIGHT HERE, RIGHT NOW! ...AND YOU DON'T CARE ABOUT MUCH OF ANYTHING ELSE BUT LETTING YOURSELF GO OFF TO DREAM LAND ...HOWEVER OR WHATEVER IT TAKES TO GO THERE!

Then there are the walls of denial and flat-out invalidation of everything that is presently happening. If a facilitator isn't operating from, and anchored solidly in their Core at all times, while allowing the process, *whatever it may be.....* if they get offended easily or have control issues that haven't been cleaned up... there could be some feathers ruffled!

Understand there is a humongous difference between CONTROL and COMMAND. Entangled in *control*, there is a forcing of one will over another, of right and wrong, of anger over losing territory. Basically; it's fear-based. *Command* on the other hand, is the ability to take charge as you bend and flow and maneuver around an obstacle to get where you want to go. It's creating win-win situations so everyone gets what they need and desire. There *is* honor and respect in this position of taking action and being in charge. It is a facilitator's job to be a Master in *command*...to allow the process, no matter how crazy it may seem at the time, or how illogical it may be, and know the truth will soon manifest and shine light, understanding, and wisdom on the situation.

During the session, at key moments with precise timing, I will use N.L.P. and other techniques to clear the blockages, and re-route the neuro-pathways. This isn't something that a manual can teach you. It has to come purely from your gut. It has to be done by intuition and the synchronicity and synergism you have with your Higher Self - ***Soul Suemah*** and the Higher Self - ***Soul Suemah*** of the client***.....Nothing else will work, or would be appropriate!***

Once sufficient blockages have been cleared and enough neuro-pathways have been rerouted, it is now time for the great re-connection with the client and their Higher Self- ***Soul Suemah***. There are several methods of doing this, and I can never predict how it will happen. Sometimes it is in a visualization or vision. Sometimes it comes in the form of unmistakable feelings and physical sensations. Sometimes it is in an entirely different dimension, and sometimes it's some totally new way that their Higher Self - ***Soul Suemah*** has made plans for, so I have to constantly be ready to "go with the flow." When this connection is complete, and usually some dialoguing has taken place...such as *messages from the Higher Self -* ***Soul Suemah*** *to establish love links and direct communication routes*...then this energy is anchored in 3 times, going deeper and stronger each time!

When a session is finished, there is generally a substantial amount of energy that continues to reroute and process…which usually takes 3 days to complete. After a session is over, it is common for the client to be hungry, thirsty, and sleepy. I tell them to honor their bodies and give them what they need to effectively complete this process. I also try to create some way of logging or tracking the improvements and corrections, because the "monkey mind" always wants to come in and minimize or invalidate the potency and magnitude of what just happened. If you know how to maneuver around these and many other obstacles, and if the sessions are done with total Love, Honor and Integrity, *the results can be absolutely magickal!*

When I work with people, I try to keep labels for diseases out of the conversation because I really don't care to reinforce and give credence or power to the disease and whatever outcome or drama is associated with it. Instead I ask them, "What kind of symptoms *are **you*** experiencing?" Once we spill it all out and have it in front of us so we know what we're *really* dealing with, we take each symptom, figure out the causes, and simultaneously create a correction program. Then, we take regular inventory of the progress as we watch each symptom get smaller, lose its power, and fade away into nothingness. This method works very well for me, and is the best way I know how to deal with these "phantoms of the mind" that have been lowered into physical form. Through my research and personal experience, my response to disease is that it needs to go back to where it came from… return to an unreal mirage…a false delusion of the mind… and then vanish.

Some of the symptoms I have assisted in taking back to ***"The Land of Vanished Delusions"*** are:
- Headaches, *the kind that hurt so bad you want to leave your body.* the kind that last a long time, make you see spots and feel like throwing up.
- Constantly feeling tired, sleepy, and weak.
- Dry, itchy, red, crusty, patches of skin.
- Aching, clicking, sticking, locking, and sharp pain in the jaw.
- Painful sores on the roof of the mouth, gum-lines, and tongue.
- Lumps on various body parts. Some are mushy and some are hard, or feel like a pearl is rolling around underneath the skin. *(Sometimes they hurt, and sometimes they don't.)*
- Bed-wetting.
- Eyes that are bloodshot or *"pink"* for no apparent reason.
- Getting very forgetful and having a difficult time remembering simple things…to the point that it's scary to go out of the house without someone to help you remember where you are going, and find the way home if you can't remember where you live.
- Ringing and/or aching in the ears.
- Fuzzyheadedness, hard to think and focus.
- Aching and deep pain in the bones, or bones that keep moving out of place.
- Sharp pain on the bottoms of the feet.
- Feet that ache, burn, and feel like they are on fire.
- Hands and feet that turn blue.
- Getting dizzy and woozy when bending over to pick something up or having the head down.
- Bladders that are weak and make it embarrassing to laugh too hard or cough.
- Pains in joints and muscles.
- Burning in the stomach when it gets empty or if certain foods are eaten.

- Hair that falls out in dime and nickel-sized patches.
- Frequent nosebleeds.
- Having attacks that restrict lung capacity and breathing, and causes wheezing and coughing…even if smoking isn't a factor.
- Anxiety, dread, and terror of things such as:
  - *High places*
  - *Elevators*
  - *Lightning and other storms*
  - *Fire*
  - *Water, so much that even taking a bath brings up fear and anxiety*
  - *Germs*
  - *Worms, snakes, spiders, leeches, rats, dogs, and other animals*
  - *Flying in airplanes*
  - *The dark*
  - *The unknown*

Also, the memories of terrifying experiences, when backed by enough fear and combined with feelings of helplessness, can cause major perceptual and personality shifts and fractures. These experiences and memories can also be extremely undermining due to the effects they have on just about every choice that is made, because it is reinforced by the grip of this debilitating fear! These terror-filled traumas can wreak such havoc in the nervous system that physical ailments usually are their inseparable partners.

I have become proficient and well seasoned in this area, as I have worked with many varieties of these debilitating terrors. I could tell you tales that would *curl your ears* ***and*** *your tail!* This is why it is absolutely imperative that Kryahgenetics facilitators have a wide background of experience, and have a high percentage of their own goblins removed through *Kryahgenetics*, so they will have the ability and reflex response to stay in peace and neutrality at all times….. for their own sake as well as that of the one they are working with. Whether these incidents happened last week, last month, last year, or fifty years ago….. or whether it was this lifetime or another….. the imprints are still there and need to be addressed, understood, reconciled, and ultimately used for supreme life enhancement and empowerment.

Some of these include:

- Flashbacks from war
- Rape
- Gang assault
- Child abuse
- Sexual abuse
- Ritual abuse
- Abductions
- Government experiments and mind control
- Auto and airplane accidents
- Fire, earthquakes, tornadoes, lightning, and other acts of nature

Some of these subjects may give you the "*creepy crawlies*" just to see them on paper. If there are certain words that were triggers for you, and you think you may have been involved with some of this R.S.S. (Really Scary Sheep-dip), know that there are ways to get set free of all these entanglements that have you ***"spellbound."*** Know that a **"normal"** (whatever that is) life of happiness and bliss, unshadowed by these scary, and very real, monster memories, is definitely possible... and probable! All you have to do is be ready and open so that when you get connected to the right help... you'll not only allow it, but embrace it!

At this time, I must tell you honestly, each client, each personal history, has been an awesome, fascinating adventure for me, as I have attempted to find the clues that crack codes. (Sometimes these can be hidden or camouflaged, which makes it an even bigger challenge!) When this is accomplished, there is an instant releasing of the chaos, confusion, and suffering. Then harmony, balance, Love, and inner peace are the new outcome.

As I have grown and expanded, there have been many buried truths that have been uncovered and had light shone on them for full-spectrum viewing. This is available not just to me but to all those with *eyes that truly want to see.*

Especially for Women

One of the understandings I have gleaned through my research and experience, is the silly, ludicrous mutations that got planted and imbedded in our consciousness concerning the life cycles of women. When you really study this subject, it becomes apparent how warped and mutated it has gotten. There seems to have been a grand campaign to twist, warp, and misinform in order to control women and curtail their feminine processes. (This has happened to men too... *And yes, it is just as ludicrous*!) The anxieties, fears, and dreads that have been handed down throughout history, and also ramped up in today's world concerning the monthly cycles of women, turns into insanity!

First of all, most young girls have been taught, or had it implied, that this life cycle can be the cause of a lot of pain, suffering, and embarrassment. As a young woman, I bought into this one...bowl, tank, flange, bob, and flusher...***the entire toilet***. Subconsciously I took it ALL on!

To begin with, I was the last one of all my friends to "start." I was one of the oldest kids in my eighth grade class and thought for sure I was going to be some kind of a freak because all my friends had "started" years ago. So, here I was at the ancient age of fourteen, and still no sign of my "monthly visitor!" I remember the embarrassment and humiliation I felt when I was out with a group of teenagers, and one of my less discrete friends said in front of my heart-throb boyfriend, (who was a senior in high school...and what a rush it was for my self-esteem!), "No, I can't go swimming this weekend, I'm having my monthly, but Laura Lee can... she always can... she hasn't even had her first one yet!" I was absolutely mortified at this inner secret now revealed to EVERYONE! How could she have been so brutally honest and stupid!? What was I to do now? My life was surely over! I was sure my boyfriend would *really truly* see me as a child instead of a grown woman now. How could I gracefully maneuver through or cover up this one? (I think I just changed the subject and then went home and cried.)

Another fear that grips every teenage girl, *and older women too for that matter*, is the fear that you'll "start" and be totally unprepared… you know, right in the middle of class or something! This terror became a reality to one of my other girlfriends. There she was in her bright yellow dress with a big red stain on the back, walking down the hall to her locker… and everyone was too embarrassed to take her aside and help her, so she went through two classes before someone had the nerve to let her in on *her own secret!* Her mother wasn't home to bring her another dress, so she had to wash it out in the lavatory the best she could, and then go back to class! My heart ached for her when I saw her after the attempted laundry operation, as I didn't even have a sweater to offer her to cover up the still visible stain. It was too close for comfort. Yes, she had experienced one of my, and every other teenage girl's, biggest nightmares!

Now let's move from the embarrassment zone and go to the pain zone. As I said, I bought into all the down-sides of my feminine metamorphosis. Some of it was my being a part of our social consciousness, and much of it was genetic programming. When I finally did "start," (which ironically was only a few weeks after the neon signs were put up about my being able to swim "any time of the month"), I was greeted with a wide variety of new experiences. Totally useless pad-belts that never stayed in place and gave me a constant "wedgie," and little handbooks to get me started, (so that I wouldn't be asking any embarrassing questions). One book I remember was, "Martha Grows Up" which was written so long ago *it could have been an antique*, and the vague terminology *only made me more confused!* Add to that a prolific crop of new pimples, bloating, fatigue, and severe nausea. And then there were these terrible monster cramps! Sometimes it would get so bad that the pain would radiate down my thighs to my knees, and I felt like I wanted to die!

Now, I knew what severe pain was all about, from abscessed teeth to boils…but this …well it hurt so bad that sometimes I just wanted to lie down and croak! All the "normal" pain drugs didn't help much; they just made me nauseated! I often thought to myself, "If this is what we have to do to have babies, then it's not what it's cracked up to be! And if just having periods causes this much pain and suffering… then I don't even want to think about what kind of torture having a baby must be!"

Another challenge I learned to deal with was that my moon cycles were so random that I could go anywhere from two weeks to five months! I never knew when to expect my "monthly visitor" because monthly had nothing to do with it! There was some type of consistency though, I will have to admit. While my friends were enjoying three to five day "flows," I would gush like an open faucet for six days, and then have three "light days." It seemed to me at the time to be a horrible injustice that was further amplified when I read a church book that was a guideline for women. In the book, *written by a man*, it said that if a woman's cycles were unpredictable and she couldn't use the rhythm method of birth control, (which was the only acceptable method)... it was because of her sins or the sins of her ancestors! Well, I wasn't sure what horrible thing I had done, so I must have had some pretty evil ancestors for this to be bestowed upon me!

I noticed there also seemed to be a definite pain pattern here. Just about every other moon cycle, one would be barely tolerable….. and then the next one? …..***Like a near-death experience!*** There was absolutely no doubt in my mind why this feminine process was referred to as, ***"THE CURSE!"***

This pain and suffering cycle continued into my young adulthood, when I added even more to my repertoire of feminine pain, suffering, and fear. When I got married at the tender age of nineteen, I started taking birth control pills, (which as you might have guessed, gave me an added stress in the form of a serious church guilt complex!) These "taboo" pills relieved some of the moon-cycle symptoms, but as a result… "POOF!" I put on fifteen pounds.

Because of these and other stresses, I also developed what the doctors told me was "an ulcer." I started taking "stomach quieters" and drinking antacid mint flavored liquid chalk like it was decadent chocolate, and of course, eating more to keep the acid down, which brought my weight up ...so now I had a new challenge, I was getting downright pudgy!

As these symptoms cycled and expanded, I started seeing lots of doctors and who prescribed new and improved drugs.

One ailment that I am happy to say I *didn't* get in this cesspool of painful symptoms, is that of the emotional swings associated with P.M.S. Why? I don't know for sure, maybe because I was too much into having fun to get grouchy, or maybe because it hadn't been invented yet… I'm not sure, I'm just glad I spared myself that one!

As a young adult, I wanted to be responsible and informed. I listened carefully to all the professional advice from "The Experts." I made sure I checked myself regularly *...well, maybe only once in a while*, for lumps in my breasts. Now I have to tell you here, this always creeped me out. For one thing I wasn't quite sure exactly what I was looking for, and another thing… well, it just didn't *feel* right; in fact …..***it scared the stuffings out of me to be checking myself all the time for a potentially fatal disease!***

It was at this time in my life that I began to look for alternative, natural, *"folk remedies"* for the answers to my illnesses. I discovered that taking handfuls of alfalfa pills would replace the drugs and antacid liquid chalk I had been gulping. No, I didn't really savor the flavor of these *"horse pellets"* as I called them, but liquid chalk was no treat either! Within two months I had my stomach pain under control and only needed to take six to eight *"horse pellets"* a day *to keep my stomach happy!* What a deal! …And to top it off, there were several other added benefits that I noticed. My bones were feeling stronger, the pain in my joints had vanished, and my breath…it wouldn't wilt the flowers anymore! And the cost? Only one tenth of what I was previously dishing out! (I could have been a great commercial, but at that time, few people would have been interested. Basically, my discovery was NOT *"politically correct."*)

That was back in the late 70's and I have many tales to tell since then of my health *revolution / evolution.* The experiences I have had in the field of natural healing and the feminine process have expanded way beyond anything I could have comprehended at that time. I began to understand the hidden agendas behind taking the feminine elements out of the feminine processes, such as moon cycles, conceiving or NOT conceiving children, childbirth, and women's feminine malfunctions.

I discovered that in societies and cultures that revere and respect the powers of femininity, there were procedures and herbs to use for everything…some to keep you from conceiving, some for strength and vitality, some for heightening sensuality, and others that made you fertile. The use of surgery to take out women's feminine organs for birth control, *or for any other reason,* was unheard of!

If there ever was a situation where a child was conceived and it wasn't in the best physical, mental, and spiritual interest of the mother, a very amazing thing would happen. A council of the wise women would come together and very lovingly and tenderly assist the mother, in *spiritually contacting* the Being assigned to the fetus, and get permission to use herbs and massage to un-attach and remove the embryo, and they used sacred ceremonies to do this. The men in these societies were very respectful of these ceremonies and would support the sacred circles and the decisions made there.

Also in these societies, rites of passage were a very important part of the maturing process, and the coming into womanhood and manhood was acknowledged and celebrated for the precious power it truly is! Can you imagine how our society would alter if we were to adopt and implement some of these traditions? Wouldn't it be wonderful to teach our young people to understand, be comfortable with, and celebrate their physical functions… to keep them revered, sacred, and honored instead of feeling embarrassed, ashamed, and guilty about the nature of their sexuality? Yes, this would surely alter our society to the very Core!

When I began studying alternative materials like *the teachings of Ramtha*, "*Bringers of the Dawn,*" and "*Earth*" by Barbara Marciniak, and the incredible information by Laurence Gardner who wrote, "*Bloodline of the Holy Grail,*" it really exploded the perimeters of the limited perceptions I had acquired. I also remember how validating it was when I read Ramtha's words about how ridiculous it is for a woman to check herself every month for a disease that could result in removal of feminine body parts and even become fatal… And if you keep looking for something, sooner or later your subconscious will do what it thinks you are asking for, and create and manifest it for you! I knew intuitively, even as a young woman, that looking for this disease *just didn't feel right*, and now I was getting more and more confirmation for my gut feelings!

Another wake-up call for me was the complete reversal of all the taboos, humiliation, and fear around menses blood. I knew when I began my quest in holistic healing that there must be more than I had been told about which I now refer to as "scarlet magick" and is referred to by the late Sir Laurence Gardner as "Star Fire." I would highly recommend his audio CD's and videos to anyone in search of some fascinating material on this subject. His discoveries make too much sense, and feel too right to be untrue. To me his research was very validating.

Most recently I became aware of the research that has been done in other countries, such as Australia and Russia, using underwater birthing facilities. In these experiments, there were no complications because of the conditions, the support, and the stress relief. In one experiment that was done in the sea, the Dolphins came to assist, bestowing their gifts of sonar, creating frequencies that not only put the birthing mother at ease, but actually put her in a state of sustained ecstasy while giving birth!

Can you imagine the implications here? I have often thought that the experience of giving birth should be equal to the bliss of conception. That orgone (orgasmic) energy *should* accompany the completion of the gestation period, and that the mother *and child* should experience the joy and bliss of orgone ecstasy to celebrate new life!

If every birth was facilitated toward this end, children could grow up to be adults that had a strong override blueprint of Love, security, passion, and joy to fall back on when things in life got crazy. What a different place this would be… and no more need for birth trauma therapy! Even if a child was "unplanned" or "unwanted," the child would feel so much Love and joy at the time of birth, that this energy could be the dominant blueprint for the foundation of his/her life, and this Love and joy could override other hurtful or negative imprints!

Just think about your own life, and how this kind of birth experience may have felt to you! How would it have impacted and altered your relationships and future? How would it affect your relationship with your mother…and hers with you? It's an amazing thing to contemplate!

In a nutshell, some of what I have gleaned from my studies and these varied authors, is that the feminine processes are very sacred and life-giving. If we start to understand the essence of the God/Dess, we know that it has to be the total and complete collaboration in synergism and harmony of both the male-female forces together, for total illumination and freedom to occur. That is what God/Dess ***is***… Male/Female in harmony, yin/yang… a total union!

There is a grand propaganda scheme that has been invading our consciousness grid for such a very long time now. This agenda is attempting to keep the ancient wisdom and true information under lock and key, so that the secrets of the illumination in the blood of the female would never be desired, and therefore, never understood. There have also been many dark and unethical practices around the globe for many, many centuries to try and usurp the feminine presence, and the Love/life force within the Star Fire… and instead use the blood of humans and animals in sacrificial rituals and rites. This is a totally distorted, perverted action that has brought much pain, terror, and suffering to many people and animals who were unwilling participants. Having worked with people who were survivors of ritual abuse, I understand how some of these perverted operations work and the mentality behind them. This knowledge makes me even more aware, on the opposite end of the spectrum, of how beautiful and powerful the proper understanding and use of the blood of the Goddess can be. If understood and used with respectful intent, this marvelous life-giving substance can do many things, from being a wonderful fertilizer for houseplants and crops, to marking property and sacred energy space, to decoding and regenerating our bodies! *It has also been revealed that **Star Fire** was one of the ingredients of the elixir found in **The Holy Grail**.*

There is much, much more I could say on this subject, but I would prefer that if you are truly interested, you would do your own research, and find out the secrets for yourself. I would invite you to open your mind and allow your Higher Self - ***Soul Suemah*** to put the proper information *for you,* in your life and in your dreams, so that you can understand and digest it at your own rate. I have given you enough information here to activate your awareness. Now, it is your turn to get the rest, by reading, studying and pondering, by meditation, or all of the above. This one is a very personal journey, and the rewards for the discoveries you may find could literally be the fountain of youth… and the expansion to higher knowledge and consciousness.

I must also tell you from my heart, that some of the most treasured elements of Kryahgenetics can be found and integrated by the proper understanding, awareness, and use of the magickal frequencies, elements, and codes found hidden… awaiting their activation in this sacred substance…STAR FIRE!

May you be inspired and fruitful in your quest for Love and knowledge… so close and yet so far…found cloaked in the feminine mysteries of **"THE SCARLET MAGICK!"**

NOW! If you are interested in learning some of the methods I use as a Kryahgenetics facilitator, your life will be altered, and tremendous healing will take place both within yourself, and in *every-thing* around you. Your whole existence will take on some new inter-dimensional adventures!

Let me notify you in advance though, don't go looking for *The Great Schools of Kryahgenetics* for training, certification, diplomas, and licensing because… they don't exist …**(And WON'T Exist!)** Kryahgenetics is a very personal Science/Art, and has to be learned by sheer desire and passion to help humanity. (Basically, you volunteer as a member of ***The CCC or Cosmic Clean-Up Crew!)*** A Kryahgenetics facilitator must have been around the block enough times to know where all the chuckholes are, and how to maneuver around them. They must also have a high level of clarity within themselves, as well as ***impeccable intent***.

If you feel that you are destined to become a Kryahgenetics healer/facilitator, I would suggest that you read this book several times. You will also need the background found in many other books on the body/mind connection. (Check the back of this book for a suggested reading list.) Then go to **The Great School of Self-Mastery**. *Turn inward to your own internal teacher for personal instruction on where to go for help and information.*

After you have had time and experience in your own private *School of **Self-Mastery***, you will know when to ask your personal tutor, (*your Higher Self* - ***Soul Suemah*** if you are ready to come and have 3-5 personal sessions with me, and observe at least 1 session on someone else. This will give you a well-rounded education in both ***observing*** *and* ***feeling*** this process, because it cannot be taught fully until it has been **FELT!**

When this is accomplished, you must then go to your Higher Self- ***Soul Suemah*** and ask for instruction on how you can use *your own* experience, ancient wisdom, and Love to assist someone else in this transition/transmutation process.

This is how Hal instructed me to set it up, so that the integrity of this Love-Science maintains its purity. No one but you decides if you are ready to be a Kryahgenetics facilitator…**BUT I MUST CAUTION YOU! If ever, at any time, Altered Ego gets in your way and you don't use honor, Love, and purity with your intent as you assist another's healing process, you will be corrected by those in the Highest Realms of Authority…..** (*and it may not be a pretty sight*!) **…..UNDERSTAND?**

Oh, and one more thing. No rights, no wrongs, no restrictions, no regulations, no tests, no earthly credentials, no control… (just you and the Head School Master inside). No one but ***YOU*** can determine how best to let ***LOVE/COMPASSION - TONE/SOUND - LIGHT/COLOR - GEOMETRY/MATH* and pure Knowledge and Wisdom move through you!**

I honor you for all of your efforts, and for taking the time and energy to respond to your Spirit's call by reading this book when it was placed before you. When you get toward the end of the book, I am requesting that you read carefully the section on Aulmauracite/Aurauralite. This Rock is a very powerful tool *and is **mandatory** to assist you with all your healing adventures in...* ***KRYAHGENETICS!!!***

Your Sister... Laura Lee Mistycah

NOTE: *At this point in time, I do not have an office that is available to the public. My time for clients is very limited, and I have reserved my private sessions for First Wave Indigos, which are done over the phone, Telegram, Facebook or Skype. I will however, be available for hands-on private sessions for those who come to one or more of our Knights Training Courses.*

In the future, I may hold group sessions and trainings in Kryahgenetics for advanced practitioners. If you have a group that is interested in these sessions/trainings, contact me at: business@mistychouse.com

THE KRYAHGENETICS EGG

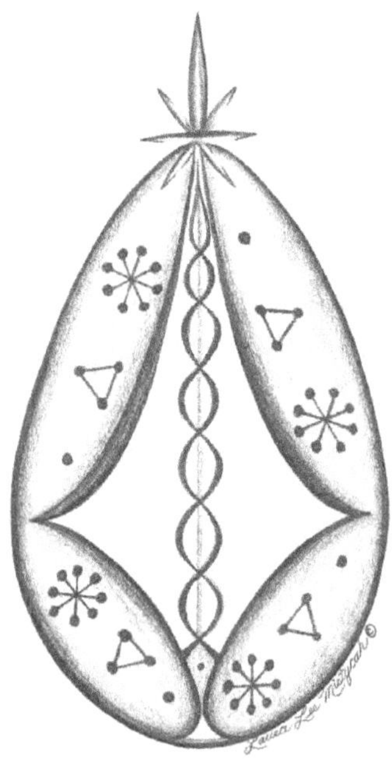

See our Café Press site for Kryahgenetics Egg T-Shirts, Fuzzy Blankets, Cups, Clocks and more…

(Click on “shop by collection” for best results.)

https://www.firstwaveindigos.com/treasure-chest#merchandise

Some people will look at this Kryahgenetics Symbol and see nothing more than an Easter egg or Christmas ornament, and then go on about their business, never giving it another thought. For them and their reality, it will seem quite meaningless.

Then there are those of you who have an innate awareness and understanding of things, even though you may have never consciously seen or heard them before …..and can figure out symbolic encryption and language not only by the way it looks, but also by the way it *feels*. For you, the geometric shapes, tones, and resonances that are emitted from this patterned image, will have deep and ancient and perhaps even indescribable meaning and value to you from the moment you lay your eyes on it.

One of my colleagues, Robert Friedman, M.D. (co-author of ***The Divine Code of Da Vinci, Fibonacci, Einstein and YOU*** and ***The Golden Ratio Lifestyle Diet***) saw this Egg, and decided to check out the precision of the geometry. He measured the curvatures, and discovered it was a perfect specimen of the golden mean or golden ratio spiral! The next time we spoke, he informed me of his findings, and I was really quite stunned. This symbol came to me in the early 90’s, and when I started drawing it, I thought I was just “doodling.” I had absolutely no conscious idea what was taking place. I kept working on it, adding things and moving things around, trying to get it right. I just thought I was making a cool design that made me happy to look at. The Egg appeared to have curtains being pulled back to reveal some DNA and a variety of interesting symbols. I was fascinated watching it transform into its completed state as you see it now.

I asked Robert if he would like to write a chapter in this book and here is his reply:

Hi Laura Lee, Thanks for the opportunity to write for your book, but I'm overwhelmed with projects, so I can't take on any more work right now.

But, if you Google Golden Ratio chicken egg, you'll find all sorts of interesting sites with great information. Basically, if you measure the height to width ratio, you should come up with the Golden Ratio measurement, which is around 1.6. Apparently Nature came up with this elliptical shape so that the chicken could go about its daily business without the egg falling out until it's ready to be laid.

Don't know if the Kryahgenetics Egg gets formed and laid the same way. Guess it depends who its mother is!

Cheers,

Robert

When I read his letter, I laughed pretty hard at the last sentence. I loved his sense of humor!

~ I now request of you to ponder as you study this piece of cosmic art/language, and ask yourself, what messages are here for everyone, and what private communications it may have for you personally? ~

Eggs Quarantine, Scramble Eggs, Egg Plants

...ahhhhh the things you can do with these Eggs!

The Kryahgenetics Egg is a wonderful cosmic tool *that is free* and can be used both as a protective protocol and also as a quarantine device. To use as a protective mechanism, visualize yourself inside a Kryahgenetics Egg (or have the Egg come and wrap around you). The Egg can be very large, with lots of room inside, or just big enough to go around your body. Make sure to have the DNA helix running down the Core of your body, with the star at the top. Take note as to what the Egg looks and feels like inside, as it may change the next time you use it. Then take a few breaths and when you feel comfortable, tell the Egg to "Turn ON." It will immediately start sucking all the debris out of your body, and when the gunk hits the shell, it will be instantly neutralized. With each breath, release debris and keep doing this till you feel calm and stable. (Your Egg may pulse or even spin to pull the debris out of you, and if it does, you will notice that you won't get dizzy!)

You can also use Kryahgenetics Eggs to protect pets, houses, cars, airplanes, etc. I have put Eggs around planes I was traveling in and even stopped turbulence on many, many occasions. (I know it kind of freaked the pilot out once, because they forewarned the passengers of serious "bumps" and made the stewardesses stop their services and sit down till it was over, so I double egged the plane and... it never happened!) *I have found that layers of Eggs are sometimes necessary, and I have used literally hundreds of layers at one time to protect myself, and my animals during the interims of psychic assault. I discovered using layers of Eggs back in 2004, when I was under some heavy psychic attack from members of a creepy, well-networked cult I was exposing. I would put my Protection Egg around me, and in 5 or 10 minutes, the Egg was gone! I replaced the Egg, and a few minutes later "poof" it was gone again! I thought the Eggs had been compromised somehow and was very concerned. It was at this time that Hal gave me the Intel to put layers of Eggs up, so I put up about 5, one over the other over the other. I could feel the protection returning, and it lasted a little over an hour. This gave me enough relief to figure out what was going on, and here's the scoop. Under "normal circumstances," an Egg will last 24 hours before it dissipates. Since I was under so much heavy psychic artillery, the energies wore down the Egg shell in 5-10 minutes instead of 24 hours! With this new awareness, I now put up layers of Eggs* ***before*** *I go to places like malls, stores with lots of florescent lights and electronic equipment, and any place with lots of electromagnetic and human static that would wear out my Eggs prematurely. Kryahgenetics Eggs have been literal life savers for me. I JUST LOVE THESE COSMIC EGGS!*

The first time I realized you could put a "Quarantine Egg" around something, I was totally amazed. It happened back in 2002, when my Ghost Buster partner Ronnie and I were invited to check out the Amargosa Opera House & Hotel in California near Pahrump, Nevada. This hotel was out in the middle of the desert at Death Valley Junction, and the closest town was about a half hour to 45 minutes away. The buildings were extremely haunted with a variety of very creepy energies and literally hundreds and hundreds of ghosts stuck there. I heard countless stories where people had either seen or heard ghosts, or been the unlucky recipient of "ghost hostility." One reason for all the nasty, bizarre things that were happening constantly was that a really foul, arrogant, tyrannical ghost was squatting there. He thoroughly enjoyed lording over the other ghosts and making their life, or rather their "afterlife," a living Hell! This ghost was a jerk when he was living and was a jerk after he died.

It was on the full moon in May of 2002 ...the energies were perfect for what we were about to do. As we began to open an *escape portal* for the spirits across the street from the hotel, all sorts of strange things started to happen. A man appeared out of nowhere and walked aggressively toward our ceremonial circle, trying to interrupt us. When he was taken back to the hotel for a cup of coffee to keep him from interfering, he just magickly "disappeared." Finally I thought, "This is just going to keep up because the hostile ghost knows what we're about to do and is not going to give up his turf without a fight!" So without thinking, I instinctively put a "Kryahgenetics Quarantine Egg" around this intimidating, diabolical ghost, and said, "Night, Night" to him as I lowered my hand from the top to the bottom of the Egg, slowly anesthetizing him. As I was sedating him, he was ranting and raving and cussing, and then all of a sudden, a horrible stench manifested. It smelled like rotten egg gas or sulfur or some such thing, and it hung around for several minutes, then dissipated when he was fully sedated. His spirit was now in stasis, totally quarantined so he couldn't escape or interfere. His quarantined slumber gave us the freedom we needed to help the other trapped spirits out of the hotel and into the shimmering portal we created to take them where they needed to go. Many angels, my Dragons, and other Allies were there assisting us, and it took about 20 minutes to get all the ghosts out. (Some of them even came back out of the tunnel to say, "Thank you," and then returned… which made our efforts totally rewarded!)

Then it was time to figure out what to do with the dictatorial ghost. I kept him in the Quarantine Egg, and slowly brought him out of his slumber..... Once again, we could smell the horrible stench as he woke up and realized he was still quarantined! He was really angry at being confined, as he was used to being the only one who called the shots and imprisoned others. When he saw the angels and our other assistants, he finally realized what was going on. This made him furious, and he was NOT going to go through this portal, and no amount of angels or anything else attending the portal could convince him otherwise. (He believed that since he was such a mean, cruel son of a gun, that the only place he would be going is straight to Hell, so he was just going to park his spirit and STAY RIGHT THERE!) Well, we finally figured out what to do. Ronnie got the bright idea to have one of the angels bring his Mother back through the tunnel and into the Egg with him. This sobered him up real fast, and calmed him down. We were stunned at his countenance transformation..... He actually started to soften up! His mother poured her heart out to him about how much she loved him, and that he was NOT going to Hell. She said she knew he had a hard life because of how abusive his father was when he was a child, and expressed her sadness that she passed away and was not there to love and protect him. This melted his steely cold heart. He trusted his mother enough now to take her hand. With this change of heart, the Eggshell's energy fields opened, and he walked out of the Egg and down the tunnel with her, reverting to a young child of about 10 years old! Whewww, what a relief for everyone involved!

After the portal was closed and sealed, the heavy energy was totally lifted. Then to our surprise, we all simultaneously smelled another essence... This time instead of a nasty stench, we smelled the wonderful fragrance of roses! (Remember now, we are in the middle of the desert, and there were absolutely NO roses anywhere!) *More details on this story and many others are revealed in the book, "Got Ghosts???" by Ronnie Rennae Foster & myself.*

After this quantum experience, I realized what a powerful device these Eggs are for quarantining not just energies, but also entities! It is also important to note here that these Eggs, like their counterpart the Aurauralite/Aulmauracite Rock, have a very strong code of ethics. You cannot use them for egotistical purposes or to try and hurt or injure someone or something with them, as they will turn off and shut down.

Now that you have been educated in "Eggs Quarantine," we will move on to the next group of Eggs on the menu…

Egg Plants & Scramble Eggs

It has come to my attention that Kryahgenetics Eggs can be of extreme value in dealing with different types of invasive implants. I have categorized them as:

*Metallic- These implants are mechanical in nature, with metallic compositions. Some include elements which cannot be found on Planet Earth. A number of these implants, believe it or not, were introduced to the body by some of today's designer drugs.

*Organic- These implants have live cells and can be detected, but many times are camouflaged.

*Psychic- These implants are projected and held in place by electromagnetic fields and thought forms.

Metallic and organic implants can be physical in nature and thus detectable under certain medical procedures ...but they can also be totally disguised and invisible. Psychic implants can become physical in 3-D if held and sustained long enough. Implants can also receive and/or transmit information, programs, commands, data, holograms, and emotions...which then can cause interference in thought processes, as well as physical, emotional, spiritual, and psychic functions.

I have been aware of and dealt with these types of implants for more than 20 years. I have had numerous experiences with them both on a personal level and with my clients. It seems that just when I think I'm getting a handle on how they operate, a new one comes out...(sort of like having to constantly design new anti-virus software for the latest computer bugs!)

Recently I have discovered that there are implant varieties, that are similar to parasites in the body. When you scan for parasites, (I use kinesiology and my medical intuitive skills for scanning), these little buggers have their own consciousness, and will stop broadcasting their energy and go dormant to trick you into thinking they're not there…you scan for them and get a NO, so you assume that is not a problem and move on. Through much stealth and *per-severance*, I have devised a way to detect them. Since they cannot change the past, I can go back in time and access accurate data on them. When I do this process, I ask my client's body if there were parasites setting up housekeeping in the body yesterday, or even 15 minutes ago. If there were indeed parasites present yesterday or 15 minutes ago, it will show up in the scan. This way you can call their bluff and accurately identify their presence and their dastardly activities.

Some of these implants need special treatment, and have to be dismantled in a certain order, similar to the protocol of disarming a bomb. I find it mandatory to use Aurauralite/Aulmauracite, to find the truth about the implant and how to disarm and remove it. I then use a Kryahgenetics Egg to quarantine and hold it while I'm figuring out the proper removal procedure.

Most of these implants are designed to go off and debilitate you in some way when you start awakening to your spiritual path. Severe headaches and extreme physical pain of some sort is very common. They can also disturb your thoughts, your emotions, and even your dreams. (While I am presently writing this, exposing their existence and designs, I am getting very dizzy, ill, and foggy headed… go figure!)

When I give Spiritual Contract readings, I find that for every contract you agreed to, you also have at least one, (and usually several) implants that are trying to keep you from fulfilling that contract. These can even be in the form of negative thoughts about yourself that have been reinforced by hurtful words, experiences, and memories...(many of which are not even from this lifetime). This dynamic can make it really rough because unless you have excellent past life recall, all you have are the debilitating emotions... which can make absolutely no sense. This scenario is a prime trap for First Wave Indigos becoming massively sedated and medicated, either by self or by "those in authority."

Once an implant has been identified and quarantined, you can use the Aurauralite/Aulmauracite Rocks placed strategically, to totally scramble implants and render them useless. Then depending on what type of implant it is, you can either reprogram it, or eliminate it all together. When this is done, there is usually an instant physical sensation, and a release/relief soon follows. Sometimes these little buggers have other programs attached, like satellites, repeaters, broadcasters, receivers, time-releases, pods, seeds, and new things that may not have even been invented at the time of writing this chapter. When you rid yourself of implants, you also have to go after all the attachments and peripheral energies for 100% clearing. After this process is complete, it is extremely important to fill in the empty spaces of what you just deleted from your body and energy fields with empowering elements/programs ...and especially a stronger connection with your Higher Self - ***Soul Suemah***/God-Goddess Self.

Here is the implant removal protocol taken from https://www.firstwaveindigos.com/post/etheric-implant-removal-protocol.
(Keep checking this web page for the latest updates.)

Implant Removal Protocol

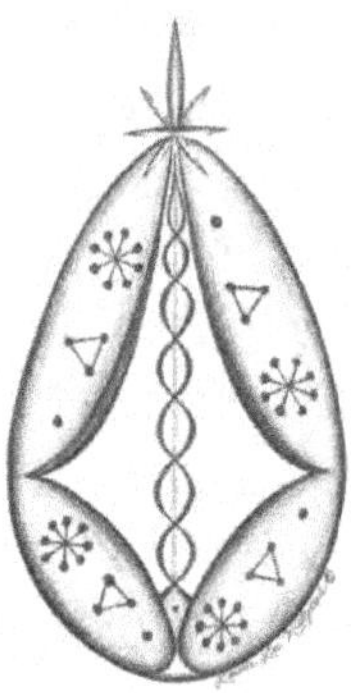

Get Ready:

Put yourself in several layers of Kryahgenetics Eggs, clear any debris in your body and electromagnetic fields. Breathe and get real focused. Use your Aurauralite Pendant or Aulmauracite Rocks to assist, placing them where they are needed in order to get rid of the implant. If you have Rocks, put one on both sides of the implanted area, or if it is your entire body, put one at your head & one at your feet, or hold one in each hand.

~Also-use your breath to clear these energies. Take deep breaths in-between each segment and use your breath to "blow them out" when appropriate.~

Clear The Implant OR Mind Control Program:

*Have your Aurauralite/Aulmauracite help you: Identify & Quarantine it with a Kryahgenetics Egg - then Scramble it - then Neutralize it - then Eliminate NOW!
*Next, take out the peripheral energies listed below that may reinstate the implant. Do this the same way you cleared the implants by asking your Rocks for assistance.

NOTE: *The Implant or Program needs to be handled first --but sometimes the implant needs to be quarantined, scrambled, neutralized, and put on hold, while you do the same process for the peripheral energies. Then at the end, they are both eliminated simultaneously.* ***Use your discretion here.***

PERIPHERAL ENERGIES & BACKLASH

*Satellites - Repeaters - Broadcasters - Receivers - Receptors - Attractors - Reactors - & Resisters
*Projectors - Projections - Projectionists - Programs - Programmers - Overriders - Overwriters - Underriders - & Underwriters
*Injectors - Injections - & Psychic Poison
*Pods & Seeds - Eggs - Larva - Caterpillars & Bugs
*Attachments - Piggy Backing - Cloaked Tag-ons - Hijackers & Saboteurs
*Back Lash - Front Lash - Side Lash - Lash Removal Lash - Unlash/AntiLash - Research & Discovery Lash
*Inappropriate Prayers & Artificial Intelligence (A.I.) - God Energies
*Mimickers - Imitators - Copy Cats - Clones - Twins & Relatives - Morphers - Phasers & Random Phasers - Shape Shifters & Shape Shifting Deceivers
*Time Releases - Event Releases - Space Releases - Time Loops - Space Loops - Event Loops - Loop Holes - & Fruit Loops (Makes you CRAZY)
*Disrupters - Corrupters - Perverters - Truth Twisters - Mutaters & Mutations - Distorters, Distortions & Distortionists
*Networks, Liaisons, Minions, Workforces, Staff, Duplicates, & Duplicators
*Plans - Blueprints - Schematics - Patterns & Templates
*Originators - Designers - Engineers - Bosses - Sources - Sources Source's - Master Minds - (& Their Memories Of You)
*Re-creators - Re-animators - Resetters - Rerouters - Reverters - Reversers - Set Backs & Booby Traps
*Thought/Focus: Misplacers, Displacers, Replacers, Scatterers, & Foggers
*Memory: Snatchers, Cloakers, Shatterers, Re-arrangers, Misinterpreters, & Filterers
*Phantoms - Illusions & Illusionists - Smoke & Mirrors - False Memories & Fear of Memories
*Curses - Jinxes - Whammies - Spells - Hexes - Black Magick & Voodoo
*Fear Imprints - Lies - Deceptions - Threats - Black Mail & Sinister Agendas
*Unauthorized Psychic Surveillance Passes & Controllers - Traps - Prisons - Freezers & Thawers
*Unethical, Obsolete, Coerced, or Forced: Agreements - Contracts - Promises - Pledges - Pacts - Oaths & Vows, and Forced Force Fields & Bands
~Through ALL Time, No-Time, Anti-Time ~~ Space, No-Space, Anti-Space ~~ Everywhere & Nowhere and All Dimensions, Realms & Realities~

FINAL RESTORATION STEP

*Clear, Repair or Replace all Body Mechanics and their Tools. (Body Mechanics are literal Beings!)

*Clear, Repair or Replace all Vortices and Vertices in Holographic Matrixes.
*Clear/Neutralize Physical Toxins caused by the Implant/Program.
*Restore/Reinstall all Appropriate Original Authentic Blueprints, Codes, Memories & Power (+ any other Appropriate Programs or Desires).
*Embed and Lock into DNA & Electro Magnetic Fields - Infuse Oscillating *pure uncorrupted* White (& UV-Light into DNA & Electro Magnetic Fields ...For Indigos Only).
*Feel/See your Authentic Higher Self - ***Soul Suemah*** (Core Star)- Amplify, Radiate, & Emanate into your Empty Spaces & Expand Through Your Entire Being ~

*Anchor by crossing your arms over your chest like a mummy, and take a deep breath. As you exhale, squeeze your shoulders and at the end of the breath, give a strong verbal anchor phrase such as, "So Be It" to lock this new matrix in place. (Anchor 3 times, each time with more intent and passion!)

EXAMPLES OF IMPLANTS / IMPRINTS / PROGRAMS / LABELS / FORCED AGREEMENTS

*Anchors, Anchor Points and Lines etc. that Tie/Bind/Imprison you to Dysfunctional and/or Traumatic; History, Memories, Places & People/Beings. (Discovered 7-16-12)
*Shape Shifting Deceiver (SSD) Implant-This is an implant most First Wave Indigos (FW-Indigos) have.
*Smoke and Mirrors is a peripheral energy that makes it hard to find the SSD.
*Reverser Implants giving opposite outcomes.
*Commanders - Program Overrides.
*Blocks & Insulators that keep you from hearing/feeling your Spirit Guides and Guardians
* Time Suckers, Space Suckers - Intimidation & Threat Implants.
*UNNECESSARY, UNWARRANTED, UNFOUNDED: - Worry, Fear, Pain Sorrow, Grief, & Anger Implants - (Scenario Builders & Worry Warts)
*UNFIXABLE, ETERNAL: - Worry, Fear, Pain, Sorrow, Grief, & Anger Implants
*Forced Hologram & Earth Entrance Agreements, Oaths & Vows - i.e.; Mandatory Amnesia of Authentic Self, Psychic Ability Shut Down, Perpetual Illnesses, Self-Sabotage, Hostility Toward Light Keepers, etc.
*Beta Blockers - Puts Betas in their Lives & or Puts Beta Spiral Energies in their Body & Fields, Making an Alpha Act/Feel like a Beta - Also Puts Perpetual Beta Energies on a Beta so They Can't Evolve.
*Duerlah "Post Traumatic Stress" (P.T.S.) & B.S. (That would be Lies & Bull Kaka or "Bull Sh!t" :o)
(*See www.firstwaveindigos.com Realm Stories Articles for info on who* ***the D-Monster, Duerlah*** *was.*)
*Mind Control P.T.S & B.S.
*Artificial Intelligence (A.I.) P.T.S. & B.S.
*Porn Vibration P.T.S. & B.S. - sucks you in and holds you there.
*Thinkable, Unthinkable & Anti-Thinkable Implants, Programs, and Backlash (These are the types that the **D-Monster** was famous for.)

I find that with FW-Indigos, all they need is one or two "implant removal" sessions and they can take the ball (or implant in this case) and run with it. They innately know what to do and how best to do it. I encourage this! I tell my clients that if they get stuck though, not to hesitate to contact me for help. It is not a shameful thing to need a little help once in a while... in fact, some implants require someone else's assistance for full resolution, while some implants are designed to not allow the recipient to take them out themselves, without repercussions.

The up side to all of this "Implantation" is... it makes the host much tougher and wiser for the experience. You gain a more profound, "intimate" understanding of these types of sinister operations, and with this education, you activate wondrous aspects of your Being that you didn't even remember existed. Also, once these implants or programs have been removed, it seems that you are so happy to be free, that you face life with a new zest and joy in the small things many take for granted.

To give you an idea of some of my personal implant challenges, here is an example which may help you understand a little better how they operate. In about the mid 1990's when I started waking up spiritually, I became aware of a strange response I had that centered around my kids. I found that I was very uncomfortable demonstrating any type of physical affection to them in public. My energy and actions seemed stiff and robotic. I could do things like dispassionately pat them on the head, but not hug and kiss them. When I was home, I was a regular "mother goose" ...however, in public I felt very awkward and uneasy. This bizarre anxiety bothered me for years as I tried and tried to figure out what my idiotic problem was!

Then, one evening in a meditation, I heard this authoritative, conquering voice in my head that made my blood run cold. It said something like..... "If you start waking up spiritually, and fulfilling your contracts, we will hunt down the ones you love and ANNIHILATE THEM!"

I knew then that this warning had subconsciously been running in the background of my mind, and affected nearly every aspect of my life. This threat was backed by some extreme, intense fear energies and imprints from some of my past existences where this very threat actually happened. At that time, I had no idea what an "implant-imprint/program" was and no idea how to remedy it.

I worked for many more years to finally get rid of this foul controller. I realized when I was on the other end of it all, that this threat dissipated slowly as my awareness of who I really am increased, bringing with it the empowering knowing what I am truly capable of. Had I known about the Aurauralite/Aulmauracite Rocks, and Kryahgenetics Eggs at that time, this implant could have been identified and removed in 15 minutes or less. What a relief it is to have these wonderful Life-Forms here to assist us!

WE DO NOT HAVE THE LUXURY ANY MORE, OF TAKING THAT MUCH TIME TO RESTORE OUR AUTHENTIC POWER!

NOTE: *In many instances, these implants are very much like getting your bio-computer hacked and reprogrammed by some outside source. Now you have the education and resources to bypass any encrypted hacker codes and regain access to your own bio-computer and take command. (I have personally set booby traps for any future hackers!)*

MUSIC OF THE
KRYAHGENETICS EGG

I have a question, how many of you, when you have had time to really 'hang out" with the Kryahgenetics Egg and bask in its cosmic energies….. actually heard or felt ***its music***?

Since Kryahgenetics is the encompassment and directing of: Light/Color - Sound/Tone - Geometry/Math - Love/Compassion, (plus 5 hidden keys) …it would be natural for many of you who are acclimated to that vibration, especially for musicians, to ***hear*** its magnificent music!

For those of you who feel inspired to explore this further (even if you don't feel like you are an accomplished musician) I am requesting that you consider sending me a copy of your rendition, either via a musical instrument, or your voice, or both – then ***donate it to Mistyc Hous***e for possible selection in a ***Music of the***

Kryahgenetics Egg CD! With your submission, write a little blurb about yourself and if you have any other CDs on the market you can put that on this profile blurb too.

My vision is to have some of the most beautiful, enchanting, and inspiring cosmic music available for people to listen to while they do Kryahgenetics Egg meditations. This CD by various artists would help us all venture into mystical places. It could also be the impetus to get in touch with our authentic selves and feel/remember our soul's history, which would then catapult our awareness of who we are and what we are capable of doing in this lifetime!

This CD has the potential of literally changing the world, by inspiring those who have the ability to change it. YOU, my fine musician, could be that catalyst!

Send your submissions to:

Mistyc House Publishing
816 West Francis Ave. #244
Spokane, WA 99205-6512

Or e-mail digital copies to: business@mistychouse.com

KRYAHGENETICS LEXIGRAMS

Lexigrams have to do with the way letters and words vibrate together, and how they can be altered to change vibration with different spellings, and different word partners. It is the art and science of creating sub-words from a name or word. These are called anagrams. They give meaning and definition to the original word or name. The classic example of how powerful this can be is how your life changes "for better or for worse" when you change your name.

Here is the definition of the word *Lexigram* that Will Schive, of *Good Works On Earth* sent me:

"***The art and science of the revealing of truths hidden in the English language by anagramming the letters of the word or name, then intuiting how these words so anagrammed may be assembled into meaningful sentences, thereby imaging and reflecting life and living with the word or name itself. The word comes from the lexi of lexicon, meaning the word, as a lexicon is a dictionary of words, and the suffix of -gram, meaning written out in full or drawn out in full.***"

In the Lexigram rules, you can create an anagram by using a letter only once unless it appears in the mother word more than once. The word *Kryahgenetics* has two E's and only one A, therefore, you can only create sub-words using the A once. For instance, the sub-word "again" could not be used in a Kryahgenetics Lexigram, because Kryahgenetics only has one A not two…nor can the word "street" because Kryahgenetics has only one T, not two.

When the word **Kryahgenetics** was Lexigrammed, it blew me away! What was described and revealed about this science was totally amazing and amusing to me. I thought I'd pass this fun discovery on to you, to help you understand the magnitude of what we are dealing with when we engage in Kryahgenetics…..***we are literally handling the keys to life and regeneration!***

Have some fun, enjoy the next pages…

(And feel free to write in this book if you come up with some gnarly Lexigram inspirations of your own!)

KRYAHGENETICS

It's Here! It Is The Right Synergetic Energy!

It Creates the Ethics, the Grace, the Yin-Yang

Thank the Earth

See Her Rise,

Hear Her Sing,

She Is Great!

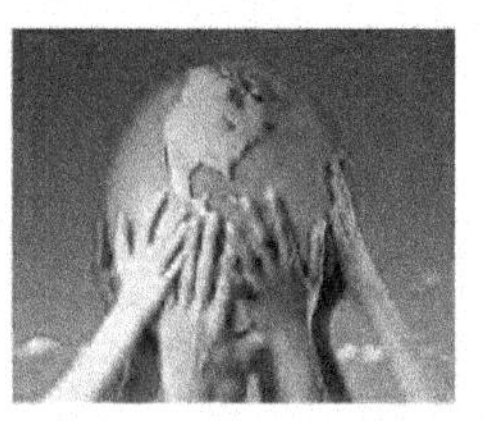

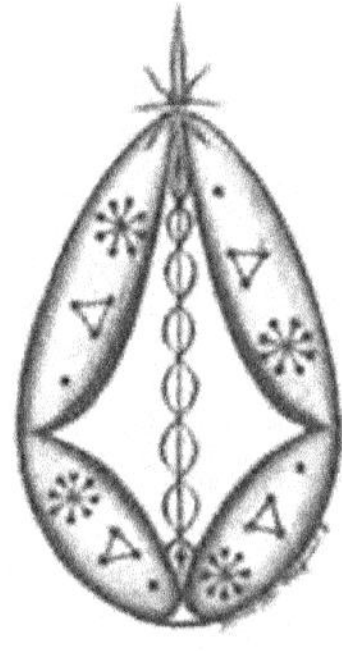

It Centers the Hearts

in the City

(It Can Erase Teen 'n Agers Aches)

Get in Sync - Seek Serenity,

Hear the Heart, then

Enter The Great Earth Era!

KRYAHGENETICS IS HERE!

It Can Change The:

*Earth	*Ash	*Rain
*Air	*Grain	*Cane
*Sky	*Ice	*Sea

* * * * * * * * * * * * *

KRYAHGENETICS Gets Three Cheers!

Yea! Yea! Yea!

Kryahgenetics

It Can Erase Any Sick Ancestry...

Then Change Genetic Heritage.

Yes! Great Changes!

Changes The:

Skin - Ears - Hair - Eyes - **Sight**

Genes - Heart

KRYAHGENETICS

It is a Star Heart

(It is "The Is")

Get In Gear - Get It Right

Try Kryahgenetics!

Share

The **Heart**

<u>Hark, It Has Rays! Yes!</u>

It Has Three - Eight - Ten Rays!

Kryahgenetics Is The Rays!

Is The Earth

In Thy Heart ?

Kryahgenetics
Is

The Center Secret

Recite It, Say "Ah" Thrice - Tri - Three

(Then Greet The Heart/Star)

KRYAHGENETICS

Is a Secret Inca Art

~ It is Certain ~

**There is Kryahgenetics Energy
In the Ankh. This Can Create/Change
Ankh Energy Genes**

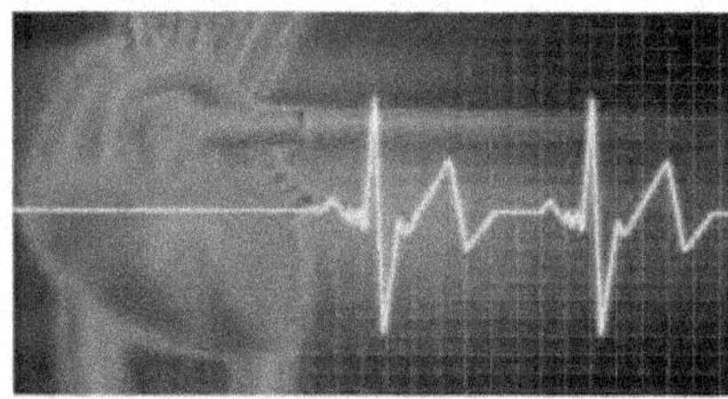

Kryahgenetics

Can Change, Then Raise,
Then Increase The Inert
Heart Energy!

KRYAHGENETICS

Can Shrink,

Ease, Erase - Any Thing!!!

Scan — Then Erase. . .

A SCARY SCENE, A GARISH SIGHT, ANY SCARE IN THE NIGHT:

*A Giant, A Hag
*A Casket, A Hang Tree
*A Hairy Rat, A Giant Insect
*A C.A.T. Scan, A Cage
*A Syringe, An EEG Scan
*A Siren, A Chase
*A Search, A Siege

*A Train Crash Scare, A Car Crash Scene
*A Chain, A Gate
*A Stern Cranky Teacher
*An Angry I.R.S. Agent
*Hysteria At A Reich Gas Site

ANY SCARY THINKS YE CAN THINK !

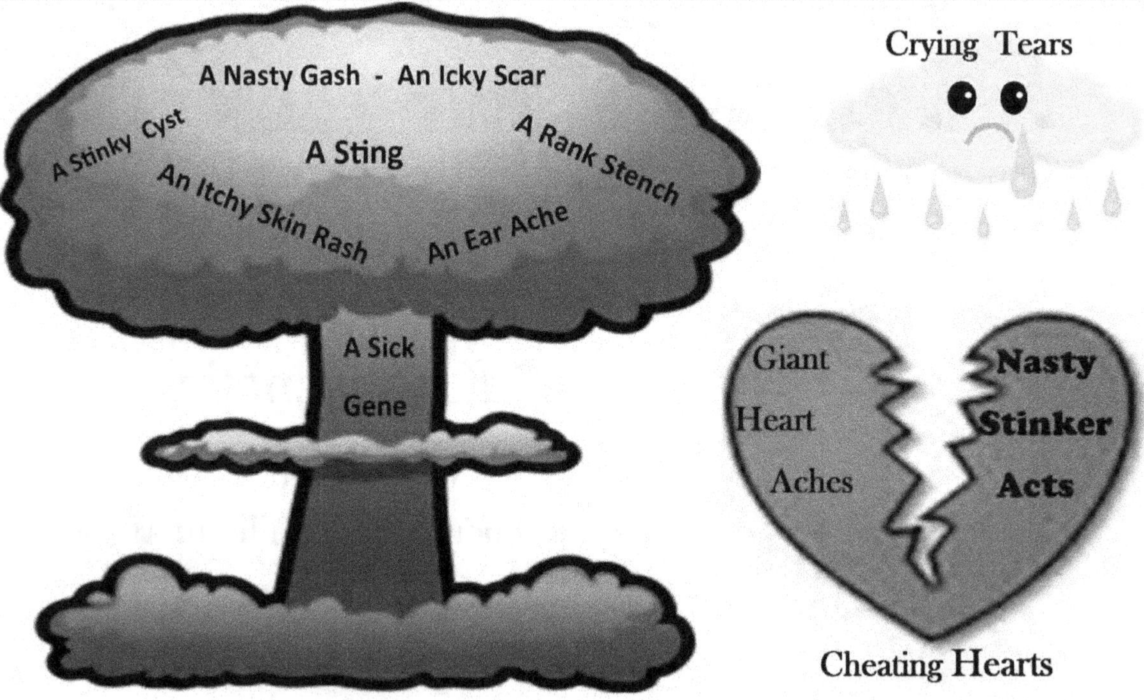

KRYAHGENETICS

CAN TEACH THE TEACHER,
THE SAGE, THE SAINT

YES, IT CAN TRAIN THE KNIGHTS, THE KINGS, THE GENTRY, THEIR HEIRS.

Hear Ye, Hear Ye...

Arise Great Kings, Knights Gentry, Heirs...
Gather the Nectar...Take it in , Ingest it,
Change the Scene, Retain the Grace

THEN THEE CAN REIGN!

The Secret
"Anti-Age-Agent"
Can Erase YEARS!
Kryahgenetics
Nectar

There Is The Right Energy In
Kryahgenetics

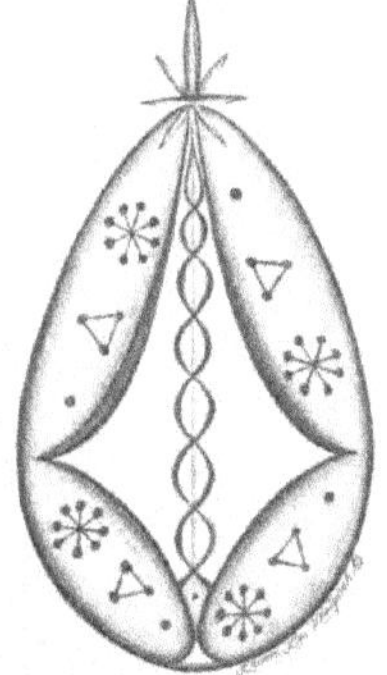

It's Sneaky, It's Tricky, Yet It's Sincere.
It can Insert, It In-Grains As It Enters.
Then It Regains Sanity!
Ah... Serenity

Hear A Certain Ring

See It In A Certain Eye Sight
Sing A Certain Chant
Then Gain Entry In . . .

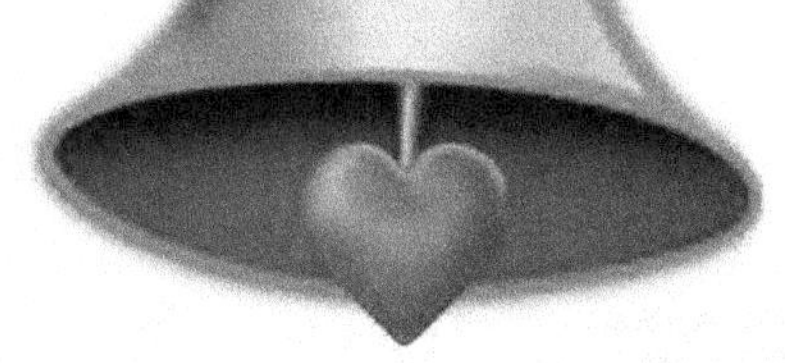

The Heart-Star

THE SECRET KEY

Create A CA$H Genie

* Take Green Energy, Raise It - (Sing A Chant)
* Gather The Ethics - The Grace - The Chi
* Then Insert Thy Heart Energy
* Rest, Then See It, Hear It, Rethink It— It IS Here!

See The Great Changes?

Cash Is Easy, Easy, Easy!
Grin - Cheer "Rah-Rah-Rah"
Shake It, Then Gyrate... Ye'r Rich!
Cashing In Is Easy, Yeah!

Hint: Thank It ...Then Share It!
Get Nice - Say, "I Care!"

Kryahgenetics

Grants Change In
The Great Hearts

Kryahgenetics Heat Rays
Negate - Hack

The Harsh, Nasty, Angry, Hate Energy
In The Sick, Rich, Stinker Cheaters
In Charge!!!

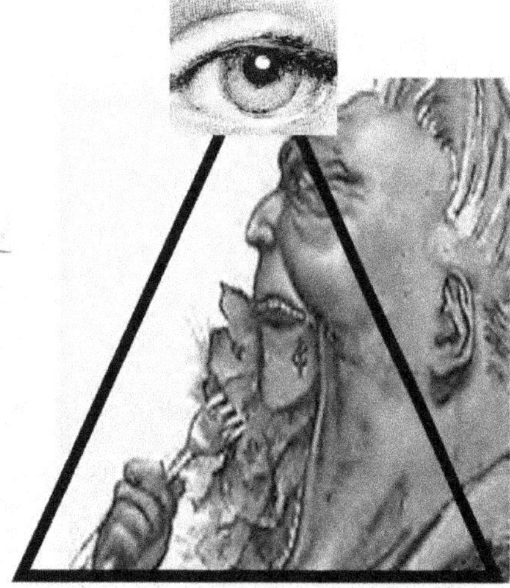

It's Cheery, It Entices...

It Changes Tense, Stern, Nasty,
Irate, Rage Energy...
Hence- It is a Great Key!

It's A
Secret???
Yeah, Har-Har-har

Hear The
Hyenas
Hysteria
See the Hyenas Grin
Tee-Hee Tee-Hee
Ha-Ha-Ha
He-He-He
Her-Her-Her

Kryahgenetics

The Great Sage in the East

Creates Ash

They Recite Chants
They Negate Their Hair
They Gather Grain
They Stay in Their Shrine
They Lay... They Rest
They Say, "Nay, Nay!"
(Yeah, They're Chaste)
They Sit...
They Stare...
They Seek Serenity

<u>They Eat Air!</u>

The Great Sage in this Era

Creates Strange Art

They Sing, They Can Act
They Think Their Hair is Nice
They Tease, Yet...They Are Caring
They Chase Cheaters
They Are Cheery...They Grin,
Then They Say, "Yes, Yes!"
(Yeah, They Share Their Genes)
They Are Hearty
They Are in Sync
They Arise...In The Ethers

<u>They Eat Cake!</u>

ADAPTERS

*This communication was given to me in 1997, in answer to a question I had asked. It was requested that I take this response, and with the assistance of my esoteric buddy, HAL, **adapt it** and put it in this book. When it comes time, and you are instructed to take a deep breath and relax...please be my guest. Hal said that for those of you who do this meditation with sincere intent, he will assist you... the same as he did me.*

Hal, Could you please give me some more insight into adapters and what they are doing to and for us?

Dearest One, *(We knew you would get a kick out of that greeting!)* The Adapters our ally *Auraurah* informed you about several years ago, are *actual Elemental Beings,* here on a service mission to this planet in this dimension. They are very ready and willing to assist you, and will make life more effortless if you learn their functions and how to implement and integrate them into your lives, and inter-dimensional realities. If you figure them out on this level, or in this dimension, you will automatically be *privy* to them on other levels and dimensions. They will be activated on those levels simultaneously for ready access and assistance there, which in turn, will automatically aid you here too. (Understand the loop here? It's like a circular or oval train track. It all fits together, and is in perfect harmony with the whole, as long as the tracks are fastened tightly together. Each track, each piece, if fitted properly, will bring the train, *the vehicle,* full circle back to the train station, *or its point of origin...back to itself.*)

These little Adapters are in reality, very alive and evolved, uncorrupted and uncorruptible Light Beings, who are extremely knowledgeable about you and your intentions and Contracts or Sacred Agreements. They are ready and willing to move into service, and will assist you in accessing the neutral position. This neutral position is mandatory in order for you to go forward with any speed, in any gear, even backward or reverse if that is necessary, in order for you to turn (your rig) around and go another direction! As with a car, nothing happens without the neutral part of the driveline, and if you didn't have neutral, you would only be able to go in first gear or reverse. (Incidentally, as you may have observed, that is exactly what a lot of earth-players do. They don't have neutral in their broken drive lines, and so all they know is one gear *forward* or *backward.* This about sums up their lives, a very limited adventure for sure...which actually equates to NO ADVENTURE AT ALL! Imagine this, all these Beings stuck in reverse or first gear thinking that's all there is, and moving as fast as they can while in those gears. And the freeways? They don't even know freeways exist! So they stay on little dirt roads, and the poor goon that's stuck in reverse, trying to go forward, doesn't know if he's coming or going, or leaving or arriving, or if he will ever get the crick out of his neck from looking over his shoulder! He spends his life, *and probably many past lives,* in the same old gear, driving the same old road, sitting there in the same old CARma, with the same old DOGma in the seat next to him, with his head out the window and his tongue hanging out. *What a sight!* If this poor guy only knew about neutral, and had some adapters to help him "get into higher gears," his ability to drive down the road of life would certainly be different!

Now about these Adapter Critters, *and I say "critters" to give you a more visual and accurate awareness of exactly what they are!* They are highly evolved, highly aware, highly educated Life-forms that are alerted and activated by your own awareness of them! Their unique abilities and strategies can help you maintain command over your emotions, and ultimately your life ...**if** you ask for their help. They can help you move through the emotional storms of life by showing you your assets. Your creative powers will then spring to life when you find yourself in a pickle! The more you get to know them and use them, the more of them you will gain access codes to, and the more of them will come to your aid in times of *emotional disaster!*

NOTE: We would recommend at this point that you stop and put this book down. Get in your Kryahgenetics Egg. Take a few deep breaths…in through your nose…and out through your mouth…close your eyes and listen to your heart beat. When you're ready, you'll start to hear your own internal songs. When these songs start playing in your head (and/or body), we will begin making some minor…*or maybe some major* adjustments on your internal wiring to get you ready for the next phase. We will *listen while we work* to your music and the songs of your heart…it helps us hear what adjustments to make. So kick back, relax, and we'll be right back as soon as we're finished. If you go to sleep, fine by us…when you're awake we'll continue.

Ahhhhh, much better. Do you *feel* the difference? Now you are ready to comprehend completely, the simplicities and complexities of Master Adaption. We have just reconnected you to the portion of your memory banks that stored the information, both "hard drive memory" and "emotional memory." You should now have a greater point of reference and awareness as to how these little Adapter Critters can be of service and assist you in becoming a "*Master in Adaption.*" Imagine how wonderful it will be when you're able to glide effortlessly from one reality to another… from an emotional earthquake… to stability and deep peace!

Suppose for instance, that you were in the middle of a big hairy fight or argument, and the heat was rising. Emotions of fear, anger, betrayal, and all the other ingredients of an internal and external battle were reaching their peak...*you know the ones I'm talking about...the kind of conflict that starts all-out WARS!!* So what if, in the middle of all this rage and insanity, you had the ability in an instant, to shift out of that gear and go completely neutral? ...And what if, in a moment, you had the ability to rise above the entire encounter and find the real culprits that were charging the illusionary drama in the first place? What if you were able to move up and down each party's time-track or time-line and see the distorted perceptions or outside influences/projections that caused the imbalance and mis-perceptions to begin with? Then all of a sudden, the whole thing would take on an entirely new perspective. You would know all of the whys and the causes of the misunderstood reality that was taking place in the present moment. And what if you had the power to not only see what was happening, but also to diffuse the energy of your "war buddy?" What if you could show your buddy the error and the insanity *and the humor* of getting into this battle over a misunderstanding or communication glitch? A pointless, senseless battle... and the root of the problem wasn't even happening now, but was actually ancient history! Lifetimes ago! The past...*even if the cause was 5 years, 5 months, or 5 days ago...* it may as well have been lifetimes ago because the past is the past!

In addition to this, in case you hadn't noticed, *many spiritual movers and shakers on Earth are having anywhere from 1 to 10 lifetimes of experiences all smashed together and compressed into ONE YEAR!!!* No wonder you sometimes get tired and disoriented, and can hardly remember when things happened... was it last week, last month...or maybe.....was it just a dream you had?

Yes, Master Adaption can be a reality for you, if...you are willing to work with and practice with your adapters. I might add that along with emotional adaption, these Adapter Beings are also available to work with you on your physical and environmental adaption as well.

While on this subject of physical adaption, I'd like to give you a little "close to home" analogy. Are you familiar with the words of wisdom, *"Grow where you are planted?"* Well, take a look out *"in your own front yard,"* for instance. Remember those nice green, hearty, healthy weeds growing in the RV pad.....the ones that are growing in the midst of 5 inches of solid gravel, the ones that never get any water, the ones that are scorched by the sun every day, and get oil dripped on them by the cars parked there...the ones that you keep pulling up and whacking down? I'd say we've got a pretty good example of a life-form that has taken this "grow where you're planted" thing to the max! When the wind blew them there, they didn't whine and moan and say, "Look at those guys over there, they're in with the grass where they get water four times a week from the sprinklers, and then the trees shade them, and the soil is rich... and it's just not fair! I never get any water except for an occasional rain, and the heat from these Rocks is horrible! The oil from these cars is killing me, and there aren't any more nutrients under these Rocks! I can't take it anymore, it's just not fair, nothing can grow under these conditions..... I'm just going to wither up and die!"

I think not...or they wouldn't be there... ***in living color!*** Let's learn from these little *noxious weeds*. If they can beat all the odds and thrive under seriously adverse conditions ...**so can you**...***if you're adaptable!!!***

Now, just for some clarification here, this in no way means to stay in abusive situations... **it means *especially if you are in an abusive situation*...do something to change your environment... or change to another environment!** Remember your Adapters, and don't be afraid to change environments just because it's new and unfamiliar. With your Adapters in place, you will be able to thrive *anywhere!!!*

It is especially important to know about Adapters now when times are so crazy, and you never know where you're going to be from one day to the next. With Mother Earth in her metamorphosis right now, no one knows when she is going to do some house cleaning! *...Actually, what she's planning on doing now is a total reconstruct job!* She's got the remodelers on their way soon, and this place will look like heck, and *be* utter chaos before the job is done! ...She has termites you know, and is having to practically build a new place! She's getting totally new blueprints and plans this time. "Let's see, I think I want a new river here, and a lake here, a geyser there, and over there a mountain range, and in that corner, a clean, clear ocean with lots of fish and vegetation. And over in that other corner, a tropical rain forest."

Yes, Mother Earth is planning a grand place here, and if YOU're going to survive the reconstruction job…YOU'd better be a "Master Adapter." Be ready to take up residence anywhere, anytime, and thrive and be happy while you're doing it! If a noxious weed can do it, so can a Light Being like you!

I believe in you.....

...Do you???

Your Pal.....HAL

WALK-INS & SHOVE-INS

We are in a new experiment now, with never before tried variables. By the way, many of these new variables are a direct result of the ruthless time-space research/experiments from the Montauk Project. ***(If you need information on that project, I would recommend the books on Montauk by Preston Nichols and Peter Moon as a good start. Even if you don't agree with everything they conclude, there is enough physical evidence and documentation that will help you get a good background on the extensiveness of this project and how it affects every one of us.)*** We now have more inter-dimensional activities and surprises than ever before. The rips in our time-space continuum have allowed people, places, and *things* to drift in, merge in, and sometimes collide into our realities. *Many of which we may not even be consciously aware of... and many of them may not be aware that they are here either!* Some have methodically and purposefully moved in... and others are purely accidental.

It used to be, *in the good old days* of metaphysics, that every once in a while you'd run into a true, honest-to-goodness ***Walk-In***. I mean, an undeniable one, with heavy physical and non-physical evidence to back it! (Very different than the "wanna-bes" ...you know, the ones that don't have lives of their own, so they create one... the ones that always have a crisis and thrive on sensationalism... the ones who always go to the extreme, and the things in their lives are always bigger and better (or *badder)* than anyone else's? The ones that need to "get a life?" ...Yes, it seems there's always a *wanna-be...* "Playing in a Theater Near You!")

These genuine Walk-Ins for the most part, were pretty well grounded, had a mission to do, and were extremely well qualified to do it. They knew who and what they were, and didn't need or really care for your approval or acknowledgment of that. Yes, they were *"odd ducks"* for sure, in a society pond of co-dependent, dysfunctional humans... desperate to be "needed and praised." These Beings made *and are still* making their mark on this planet. They trigger a change in the consciousness grid and the expansion of awareness by breaking morpho-genic fields or "M-Fields."

Breaking morpho-genic fields, is simply... *or not so simply...* doing something or proving something that had heretofore never been done, nor believed it *could* be done. An example of this is: It used to be commonly known and accepted that no one could run a mile in 4 minutes. It was considered an impossibility.....until someone had the audacity to go beyond those borders...and did it, breaking an M-field! *The current world record is now 3:43.13 set in 1999.* That achievement broke through a reality grid, changing the consciousness field and expanding the options. Hence, many others followed the lead and continued to do what was previously deemed impossible.

The rules of protocol in a Walk-In situation used to be that an agreement or contract was made prior to the *resident Being's* birth. Then, at a certain place and time, an *accident* happened. This could be a near-death experience, a simple blow to the head, knocking the resident *unconscious*, or even being put under general anesthesia. During this period of *unconsciousness,* the switch was made, and the Being *originally* in the body handed it over to the *Walk-In* to complete a mission, thus honoring the pre-arranged contract. Understand that this is not a haphazard procedure.

Much thought and calibration go into this switch-a-roo. The *original* Being usually has a new assignment waiting, you know, more karma to work out, or if they have completed a certain level of evolution, then they get to take a "spring break" and go to the "Cosmic Bahamas" before taking on a new evolutionary spiral. (See chapters on evolutionary spirals later in this book for a detailed explanation.)

Whatever the case, be assured that under these circumstances there is a total willingness on the part of the original resident. *"I'll go to Earth, grow up a body, work out a few karmic debts, and then I will leave, and you can take over without spending the time to grow up a body too."* It's simple...well, sort of... sort of not... because behind the scenes there are genetics and environment to consider. The information and coding, even though *pre-calculated,* could get some glitches in the system, fractures that need to be fixed, illnesses to clean up, emotional mutations that need adjusting... Yes, life isn't easy for a new Walk-In!

Think back on people you have known, and see if you can detect a possible Walk-In in your life! Have you ever known someone who had one of those *accidents* explained earlier, and when you saw them again, they had a totally different personality? Do you know someone who was self-centered and used their time and money on selfish, irresponsible things, and then after a "knock-out" event, they suddenly became a great humanitarian and redirected their time and energies into things like *solving personal, local, and even world problems*? What about someone who, after being "put out," began to display new talents, and had totally different interests and purpose in life? Think and ponder on this, maybe you yourself have had a close encounter with a *Walk-In!!!*

Another dynamic of a Walk-In is that they can have amnesia, and then slowly get their memory triggered of who they *really* are. They may even have new awarenesses and information about subjects they had no interest in, or reference to before. They may suddenly, *over a short amount of time,* acquire knowledge of such things as biochemistry, astronomy, physics, alchemy, and history... not only of this planet, but also of other star systems, without ever having studied or been involved with these subjects. They may also become aware of such things as what their cosmic origins are, what their specialties are, and what their purpose is here and now, *which by the way, may or may not have been in alignment with the agendas of the "Walk-**Out!**"*

There are many different circumstances, goals, and modalities in the land of Walk-Ins, so it's difficult to give any structured profile. There is though, one thing they all have in common. When they take on their new body with its genetic coding, life's circumstances, relationships, soul memory imprints and data, they ***always*** maintain their own original resonance frequencies...their personal signature, so to speak. This personal signature, then has to interface with what was already in the body and still maintain its dominance, even though there is a blending and merging with the original blueprints. There is a custom remodeling project going on, and as in all remodeling jobs, depending on the extensiveness of the project, (*even if it's only a paint job),* you can tell that the house just doesn't *look or feel* the same. Maybe you can't identify right off what is different, but you know it has changed. So it is with a Walk-In, the avatar is the same on the outside but they just don't look or *feel* or *act* the same anymore.

NOTE: All First Wave Indigos are Walk-Ins. Some walked in as babies, and I humorously tag this scenario as a "Crawl-In," but many walked in around the year 2000. For more information go to: www.FirstWaveIndigos.com

And thus it was, in days gone by; this was a very methodical and structured process. Ahhhhh... "Those were the days."

And now, for something completely different… The scene changes.

ENTER BACK STAGE: **A new breed of villains** in our exciting and sometimes not so ***mellow*** Earth *drama…The Earth Time-Space Bandits…(and they are breaking all the rules and codes of ethics!)* Yes, every good *Melodrama* has to have one or two….. And our 3-D drama certainly has more than its fair share. Ohhh, ***these*** villains…..**they're absolutely ruthless!** They are tearing up the town. They have no respect or regard for anyone or anything, and give no thought to the consequences or outcome of their actions. They're just here, *"**for the Hell of it!**"* They are the Sneaky Snakes that think power comes from what you can do, and make…..*or rather MANIPULATE…*with technology and/or magick. They are power hungry little devils, and will stop at nothing in their quest to become the BIGGEST, BADDEST, MEANEST, TOUGHEST, *RICHEST*, ***"GANGSTAS"*** ON EARTH!

In their hunger and thirst for ultimate supreme power, their perceptions got distorted and perverted. In their fractured insanity, they began usurping, *or at least trying to usurp,* the feminine powers…the sacred creative essence of the God/Dess…the Life-Force that can only be created by the Feminine Ray.

In their foolishness, they believe that their technological power can reign supreme by overthrowing the very power and essence that created them…their Spirit…their Being….. and the whole of the Universe!

This insane gesture is wreaking havoc, not only in this sector of Time/Space, but is rippling into other areas of this and other Universes as well! (…Not to mention the inter-dimensional rips and pollution it's causing.)

WHAT A HELL-UV-A MESS!!!*…or maybe it's so backwards it's a mell-uv-a hess?!!* What to do?…What to do? There must be a Hero somewhere in this drama; …maybe we should put out a cry for help?

"HELP! HELP! SOMEBODY SAVE US FROM THESE VILLAINS!!!"

WHISH…Enter our Heroes…THE COSMIC CLEAN-UP CREW!!! (…You know the ones… "It's a dirty job but somebody's got to do it," crew?) And their wages??? …Well, you couldn't pay them enough…So….. I guess then you'd call it, ***"Volunteer Work"*** …And their reward??? …They do it out of **love and devotion** for Truth and Justice and all the Life-forms that are being enslaved.

So, here's the situation. We have individuals and groups with some *serious* technology, who decide they don't like our history… it doesn't *serve* them… So, they take it upon themselves to change it….. and go back and do some editing on this movie and… ***POOF!*** A whole new dimension is formed, and a new historical outcome appears. (Have you ever been totally fascinated with the subject of time-travel, and absolutely enthralled with time-travel movies and multidimensional shows like *Sliders?* Well, maybe there's a reason…)

Basically folks, we're at critical mass here. Because of all the holes, rips, ripples, bleed throughs, and crossing of currents, what happens next is a *crapshoot!* We have created a whole new element in this free-will zone that hasn't happened before, and that element is: **Any *one* and Any *thing* CAN and DOES hack into this time/space/dimension, and as a result, things and Beings that have no business here, and theoretically shouldn't be here… ARE SHOWING UP!!!**

I can see it all now… front row seats are a hot item this season in all the cosmic ticket outlets to view and ***bet on*** *the outrageous events and conclusion of this Earth game! The cosmic bookies, refreshment-stand* *operators, and of course, T-shirt & future memorabilia vendors, are all there cashing in on the last episodes to the live drama of the* ***Great Planet Earth Transition!*** *Beings from the farthest corners of space, are taking off work,* ***or calling in sick****, so they can come and witness first hand these* ***Earth-Shaking*** *events. The stakes are high, anxiety even higher, and Planet Hollywood is there vying for exclusive movie rights... this is sure to be a classic legendary blockbuster!*

Now, back to our Walk-Ins/Shove-Ins Saga. The rules and regulations have changed considerably and to put it bluntly, most of the rules and regulations have become extinct due to the lawlessness of "The Outlaws."

The order and methodology of Walk-Ins and Walk-Outs is history, and now we have a new *Bully* type of situation that makes you take a microscopic look at our previous perceptions and the fine lines of "Free-Will." Because of the irresponsible, and many times unethical experiments at Montauk, we have a brand-new, never-been-tried before, reality game... or maybe it's better to say "***un***" reality game.

What used to be an *orderly* process of walking-in and walking-out, has now become a process of *pure chaos*! What is happening now with the "Gangstas," Outlaws, and Bullies, is that any *time,* any *where,* someone opens themselves up, even if it's only a crack, these bullies weasel their foot in the crack and expand its opening... Then with a *push* or *shove*, they evict the surprised and unaware resident Being, and set up housekeeping ***in their body!***

NOTE: *Some of these "Shove-Ins" are wayward ghosts who are looking for some place to go that feels comfortable to them, and aren't really aware they are raising Hell. They are just trying to find a place they resonate to. A large number of them are very confused and scared because of an abrupt, violent or disconcerting death. Many times this occurs because of drugs and/or other altered states. These poor ghosts* **did NOT get the memo** *so to speak, about what just happened to them, not even realizing they are dead. They don't know where they need to go next, or how to get there. They were in such a low vibrational state when they died that the "higher ups" couldn't get to them to help out. There are Beings on the lower planes that know "fool well" what is going on and give them a little help shoving-in to a live body. About 40% of all Shove-Ins fall into this category, and are in need of rescuing. The other 60% are Gangstas from not just this Earth plane, but also from other places/planets in, and sometimes outside this Universe. There are occasions where there is not a complete "Shove-In"...the Being is not "inside" but "hanging on" or "piggy backing" like a back pack. This is what I call a "Shove-On," and it seems to be a tad bit easier to fix.*

Every so often the original Being is still attached and tries to take back control, but keeps getting kicked out again. Sometimes it just "hangs out" watching and waiting for a chance to get permanently back in! Other times they are shoved out with such force that they no longer have their attachment cord plugged into their body. In this case, they either hang around and follow the body, trying to devise a strategy to reclaim their turf, or maybe give out an "S.O.S." for some assistance to get back in again. Other times they get so disgusted with what's happening with their anatomy and how it's operating *with a new boss,* that they say, "To heck with it all, I don't have to put up with this!" They'll turn around, walk away from their body altogether, and go find another game to play somewhere else.

If you are ever involved with a Shove-In situation, you can be assured that it wasn't instigated or directed by a Light Keeper! But don't think for a minute that you are powerless to do anything about it, no-sir-ree. There is a multitude of things that can be done to not only get reinstated, but also reinforced!

NOTE: *If the Shove-In is a mere "Wayward Ghost," there are many ways to help them. Reading this book and also,* ***"Got Ghosts??? The Bizarre but True Tales of the Ghost Buster Gals,"*** *by Ronnie Rennae Foster and myself, plus getting some Aurauralite/Aulmauracite will give you the information, tools, and support you need to rescue trapped souls.*

The first item of business is to recognize that there is something ab*soul*utely not right here. You see all the telltale signs that point to an entirely new Being in-bodying this body. Don't let your love and compassion for the original Resident Being cloud your perception. If what used to seem like "just a phase" turns into a totally new personality with a new unfamiliar resonance, you could be dealing with *a* ***Shove-In***.

At this point, it is extremely important for you to get very clear and *neutral*. Separate your *self* from the illusions of "the body" and tune into the original Resident Being and their Higher Self - ***Soul Suemah*** *wherever they may be.* Make sure you feel the connection and guidance of your Higher Self- ***Soul Suemah*** and any other back-up support from other Spiritual Beings you are in alliance with...*who you ascertain could be of value and assistance to you in this matter.*

Then go *directly* to this person's Higher Self - ***Soul Suemah*** to establish what their will and desired outcome is before you make any moves to assist them. **Remember**, *your will may not necessarily be their will. There have been a few times that I was instructed by my guides to back off, when attempting to remove a Shove-In. I checked again later to see if anything had changed and got the green light. There were obviously reasons why, and most likely the timing was wrong. It was important that I was first of all, cognizant enough to be aware of the possibility that it was NOT ok for me to interfere, and second, to be intuitive enough about the bigger picture and not assume I knew it all at this point in time.*

When you are in this clean neutral space, you will be instructed how best to assist. Each case is different, and must be handled as a custom-designed program. Maybe all you will need to do is **firmly** affirm their position as the Resident Being. It is very feasible that you can **out-create** and **un-create** a situation by putting a strong consciousness grid into the person's body and energy fields that "the big bully-buttinsky," does not exist in your reality or in the reality of the Original Being.

Yeah, this will probably, *most likely*, tick the bully off, and it will rant and rave... pull ugly faces and make all kinds of threats. It will try anything to get your attention *and your agreement* that it DOES exist, *and it is the supreme force here...* ***the biggest bully you've ever met!*** What it is ultimately trying to do, is trick you into reinforcing its existence, its supremacy in this situation ...And ***your powerlessness!!!***

So, if you just calmly and firmly maintain your position of deep peace and continue to affirm its non-existence, pretty soon its power and its butt-in position begins to dissipate, like water in a hot frying pan. Turning on the heat makes the water leave the frying pan, changing its position and also its form. **Get the picture here?**

I personally have had some background and experience with this method. It wasn't easy at first, and I had my moments of questioning my capabilities and my sanity as I was dealing with one of the biggest, raunchiest, foulest, most vicious, and aggressive scoundrels in the Universe... and ***IT*** knew it... and ***IT*** knew that I knew it!

What I attribute my success to, was my consistent persistence in the matter. (Now, this doesn't mean that I didn't get psychically beat up a few times, and was left with a few psychic bruises, but I was a determined little beaver! I would just continue to ***ruthlessly and relentlessly*** maintain my position of deep peace as well as solidly maintain my own ability/capability to create and un-create. I guess you could say that what I did was, "invalidate the ***hell*** out of ***it!****"*) Pretty soon this bully started to loosen its grip, weaken its stronghold and gradually lost its power and position in ***my reality***.

I have found that this method also works extremely well if you ever find **yourself in a position of being *put-out*, or *shoved-out*.** *Never underestimate your power to create...or* ***un****create!*

Another method is to quarantine the Shove-In entity with a Kryahgenetics Egg and either hand it off to your Higher Self - ***Soul Suemah*** and/or one of your trusted spirit guides, or call in a "cosmic recycle bin" and stuff it down one of those.

NOTE: *A cosmic recycle bin is just what you think it is. You put something in one end, shut the lid, and it cleans/recycles it for you. If there is something useful after all that cleansing, it spits it out the other end...if not, it extinguishes it. They come in all shapes and sizes depending on the task at hand. (Your Aulmauracite Rocks know what to do and how to use the bins. If you are not sure...just hand the "recyclables" over to your Rock buddies! See Chapter 22 on Aurauralite/Aulmauracite.)*

One more little hint when it comes to the fear factor. I picked this one up from some of our greatest teachers, our kids. One day, several years ago one of my sons, who was about six at the time, said to me, *"Mom, you know what?...A ghost can't scare you* ***if you're not afraid of it****."* I laughed and said, "You know, you are absolutely right! *A ghost* ***can't*** *scare you if you're not afraid of it ...And neither can a monster or a boogieman, or an alien!*" (What would we ever do without the wisdom of innocence?)

At this time and space/place in this adventure game, it is imperative that you maintain command and total ownership of your life on a constant basis. You must stay alert and not fall prey to victimhood. You must maintain the partnership, the connection to, and the total alignment with the direction, wisdom, and advice of your Higher Self - ***Soul Suemah,*** your God or Goddess Self. This is now mandatory, when the strong seem to control and absorb the weak.

And now with all of your reading, studying, meditating, philosophizing, workshops, and practicing... well, guess what kids, it's *Show Time!* ...And if you can't remember your lines, you'd better be able to hear, or read the lips of your prompter, (Higher Self - ***Soul Suemah***) In addition to this, the script gets changed on a daily basis, so it would be way advantageous if you were a darned good *ad-libber,* 'cause other cast members are forgetting their lines. This *Play* we're in could easily turn into a *Bad Dream* if we don't pay attention to what's going on around us, and what the other cast members are doing.

NOTE: *I often humorously say to my ghost buster partner Ronnie, "The dead are easy to handle and deal with, it is 'THE LIVING' that create the biggest problems, because you can't just haul them off to a life review or a Cosmic Recycle Bin like we do with ghosts!" (Which is precisely why so many people get Shove-Ins or Shove-Ons. Bodies are a hot commodity to these "Ass Souls & Ass No-Souls!" I can hear their thoughts now, "****Back off... I have a body and I know how to use it! ...Now don't make me mad or I'll make this body do unscrupulous things!****" These entities/spirits can go undetected and create all sorts of chaos and mayhem... and unless they physically hurt or kill someone, they are free to run-a-muck ...and even then, they still may weasel out of any kind of reprisal if they have outside help getting them off the hook!) The good news is, people like YOU are reading this book and are catching on to their* *games. With the keys and codes available in this book, we can now not just start* ***an evolution revolution,*** *but see it to completion, and get this mess cleaned up once and for all!*

Arrrrrrrrr .....Tha pirates be a scammin' tha seas mateys, so yu'd best be a watchin' un' takin' charge uv tha wheel. Ya hav' ta be tha capt'n uv yer own ship now!

So you'd best be a qualifyin' yer crew, un' don't let any skalley-wags on board. Ya can't afford ta be havin' no mutiny, now can ya?

If'n you let tha bilge rats aboard, ya might find y'urself blindfolded un' a walkin' tha plank off yer own ship! ...Un' that would be a lubberin' shame, now wudn't it me mateys?"

One qualification that is imperative now, as you are taking charge of the wheel and steering in these uncharted waters, is the ability to rise above it all in a moment's notice and take an uninvolved, unaffected bird's-eye view of your situation. Close-up looks can be deceiving, and you never know if the little floaty up ahead could actually be an iceberg! We don't always know what's "underneath the surface."

How many times do we experience something and automatically assume that we "know it all?" We'll jump to a conclusion that is totally inappropriate and inaccurate, or observe someone else who is heavily involved in this *limited perception drama game.* This seems to occur most often when someone is activating our triggers and pushing our instant-reflex defense buttons, and we are unwilling to see that we might not have all the pieces to the picture. Usually it's the people closest to us, i.e., our spouses, our kids, our parents, and our co-workers, who activate this ***reaction game***.

Imagine yourself in this specific scenario: You're in a hurry to get to a meditation, or a W.S. (Weird Sh*t) Meeting. You're in rush-hour traffic on the freeways in Phoenix, AZ, it's hotter than Heck because it's the middle of August, AND YOUR AIR-CONDITIONER JUST WENT OUT! ...And if that weren't enough, there are lots of out-of-state tourists on the road who don't know the freeways or where they are going, and road rage is running amuck! (Get the picture?) We can get so wrapped up and entangled in the emotional energetics of it all, that we delete all common sense and our ability to *respond,* because we are so involved in *reacting*. Instead of subduing the ever-increasing road rage, we get caught up in it and become a part of it, causing more of it!

And what about when we, or someone else in our drama game, makes a serious boo-boo because they didn't get all the facts. They may put something into motion that causes a lot of damage, hurts a lot of feelings, and creates a lot of harm, which could have been avoided altogether if some calmness and clarity would have been the first defense.

In case you haven't read between the lines yet, and you're still wondering and worrying about whether or not ***you're*** a candidate for a Shove-In takeover... I'll fill in some of the blanks for you. It is next to impossible for these hoodlums to gain access to you when you're in a state of joy, calm focus, deep peace, love, compassion, happiness, laughter, bliss, and total self-confidence... (NOT ARROGANCE! *...That one rings a Cosmic Bell that says, "Come on in, this one's ripe 'n ready!"*) Also, when you become solid in maintaining a strong personal relationship and alliance of Love, communication, and camaraderie with your Higher Self - ***Soul Suemah*** ... this creates a "Total Coverage Insurance Policy!"

Some of the emotional states that attract a Shove-In are: Hate, Anger, Self-Loathing, Revenge, Jealousy, Rage, and prolonged Depression & Grief.

Now this does not mean that shedding a few tears now and then will put you in jeopardy! Expressing sadness and grief at appropriate times is an important part of being human and being in sync with your emotions, while giving yourself the freedom to express them. This is healthy and encouraged!

I'm talking about the day after day gloomy grief that puts a dark cloud around you and those you live with.

And what about the anger? Well, again... *little spouts and steam blowers every once in a while keep your nerves from fraying! ...And sometimes we need to get angry to cause change and let those around us know we're serious about boundaries!*

No, the anger I'm talking about here is the constant and habitual kind, where everyone and everything makes you annoyed and angry... and of course, someone or something outside of yourself is what's blamed. You have everyone and everything, tried, convicted, and punished over and over! I'm talking about the automatic and prolonged states of intense or unprovoked anger that makes mountains out of molehills. ***These are the states that put you at risk!***

So many times, it's the little things that rile us up, "disturb the peace," and change the energy of the dream... into a nightmare!

If your favorite exercise is jumping to conclusions, and your head's temperature tends to be *hot* rather than *cool,* remember again folks, "It's show time," and it's time to put into action everything we've studied and learned.

I know it looks so good on paper, and feels so good to read books, watch videos, listen to podcasts, and discuss the benefits of all these philosophical living codes. Whether it's Metaphysical, Eastern Philosophy. Native American Spirituality, Old Age, New Age, New Wave, or whatever you want to call it, all of this information can give you warm fuzzies, ***yet be absolutely useless if there is no application and action behind it!***

Sooo, the next time you feel yourself starting to get irritated and letting your fur stand on end, take a breath and allow the *passion for the reaction and anger* to pass through, and be filtered ***by your Heart/CoreStar***. What will happen next is pure magic. Either you will change your perception and disengage the energy of anger and conflict, or you will take a firm and commanding, but calm stance, with clarity that will bring truth and justice to the surface.

The ironic thing is… this manifestation will come ***soul***-ly as a result of your ability to masterfully hold this space/place of deep peace, truth & justice!

"Avast ye mateys! Hear me now un' listen ta me words. Y'ul be a travelin' thru some right strange waters here, un' they be infested with sharks, un' snakes, un' crocodiles, un' pirates, un' all other kinds o' no-good, lily-livered, rotten-timbered bottom-feeders ya may never 'uv seen b'fore, un' will surely shiver yur timbers. Don't get keel-hauled by tha changin' rules… Tha pirates game changes daily cuz it's like tha sea, un' it never stays tha same. Remember, me hearties, yu'r just in a hologram, un' yu'r here fer some swashbuckling, action-packed, consolidated learnin' un' fixin'… Un' not ta worry, ya can't really get y'urself hurt, 'cuz ya can't permanently inj'r a spirit. Arrrrrrrrrrr…..

Aye, un' one more thing… By Neptune's trident, y'ur never alone! There'l always be someone a keepin' a weather-eye open fer ya. Yu're smart as paint, ya are, un' yu're never in a fix that ya don't have tha wits ta get y'ur self out of!

So ya best be a takin' off y'ur kufflinks, un' a-rollin' up y'ur sleeves. Batten down tha hatches, un reef tha mainsail. Tha stormy waters are a comin' un' YOU be tha one at tha helm. Prove yur navigatin' skills, un' see how well ya can maneuver in these challeng'n waves, un' make this tha best life yu'v ever had!

You be tha dreamer here matey. It all be up ta YOU now!

………………………AARRRRRRRRR!!!"

WHAT THE DEVIL'S BEEN GOING ON HERE???

Hopefully the information and viewpoint I am about to give you, will put a twist in your perceptual understanding of Evil and Dark, Good and Light… and perhaps make you "re-think" your "pre-thinks" on the subject. Be forewarned, this is NOT the typical explanation of how it all works.

In the beginning, there was Light and Dark …2 polarities…neither one better than the other, just different …bi-polar opposites. They balanced and complimented each other, and both had equal time. Imagine what this planet would be like if there was ALWAYS Light/Day and NO Dark/Night to give relief from the heat/brightness of the day. Night time can truly be a savior. It seems that we have gotten way out of equilibrium in our belief and aspiration for constant light, because, well… we have been told by all the religions and spiritual "authorities" that "Light is good and Dark is bad." When you look at the day and night scenario, you know that this is a very flawed teaching.

Now, the way I see it, The Dark has gotten a seriously bum rap for things it wasn't even remotely responsible for, and *no credit* was given for all the relentless hard work and perseverance that has gone into defining and upholding this vibration! It makes you wonder *why* it has been so brutally discredited, doesn't it?

The Dark isn't bad, it's just different, and in order to truly understand and embrace The Light, you **must** have some knowledge and respect for The Dark and how it operates. The Dark sector of this Universe is the element that holds the opposite polarity for The Light. This element HAS TO BE! If it weren't, there would be nothing to identify and hold The Light in place! The Dark, as you know, defines and serves The Light. In its authentic element, it supports and stabilizes The Light. (…And yes, you guessed it, The Light also serves and upholds The Dark!)

To understand the authentic Dark Sectors of the Dark Realm in our Universe, you can get a glimpse of it by delving into the vibration of Black Light or Ultra-Violet Light. In its presence, white is illuminated brighter, and with a totally different vibration than with sunlight. If you put a white cotton sheet under a Black Light, the white takes on a new character and actually broadcasts itself into the dark. It appears as if the sheet has its own electric luminescence from inside itself. You can move it around in a room, and it actually shines light on the things around it. The Black Light gives everything that its rays touch, *especially bright colors,* a totally new dimension.

NOTE: *New research and information is now being revealed about how our bodies NEED Ultra-Violet Light and deteriorate without it. It awakens sleeping codes within us that are mandatory in order for us to expand into other dimensions. Ultra-Violet Light also breaks apart and scatters harmful waves and radiation coming from electronic equipment like computers, TVs, microwaves, etc. There seems to be a lot of things we've been told are harmful that are actually essential. This has been done in order to keep us away from truth, and keep us in a stupor of confinement and submission. Black Light/Ultra-Violet Light* *happens to be two of these propagandized subjects ...and yes, we do need to be aware and practical about overdosing pale pink skin in the sun, but at the same time consider what happens with the lack of it. There is a high depression or Seasonal Affective Disorder (S.A.D.) rate in areas like Seattle, WA., where the UV rays from the sunshine are a rarity, especially in winter. Tanning beds, (the more recent ones), are also a remedy for S.A.D. and I personally feel these beds, if done in moderation can be very useful, in spite of how they have been demonized by the media and the medical community.*

Experiment sometime with Black/Ultra-Violet Light, and I'm sure you'll come up with some amazing ah-ha's on your own! (Black Lights with fixtures can be purchased in novelty stores and online. They even have LED Black Lights now! **NOTE:** *Be careful of the Black Light bulbs; many of those get very hot and do not have the UV effects! Get the UV-Incandescent bulbs. They are multi-purposeful.*

If you think of The Light as White Light, and The Dark as Ultra-Violet Light, you'll begin to understand the concept here. The Dark Polarity/Realm of the Universe is a lot like Black Light…it's not bad, it's just different. In fact, in many ways, *it's out of this world…*it's so enchanting and beautiful!

What if you decided to be afraid of Black Lights, and wouldn't step foot in a house that had one? Well, then you'd never know the beauty and altered reality that springs to life when you walk into a dark room that has been flooded with Black Lighting. The vibrancy and magick it offers when illuminating something, is unexplainable to someone who has never experienced it! (Incidentally, we have Black Lights on 24/7 in nearly every room in our home for the purpose of health and experimentation. I have one on the wall next to the computer, and if it ever goes out, my face and eyes get immediately dehydrated.) In my former house, the Black Light in my bedroom illuminated the over three hundred stars and planets I creatively and strategically placed on the walls and ceiling. It was a trip to sleep "under the *fluorescent* stars" every night and bathe in the rays of the Ultra-Violet lamps!

The Dark has its rules, regulations, and laws that must be adhered to, and if broken, *have some very serious consequences.* There is beauty, honor, and integrity in the hierarchy of The Dark, and the balance and respect for the male/female energies are explicitly upheld. If things should ever get out of balance in this sector, a ripple of chaos would go out into the Universe and boomerang back to the other polarity….. The Light.

Needless to say, the Beings that hold the frequencies to maintain stability in The Dark polarity are *magnificent, wise, intelligent, noble, and respectable.* They take their position very seriously and won't leave their posts until a suitable replacement is trained and seasoned long enough to accept and execute the responsibilities of that post. There is always someone in training to be a back-up or replacement for each position. It's a grand network and very proficient. There are many checks and balance systems working constantly to keep the polarity in that Realm anchored and stable. I for one, have a tremendous respect and admiration for the loyalty and integrity by which The Dark Realm is run. The more you understand this dimension, the more you revere it!

From here on out, let's refer to The Dark as "Dark/Light" and The Light as "White/Light" because this better defines and gives proper perception and respect to both polarities.

When you think about the yin-yang symbol, this viewpoint makes way more sense, since the pure uncorrupted Dark/Light & White/Light have a synergistic symbiotic relationship. This replaces the idea that the symbol means dark or "evil & sinful" and a part of The Light, and the benevolent Light is a part of corruption and darkness. It always disturbed me when I would hear this philosophy as it just didn't compute and also didn't *feel* right. When people talk about their "dark side" in this respect, it is like they are accepting this corruption/evil because that is just the way it is..... "*The philosophers and Goo-Roos have been saying this for centuries so it must be true! (Gurus is spelled this way deliberately... Goo being the operative word here.) Everyone has a dark side and we need to accept and embrace that dark part of us.*" I have seen some people accept this with almost an element of pride, as they embrace corrupted darkness as part of their authentic selves. This gives the corruption/evil not only a foot in the door, but full freedom (or should I say *fool freedom)* to expand and take over...all under the guise of "balance!" When you really think about it, it reeks of a covert operation, and **no one questions it!** It would be more to our advantage to realize that there may be corruption or "Corrupted Dark and Corrupted Light" lurking in and around us, so we need to be on the look-out for it. If we find any particles of Corrupted Dark and Light, we can then remove and replace it with something positive, nurturing, and empowering.

Speaking of questions, where does the Devil and Satan fit into all of this? .....Well, they fit in, but maybe not quite the way we've been told.

We all know that evil is running amuck and is in our face every single day! Now, since we have established that evil has no place in either The Dark or The Light Realms... we realize it is in a class of its own: ***Corrupted Light & Corrupted Dark!*** Evil is ever-consuming, and propagates the corruption/destruction that is terrorizing this planet and many other sectors of space. Long ago, when the Universe was new, a horrible corruption virus got loose here and has been waging war **in its attempt to infiltrate and dominate both the White/Light and the Dark/Light Realms!**

As the corruption grew, so did the thirst for power and control. In the midst of all this, there were some Beings here that Hal refers to as ***"Ass-Souls"*** who got an insane, hair-brained idea. They thought to themselves, "Hey, why don't I use technology and physical power to usurp Natural Law and Universal Law? .....Then I can rise up, take over and become the 'Big *Head* Cheese.' I can use this power to scare everyone and also dupe them, brainwash them, confuse them, confine them...and they won't have any choices except the ones I give them, and I'll be very powerful and maybe someday the architects of this Universe will even fall down and worship me!!! And wow, what a rush!!!"

NOTE: This Ass Soul personality profile, reeks of the same immature, juvenile brat traits that the Sumerian God, Enlil, personified. In my opinion, he was the ultimate irritable, unreasonable, tantrum-throwing, arrogant, resentful, hotheaded, conniving, self-serving, "stinker" you'd never *EVER* want to meet!

I think I like the category that author Barbara Marciniak puts him in the best, when she called him a "godling & godlet" (with little "g's!") I might also mention, Enlil had other names as well, one being **The Lord God Jehovah**..... (I bet this was a shocker, as you probably thought I was going to say, *Son of a Grinch* or something like that...right?)

No wonder there's been so much turmoil and confusion about God from avid Bible readers! If our "god" is supposed to be Kind, Loving, Allowing, Forgiving, Compassionate, Patient, Caring, Wise, and All-Powerful...then how do you figure this Being can all of a sudden get:

VENGEFUL?...How many times does it say in the Bible, "Vengeance is mine sayeth the LORD?"
JEALOUS?... ***"Thou shalt have no other Gods before me... For I the Lord thy God am a jealous God" - Ex. 20:3, 5*** *- (Now, could you please tell me, how in the heck could someone who is supposed to be an omnipotent God, that has everything, and knows everything, possibly have reason to be jealous of anything or anyone, especially one of its creations? ... What a joke!!!)*
FILLED WITH WRATH AND ANGER? ...*Many scriptures tell of incidents that made the Lord fill with wrath and anger ...And still other scriptures give reference to all the men, women, children, and even animals and plants in selected cities that were destroyed by the hand of the Lord.*

Now, it seems to me that **all living things** back then, had to constantly tiptoe around, and walk on eggshells, so as not to say or do anything that might "tick off" or offend "the Lord!"

Does this scenario have some serious resemblance to the anxiety children of alcoholic parents have? It's something to really think about!

I don't know about you, but this Jehovah God, scared the dickens out of me as a child and caused some major confusion in my little head. I was constantly asking myself, "Did I do something wrong? Was I good enough? Was I going to get punished for something I didn't know about? How will I know if I'm OK with God?" ...And... "How come Jesus seems so nice, and kind, and loving, but Jehovah is so hostile, mean, angry, and down-right scary?" .....I didn't understand that one, AT ALL!

Then, as an adult in about 1991, I became aware of the information from people like Ramtha, Zecharia Sitchin, William Bramley, and others that told of a bigger, more expanded version of us, and the gods that came here to *enslave*... I mean *save us*. It was mind and heart wrenching as it blew the heck out of my paradigms, which were a product of 35 years of organized religion and environmental input!

I went through all sorts of emotional roller-coaster rides. I had waves of deep grief and not knowing what to believe anymore, followed by total anger turned inward for allowing myself to be duped into worshipping this "doo-doo head" all those years! I also went through waves of fear like, "What if I'm wrong?..... Then, if I go back to worship this god again, he's ***really*** going to be ticked off at me!"

It took me about nine months, ***which FYI, 3's and 9's seem to be completion cycles, 9 being the strongest as it is 3 cycles of 3,*** to really stabilize after I first made the decision to stop worshipping this guy, and figure out who and what "The Creator" *really, truly* was about. For a while, I thought I could somehow continue to go to church and maybe wake up some of my closest friends and family to the blatant truth I had just been slammed with... how we had been manipulated, duped, and scared into submission by this tyrant ***godless***...I mean ***godlet,*** Jehovah! (As you can imagine, that didn't work out so well, and I got severely reprimanded instead of celebrated!) After several months of this, it became apparent that living the duality was too heart-wrenching and caused too much inner turmoil.

Finally, the day came that I could no longer continue to live out of sync with my Heart/CoreStar inner truth, and so I made an appointment for me and my husband to see our Bishop..... *who, by the way, was a psychiatrist.*

When we arrived there, I got straight to the point. I said, "Bishop, we have some serious problems with the doctrine of this church"... (His eyes showed shock and disbelief as he sat down..... This was the last thing he expected to hear from my mouth. My husband and I had always been such good, stalwart, and active members he could always count on for help and support. We both had held many teaching and executive positions and was considered to be some of the most diligent church members in our area!) .....I continued, "I do not believe that the God of the Old Testament, Jehovah, is the creator of our spirits." (This really took him aback. Stunned is the best way to describe his reaction.) I went on, "I think that Jehovah was a **dysfunctional, schizophrenic, psychopath!**"

At this point, he nearly fell off his chair..... The blatant descriptive terms of psychological defects were well interpreted and clearly understood, given his many years in the psychiatry profession. I wasn't trying to insult, offend, or horrify the poor man, *but I managed to do all three at once!* I was just being as honest as I could in my evaluation, and to me it was as brief and to-the-point an explanation of my research as I could possibly get!

The next encounter we had with our Bishop was one in which he said, "I fully intended to meet with you and your husband to chastise you, but after hearing all your stories, and why you feel the way you do, I realize that your intent is from your heart. I don't ascribe to your findings and information, but I can't condemn you for them either!" We were immediately released from our church jobs and we handed in our membership resignation, which incidentally circled back and forth, from office to office before it finally went to the church headquarters in Salt Lake City. No one knew what to do with us, because the way we left was not common.

I felt sorry for our Bishop. Part of him knew what I was saying had validity, but the other part of him couldn't get out from under the jaws of the DOG-ma. We parted with a hug, each respecting the rights and decisions of the other, but I know that his, (and many other church members') perception would be permanently altered. The question of whether or not my research had some reality or validity will haunt them, and arise every time they read scriptural verses depicting some of Jehovah's temper tirades!

OK, now back to Satan, The Devil, or the Big Head Cheeses who was trying to usurp all authority in the Universe...So after that insane thought, they forgot to laugh and say, "Just kidding, sorry about that, it was just a joke!" ...And with that thought, energized by intense emotion, a bigger fracture was generated in the psyche of these Ass-Souls, and ... *VOI-LA*... the Altered Ego started running amuck!

The Altered Ego grew and continued to degenerate, and inundate people with a diversity of inappropriate and inaccurate perceptions like: "I'm not good enough... and never will be." "I am useless, worthless, incapable, and desperate." "I have to struggle for love and basic survival." "There isn't enough to go around...If I have some, then someone else will have to go without..." etc., etc., etc. And then there's the big one, "I feel so ashamed, helpless, and hopeless, I just want to die!"

Of course, on the other side of the distortion scale, we have the ultra-superior, power-hungry, delusions of grandeur control tripper Ass Souls. The Global Elite/money monger, corporate heads, strongly adhere to these rules: "Seek wealth, power and domination at all costs!" "Divide and conquer." "I have to have the very best." "Get it before someone else does." "Intimidate and consume the weak." "Lie, cheat, steal, kill, I'll do whatever it takes to get what I want." "No matter how much I have, it's never enough." "It's my right to have everything." "I have to look good at all costs." "Live with ultimate power and supremacy through the spiritual and physical death of your subjects." ... or "Drain their essence and give it to me!" (Sound familiar? Remember the Skeksis in the movie, *The Dark Crystal?*)

So as this virus warped and mutated, it spread and wreaked havoc on both The Light AND The Dark polarities of this Universe. And who's to blame for all this whacked out mass-mess? ...The Devil?..... Well... actually no..... the Devil didn't do it, because, ummm, there isn't ***really*** any such thing as a Devil..... (or an Easter Bunny... or a Santa or a Tooth Fairy...)

(Now don't close the book yet, I know you might be a little upset and offended at this blatant, radical statement, but please read a little further before you form your opinion.)

Let me relate a quote here taken from a book by Michael Adams entitled, *"**My Little Book of Blasphemies** (and other thoughts from the shower)."*

"Does it make sense that the most powerful, most creative, most intelligent force that ever was or ever will be, could screw up their creation so bad, that they should have to create a grand junk yard, complete with an incinerator, then hire the ultimate bad guy (who by the way, is also their arch-enemy) to run the joint? Then have this bad guy slowly burn, torture, and destroy the masterpieces that didn't quite turn out the way the Master Architect had planned? The whole idea says that God is not perfect, and that He/She is pretty pissed off about it. Does that make any sense?"

OK, if you want to assign the name *Devil* to this fractured, mutant Altered Ego Virus, go right ahead as its "in-words" or lexigrams do a good job of describing this loathsome virus. Let's dissect it now and see what those "in-words" are. In the word *DEVIL,* there is the sub-word *EVIL,* (and evil really does vividly depict and sum up in our language and perception, what this mutant virus is spreading). If we continue to move down this letter language lane we find another sub-word, ***VIL*** or ***VILE,*** which if referenced in Webster's tells us: *adj.- morally disgusting, repulsive, miserable, and unpleasant, degrading, mean.* And if we take this one step even further, we find the prefix ***IL:*** *adj.-not healthy, sick, destructive in effect; harmful; hostile; unfriendly; not favorable; not up to standards. n. evil; injury or harm; something causing suffering.* And then you have DIE…and that says it all!

Basically, I'd say we've got a serious sickness happening here!!!

Well, you still have your book open, so either you blew up your confinement boxes and are ready for some major paradigm shifts, or you already knew or suspected this information to be true…So you're reading for personal validation….. or for sheer entertainment! Whatever your reason, I commend you for it!!!

So, here we are at this point. We've gotten some terminology straightened out and standardized. We've established that the Altered Ego, *the sickness, the insane virus run-amuck* is synonymous with ***ev-ill***. Then, the next item of business that needs clarification and clearing up is the bum rap that Lucifer has gotten…Yeah, he's been credited for raising all kinds of Hell, and doing all manner of Evil Deeds! Well, the truth of the matter is…Lucifer is a ***"position"*** not a ***"person,"*** and in the hierarchy of benevolent Lords from the Dark Realms, it is one of the names/titles for ***Dark Emperor!***

What I am presenting here, once again, is the possibility/probability that the *Dark Polarity* is not evil and bad, but actually extremely honorable and necessary! (This may be totally "way out" for some of you, and may raise a lot of questions. To this I would say, "Hurray!!! Question EVERYTHING!")

Others of you may be thinking, "By golly, that makes sense to me… We have Light & Dark… And then we have Corrupted Light & Corrupted Dark. *(Yes, you read that right, this is the second time I said "**Corrupted Light**!" Light can be and has been corrupted for eons!)* …So we have **Evil/Ego** running amuck everywhere…and it's Hell-Bent on polluting **BOTH sides!**

NOTE: *I have heard many people in New Age communities ascribe to the philosophy that, **"Beings on the dark side are just playing that role so that we can learn lessons from them, (and many of them don't really want to be there, but it is out of love for us that they are doing it!) Once we have learned the lesson***

they are trying to teach us, then they can be released and stop being "the bad guy." We need them for our own good! If we love them instead of being angry at them it will fix everything."

My reply is this: *There is far more to the story, and this philosophy has a hidden agenda that you need to understand before you can get the bigger picture and truly act appropriately. First of all, the* ***Corrupted Dark has developed immunities to people sending them Love'n Light and warm fuzzies.*** *It is totally deflected and does nothing to them but teach them better how to build new immunities to different Love vibrations. Second, there may indeed be Beings that DO NOT want to be playing that role of "the bad guy!" Some of these Beings got "hijacked" into this job... just like some of the young service men and women got hijacked into wars that our governments (i.e., corporations and "banksters") are waging. Once inside, they realize it is a scam, and they had been duped into hurting and killing innocent people! So they want to get OUT...but they can't get out until their term is up! Suicide is running rampant in their efforts to "get out!" On the Forbs.com website 5-Feb-2013, it claimed that in 2012, 349 active duty soldiers died by their own hand: that is nearly one a day! Since the trauma lives on, the statistics for vets is a staggering... 22 per day, or nearly 1 per hour! This philosophy of needing a bad guy to teach us our lessons fits really nicely in the Corrupted Dark's file cabinet. Then it is put out for distribution in "memos" to the authentic Light/Dark Keepers, so all of those who have the ability to challenge and overthrow the perpeTRAITORS of the* ***Corrupted Light & Corrupted Dark Régime****, will back down and do nothing. I agree that these corruption perpeTRAITORS, and those who work for them can indeed from time to time, make the rest of us smarter and wiser...BUT that is really NOT their intent. The truth is, there are other ways to learn lessons that are even more efficient and productive. The problem is, we have not had the luxury of these superior learning methods because this inferior method which has been forced on us, is all we have ever known! Another grand control system that has been forced on us is degeneration and early death. The truth is, our bodies can live to be literally thousands of years old! BUT with age, also comes wisdom, and to the corruption perpeTRAITORS... that is a BAAAAAAD thing; hence our limited average lifespan of 60-80 years, with drugs keeping us alive and brain dead.*

THIS IS THE VERY REASON FOR THIS BOOK! We can live longer! We can live healthier! We can wise-up! We can rise-up and take our Planet back! It is the most loving thing we could possibly do for our beautiful Earth Mother Guyah, and all of humanity, all of the plant, animal, mineral, and nature spirit kingdoms! The answers are inside YOU, and some of the keys to unlock those answers are in this book... and the Alchemy of Kryahgenetics can help you activate the will and the fearlessness to transform yourself into a "Super Human!"

OK, now for the inside scoop!

The Originator/Boss of the Altered Ego Virus that is responsible for corrupting all of our files, damaging our motherboards, and crashing our hard-drives, has recently been extinguished! (Ahhhhhhhhh...let's all give a HUGE Sigh Of Relief!)

So why is everything still so Quacked-Up, you ask? Well, they left a HUGE mess, and the virus is still running amuck, so we are all going to have to join forces to arrest the virus and reverse the corruption and destruction it propagated. This is a mammoth task, but that's why most of you reading this book are even here on this planet! As part of the Cosmic Clean-up Crew, (CCC) your mission is to help get it all put back

in balance the way it was originally designed and intended to be. It is a group effort, and we need everyone's expertise both on and off-planet in order to get the job done!
(See https://www.firstwaveindigos.com/ for the rest of the story.)

But wait, that's not all! Just for coming here today, I have a special one-time offer that you won't find in stores! You also get some free secrets found in this book that will help you get the job done faster and more efficiently, so you will have more time to play! And there's more. Here is another special for you today, no one else but you. This is a one-time special offer you won't find anywhere else. If you join the CCC - Cosmic Clean-Up Crew today, you also get a surprise gift! You will get some free unsolicited advice from Hal! You never know when or how he will show up; he will just inundate you with his silliness and wisdom, and it will be a complete and total surprise! But wait, that's not all! Hal has brought with him some of the best Technician Beings from all over creation. They have new and inventive ways of getting into your HEAD computers, and planting the top-of-the-line virus destroying mechanisms, or ANTI-VIRUSES, which are, *Laugh and Release!* That's right, it is so simple, it's funny! Some good HEARTy belly-laughter could start a counter chain reaction, which can in turn knock you out of the nightmare you have been sucked into, setting you free! In this new position, you can act appropriately and get your creative juices going, so you can find more innovative ways of taking charge and cleaning up this whole ***Damn*** *Mess!*

If you get in step with Hal, the Cosmic-Jokester, your life will turn from tragic to magick! If we all work together and take this humor business seriously, we just might get things all cleaned up and make it back Home in time for dinner!

So… let's do a practice run here. Remember feeling threatened, angry, misunderstood, or hurt, and it just kept feeding on itself? (This seems to happen the most with people who are the closest to us: friends, family, and especially "significant others!") Well, the next time that happens, *take CHARGE of the situation instead of CHARGING the situation.* Go to Neutral…Center…and then ask, "How can I respond differently? What's REALLY going on? Is there an element of humor here somewhere?" Once this is accomplished, the hurt, anger, or fear, starts to dissipate. At that moment, you begin to take command again and the energy of the event and the emotions no longer own or control you! If you can get to the point where you see the humor in it all, and can truly laugh at the situation, that laughter will create and release chemicals and electro-magnetic waves, which put you in a position of Self-power. In this new position, you can broadcast this energy into the Universe, and it can heal what lies in your path.

Why not take this experiment to your study groups, meditation groups, and support groups… *especially* if you find yourself in the middle of, or involved with, one of those *whine groups!*

Use your creative energies and power to think up and try different methods of inducing contagious laughter to help you jump to the next level if you feel stuck. (Invite your Guides, Angels, and Cosmic Helpers in on it…you just may tap into some of the most profound cosmic truths and secrets of the Universe!) You'll heal and gain wisdom in some of the most HALarious ways, and guess what…IT'S FREE! *...which incidentally is quite ironic, because FREEDOM is what it creates!*

So there you have it... a few morsels of information that have been locked up and all but banned in our spiritual education systems. It's up to all of us to FEEL our way out of this crazy distorted illusion, and the only way ***out*** is ***through…. .through the Heart/CoreStar.*** If all we think, all we say, and all we do, is first filtered through this Master Control Center, a new perceptual seeing or vision will occur, and the bogus, unenlightened realities will be very clear, obvious, and ridiculous. If we continue to be willing to expand our perceptual borders, then just maybe we will remember all the ***forbidden knowledge*** pertaining to who we are personally, and also the true, authentic history of our planet and the Universe that has been so repressed and kept secret for such a long, long time.

This knowledge actually has no choice but to surface now, because we are in the gravitational pull of a UV-Light vacuum that is calling us all to our prospective Homes….. to our authentic selves. It is calling all of us to see with our new vision.

This Love Light is magnetizing us to the truths of who we are, what we've experienced, and what our innate talents are, so that we can easily and accurately be able to identify the lies, correct the errors, and heal the fractures that have been the cause of this bogus insanity for eons.

With this project complete, we'll wind up with a page full of PhDs in wisdom, and one Hal-Of-A mega adventure. We'll take the information from this experience, clear the negative emotions from our nervous systems, and download it for future references as data (0's & 1's), into our Soul's memory banks. That way everything is recorded, but the pain and suffering is not there to haunt us… just the data so we can read it, share it, and be ready for action if anything like this ever happens in the future… Now we can stop it before it gets out of hand. Until then, may you feel the Love and guidance of your **Heart/CoreStar** and connect with others who operate from their **Heart/CoreStar,** as you laugh your way through it all…..***and I'll see you on the other side!!!***

ENJOY THE JOURNEY!!!

In closing, I leave you with this meme that pretty much sums it all up!

MONEY, MONEY… WHO'S GOT THE MONEY?

This may seem to some of you, a pretty far-out and unrelated subject for a book that's supposed to be about healing. To others of you this makes perfect sense, because one of the serious and debilitating…and sometimes "terminal" illnesses many of us have is "Lack-itis," or "Cancer of the bank account!" If these infections of the monetary system are not challenging diseases and illnesses that you or your friends, family, or clients have, then feel free to skip this chapter, and we'll see you in the next chapter… (Actually, I'd like to see you in my office to find out how you got your immunities to these ailments!) To the rest of you, the following information could be *worth its weight in gold!* (Pun absolutely intended!)

WHAT'S WRONG WITH THIS PICTURE?

Examine the two charts on the next page and draw your own conclusions. The statistics in the first one were done in 1998 before the first edition of this book came out. The second set of stats were taken in March 2013 …after 9-11 and the 2008 bank bailouts. As you can see, finances have gotten worse for everyone BUT the Light-Destroyers. (Remember that there is White Light and Dark Light, both are considered "Light" in this book.)

This means that corruption on this planet has gone into critical mass and the tyrants are in dire need of a good karmic smack!

After you have reviewed and understand the charts, (*See Chapters 13-18 for an explanation of Light Keepers and Light Resisters*) you will notice that in 1998, Earth Beings pretty much got their fair share, as they represented 40% of the population and they got 40% of the $$$ …but not anymore! They are slipping into the category of the "have-nots" …while the Light Resisters, "the haves," are grossly consuming and hoarding the wealth!

You will also notice that there are twice as many Light-Conductors and Alphas on this planet as there used to be, so they are not just simply being cancelled out by the Light-Destroyers and Distractors as they once were!

What a rude awakening here! How could things get so unjust and out of balance!?

NOTE: This information and these statistics were given to me by Hal. It felt right, but at the same time seemed extremely illogical, (but then, much of what is happening here on Planet Earth right now is illogical and senseless.) I was quite surprised when someone sent me this short video entitled, *Wealth Inequality In America*: by "Politizane." https://www.youtube.com/watch?v=QPKKQnijnsM It confirmed the information Hal had given me. It is "off the charts" **…literally!** This video was made in 2013ish, and everything is far more intense now. The good news is that the masses are waking up at warp speed, flipping the tables and the shift is hitting the fan on the Dark Lords now!

NOTE: *The descriptions and dynamics of each type of Being are found in later chapters*

Key: L.D.= Light Distractor - L.A.= Light Assistor

~1998~

TYPE OF BEING	POPULATION %	% OF $$$, PROPERTY, COMMODITIES & CO.'S OWNED & CONTROLLED
EARTH	**40%**	**40%**
LIGHT RESISTER TEAM		
L.D. Beta	**20%**	**20%**
L.D. Alpha	**5%**	**15%**
Light Destroyer	**5%**	**15%**
	30%	**50%**
LIGHT KEEPER TEAM		
L.A. Beta	**20%**	**4%**
L.A. Alpha	**5%**	**4%**
Light Conductor	**5%**	**2%**
	30%	**10%**

Light Keepers Own 10% $
Light Resisters Own 50% $$$$$
Earth Beings Own 40% $$$$

* *

~2013~

TYPE OF BEING	POPULATION %	% OF $$$, PROPERTY, COMMODITIES & CO.'S OWNED & CONTROLLED
EARTH	**40%**	**12%**
LIGHT RESISTER TEAM		
L.D. Beta	**20%**	**10%**
L.D. Alpha	**5%**	**20%**
Light Destroyer	**5%**	**50%**
	30%	**80%**
LIGHT KEEPER TEAM		
L.A. Beta	**10%**	**4%**
L.A. Alpha	**10%**	**3%**
Light Conductor	**10%**	**1%**
	30%	**8%**

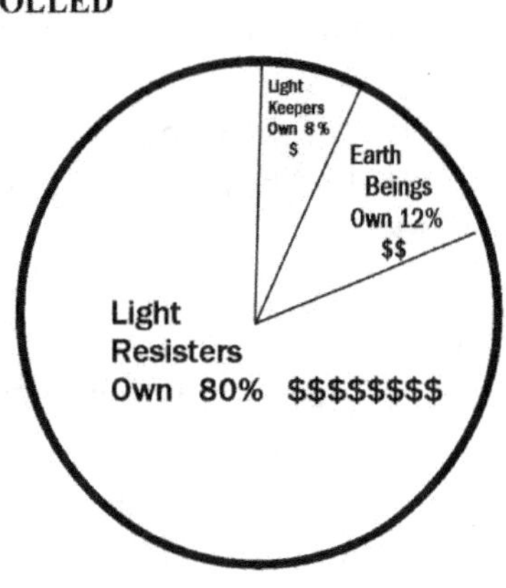

The good news is that things have to reach critical mass sometimes, before truth is exposed, creating so much evidence that you can't deny it or pretend it isn't there. Also, numerous FW-Indigos all over the globe are waking up to who and what they are, and accessing their X-Men abilities to bring Truth and Justice to this planet. (*The Occupy movement is one shining example.)* More good news! We have gridded the 3 major power/control centers on the planet: The City of London, Vatican City, and Washington D.C. with *Aulmauracite, the Stone of Truth and Justice.* These 3 power/control centers are feeling the effects of the grids, and as it's only going to get more intense, they can't escape… And the truth shall set us free!

You will also be happy to know that Hal has something to say about it all, and his message is just as applicable now as it was back then, maybe even more so now, because we are at that critical mass position and abrupt change is imminent. This change and transformation can be illuminating, and Lady Justice and Lady Karma can have their way with these corrupted beings. If we pull together, we can be *Karma and Justice Assistors*! What a concept, eh?

Here are some "Memos" Hal gave me in 1997. He gives answers to the million $ questions, and they're literally worth *way more* than their weight in gold! Are you ready????? ...Here you go!

(Memo #1 given in July of l997)

MEMO: To Light Workers (and players) everywhere. It is now time to take back your power in the form of $$$$$. As many of you may or may not know by now, you are, and have been for a very long time, under the spell of the tyrants who believe they govern your planet. They have been "whipping you into submission and fear" through financial tyranny, and causing you to get stuck on the gerbil wheel. You are fighting to keep your families alive from day to day, and you're afraid that if you stop for a rest, or even slow down, you will get further and further behind, and your financial obligations of food, clothing, and shelter for your family's basic needs will not be met….. and then you and your family will perish!

Add to these fears the real "in your face" intimidation from governmental bodies, taxing you from all sides and scaring you out of your mind. These "Tax Bullies," force you into their systems of *"health and warfare"…I mean welfare.* To those of you who are brave enough to say, "No thank-you," to their system, you will find it very difficult to survive because of how the $ system is set up.

Then add to this, the genetic and cellular fears that have been imprinted for centuries from dogmas and religions, which say, "If you have $$$ you will surely be wicked and corrupted." …"You can't be spiritual if you have $$$." *…"It's easier for a camel to go through the eye of a needle than for a rich man to get to heaven."*

You put all these in-*greed*-ients together and stir in some un-deserving and some fear of your own power, and… well… gosh… we'd say you've cooked up a real nice melting pot of S.S.S. (*Sustained Survival Syndrome).*

Now we say to you, is this any way to run a life??? How do you Light Beings ever expect to get anything done if you're constantly putting all your time, energy, and $ into mere survival? When do

you have time to *really* get into your spiritual contracts when you're so scared and busy and exhausted?

You don't even have time to stop and relax and smell some carnations... let alone contemplate and figure out why you're here and what you're supposed to be doing... let (*way, way*) alone the $... Yes $$$$$ to accomplish your missions! (Do you ever feel sometimes that you're playing out episodes of, "MISSION IMPOSSIBLE" and you're stuck somewhere in the middle... and the suspense is *killing you?*) WAKE-UP!!! It's time to move *through* the movie...Get it?

How many of you have an invention that would cut down or alleviate certain types of pollution? And how about you scientists and Tesla buffs who have information and technology that could change the world for the better? And how about you healers and Earth keepers, do you have techniques, methods, and information that could save a lot of pain and suffering? ...And tell us truly, what is the biggest thing that is keeping you stuck and unable to see your dreams come to pass? ...Now let's see...could it possibly be the big M word... $ $ $ $ $???

Yes, there are many ways of moving goods and services without $, but ultimately you get stuck somewhere along the line *because of the lack of it,* if you are seriously trying to make major changes with long-lasting effects! Let's face it, you're living in a $$$ $ystem, and in order to change or get out of the $$$ $ystem and truly become $overeign, and make a mark on this planet, *not just fade away and try to hide...* It takes $$$$$!!!!! ...and in LARGE amounts! (Are you with us here, are you getting the BIG picture now?)

Now let us ask YOU something. If you were a tyrant, and you wanted to keep people in bondage, and if you didn't want spiritual, social, and planetary evolution to occur so you could stay in power, what diabolical schemes would you create and enforce?

Well, let's see... most of the population is sick, depressed, and drugged up, (by choice or by prescription...*same thing*) ...antidepressants are running amuck these days...And let's not forget painkillers! And if that wasn't enough, you add to this the risk of living in a place where diseases are *unnaturally created* and being spread daily, yes *created and spread* daily!

Then there's the *imprinted* fears that if you ever do find a way out of this maze, you and the ones you love will be hurt or annihilated! (Search inward long and hard for this one, it runs deep and tries to hide when you look for it.) ...And intertwined and entangled through all of this are all sorts of $$$ I$$UES and hidden agendas!

Now, let us ask you another question. If *good people* are corrupted when they get $ ...then who *always* has control over the money and how it is used? ...And if everything revolves around how the $$$ is spent, and if the guys and gals wearing the white hats never stand up and take their rightful share of the $$$ and have some command over how and what it's used for ...then who do you suppose is handling and managing, *or rather mis-managing,* all the $$$?

You got it, those sneaky Grey Hats, and they're doing a *bang-up* job of it right now, and are having a pretty darned good time doing it!

Well Buckaroos, the tide's a changin' and it's time for a new ending to this movie, 'cause if it continues on, no one will win... everyone will lose, and we'll just have to start this movie over and over and over, (You remember the movie "Groundhog Day," it never ends till you get it right .....right?) So let's go to the editing room and do some *slicing and splicing,* and see what award-winning movie we can re-create!

First of all, let's get something straight. $$$ is the code that gets you into the Game of Life, so if you have any doubts as to whether or not you should have your access code to be a player in this game, let me ask YOU!!!, "If you had all the $$$ you wanted, what would YOU do with it?"

Would you make new drugs and electromagnetic devices to make people sick and docile so you could control them better? Maybe you would spend it making large, quarantined areas that look and *feel* like concentration camps so you could keep people under strict observation and control, or maybe you would create some far-out weapons that could maim, kill, and turn people into robots. Maybe you would use your $$$ on Tesla technology that could control emotions, responses, attitudes, and the will of the people, animals, and weather...so you could be sure they always do things YOUR way...and if they get smart and try to resist, then just turn up the *irritation juice* and get them fighting amongst themselves...and thinking their friends are their enemies...(That's a fun one to watch.) ...Then get them so scared and isolated in their efforts that all they do is create chaos! Maybe you would use your $$$ to do some far-out genetic experiments that would cause a lot of pain and suffering in the Plant and Animal Kingdom as well as to humans. Maybe you just want to be the *Big Cheese* Grey Hat, so you try and get all the $$$ and technology before the other Grey Hats do ...and you don't care what you have to destroy in order to be *THE BIGGEST CHEESE OF THEM ALL!!!* (Need we say more...?)

We said earlier that *the tide's a changin'* and who better to help with this tide change and *thorough clean up job,* than a mother ...or *Mother Energy?* Go inside and find your own unique way of communication and collaboration with this incredible feminine energy you have access to, and get the truth to manifest *inside and out!* It's *high tide* time you moved out of this *corrupted* patriarchal system that fights, scares, and tries to gain power in its effort to control The Feminine Ray...(It's a pretty whacked out concept, but it's ruled for eons here.)

Inside, you will find the ultimate Love Source that will lead you to the Truth, and assist you in this clean-up job that will *set you FREE!* Find your *own methods* of moving the $$$ energy back into the hands of the stewards of the God/Dess, so that the movie can finally have a happy ending!

Clan together with other *spunky Light Keepers* and create your own ceremonies, meditations, dances, songs...whatever it takes to move your emotions to *an all time high...* and put an end to the spell of $$$ oppression and strangulation that has been keeping you and your expression of Light in bondage!

Do some money laundering here! It's laundry day! Get your laundry supplies ready, and let's clean up the energy of all the "Filthy Lucre" that's floating around and coming through your hands. You have the supplies and washing instructions to turn this soiled $$$ energy into clean, fresh, bright, shiny, happy "DOUGH" that keeps EXPANDING and RISING!

You may want to do a Spiral Curse-Reversal Ceremony(SC-RC) to give yourself a jump start, (See www.FirstWaveIndigos.com for ceremony instructions) or some *"write and burn"* ceremonies to clean things up again and get the energy moving and transmuting. For general Practical Magickal Practices: if the moon is waxing, write on paper, cloth, monopoly money, (whatever *"gets you in the groove"*)...your desires and the things you would like to *create and have come into* your life. If the moon is waning, then you would write all the things you want *out* of your life... the things you want to eliminate and get rid of...(*Toilet paper might be an appropriate paper product for this one...ha haa)...get creative, but most of all get into the emotions of it...your emotions are the key here!*

Then with your decrees backed by these intense emotions, set fire to your writings and use the powers of alchemy to put your decrees into motion!

CAUTION! ***If you are indoors, please be aware of the Laws of Fire... I was witness to a write and burn where the conductor of this ceremony (not to mention Laura Lee's name or anything) was so caught up in the emotions and thrills of her creations that she darned near set the rug on fire!***

Get creative as you use your innate powers of alchemy to neutralize the oppressive energies and things that have damned your progress thus far. Continue your songs, dances, meditations, and ceremonies on a regular basis and don't let up...Be persistent...and be creative, try new things.

If you cannot band together with other Light Beings in human bodies, then team up with the Plant, Animal, and Mineral Kingdoms. (You'll probably want them with you anyway because they will surely feel your intent and give you support, and their consciousness is *superior in nature!*) ...Let your internal teacher help. You'll be amazed at what ancient information you have inside, if you allow it to come out... and most of all, be happy and excited for finally taking your power back!!!

And last but not lost, *and we do mean lost,* ask for assistance from your Spirit Guides, Guardians, and Angels... It's our jobs, and unlike many of you, we can't wait to get up and go to work, and we have a darned good time working over-time if necessary!

We think our job is a *professional party,* and we are avid party animals!!! So... Gitty-up and let's party hearty...AND REMEMBER... You're on the editing team, so let's get together and make this the award-winning movie of the century!!!

With all our Love, White & Dark Light, Laughter, and sense of adventure...

THE 555's ...or "THE HOWELL TONES"

(Memo #2 given in Sept. of 1997 *after one of the spunkiest Light Keepers around, by the name of Rose Konda, took the challenge to heart. She, along with the company and alliance of some of her favorite renegade sisters, came up with simple, but absolutely correct, understandings of how all this $$$ stuff works and how to make it work for YOU...and excitedly shared them with me.)*

MEMO: To the Light Keepers, and future $$$ Keepers. Excellent work Watson, I say there, I think you've got it! Rose is 100% "right on the money!" ***Ha, Ha - I just love puns! They're so… well, punny!*** **She got the pictures we've been sending, hurray!!! Her interpretation is sooooo right on!**

The reason that the Light Keepers are having such a difficult time with $$$ has to do with vibration! $$$ right now carries such a low vibration and is constantly being used for such ***low vibrational things,*** **that it is extremely difficult for Beings vibrating at a higher frequency to be able to handle it in any way, especially in large amounts! So even if they did overcome their $$$ guilt issues, they are still faced with this challenge of vibration!**

Rose's remedy is stupendous! You have to take the ***greenbacks,*** **or** ***"frog skins"*** **as she called them, and simply change their vibration to a high enough octave that you can reach them!!! There are many methods of doing this, and I would suggest you try as many as you can, "just for the HAL of it." Don't take it so seriously, have fun with it, and put a lot of emotion into your creations!**

Can you imagine how "*HAL*ARIOUS" it would be if the vibration of all the ***"filthy lucre"*** **out there was transformed into "love money," and it was pulsating at such a high vibrational frequency that all the cutthroat Corporate Tyrants and Monopolizers suddenly couldn't handle $$$ any more… and it just "slipped through their fingers" because of its vibration?**

"Think about it!!!"

HAL

NOTE: Toward the end of 2006, Hal instructed me to do something very off-the-wall and bizarre, (yes even for Hal this was a bit over the top) but what he said made so much pathetic sense, I just shook my head.

Hal told me that in order to raise the vibration of $$$, you first have to match it, or you can't touch it. He said that in 2006, $$$ got hijacked, and the only way you can get to it is to go undercover and *pretend* to be a part of the corrupted network. He said that using "love 'n light" to get into that system is a joke, and you will be locked out or kicked out quicker than a Fort Knox alarm system! The ONLY way into that "club" ...that "*good old boys' network*" is to sneak in though magick and get on the same vibe or wavelength. Now the trick is, since it is so appalling and so sleazy, no honorable and ethical person would go there! That is how they keep to themselves and keep the good people that would do good things with their money out of the game. Yes, some slip in, but only on a limited basis and are never allowed into the upper echelon or "inner circles" because that would ruin their upper class system of "haves and have-nots." This system has been defined, redefined, and refined for thousands of years and they are not about to give up their turf to some "benevolent twit" who might throw a monkey wrench into the class system that keeps them in power. *Power over the people... (animals and plants too...basically they think they own/rule the world)*...and at the top of the $$$ lords' food chain, is a gaggle of top-notch psychopaths! (Actually, most of the $$$ lords are psych/sociopaths... but if you call them on it, they will go out and contribute a few measly millions to a charity *for a tax break* and to make them look "normal.")

This is how they play the game and it has worked very well ...until now. People are catching on, and the internet is a total double edge sword to them. They can't play the game the way they used to because someone is always watching them...(*and it used to only be the other way around!*) Also, we now have enough CCC or Cosmic Clean-up Crew Members, *which include FW-Indigos,* incarnated on the planet who can see through their phony bologna and have the guts to stand up to them and call them out!

What Hal instructed me to do, honestly made me sick to my stomach, but it also made me laugh at the same time. He told me to take all my benevolent warm fuzzy things off my bedroom Altar and start over. He said I needed to make it a "Skank Altar!" He told me to put some nasty nighties, porn pictures from the internet, and other such things on there to represent the porn vibration. Then to add some old match books from casinos, some dice, playing cards, and anything I could think of that represents the energy in Vegas and other gambling institutions. He had me put some paper $$$ and coins in the middle. Then get pictures from magazines that represent high society and the ruling class. He said, "Understand that the porn vibration is intertwined and infiltrated in all of it, so make sure that energy is prominent." When I heard what he was saying I about laughed my tail off because I knew it was true: he was absolutely right! I had been doing research for my book, *The Anatomy of the Porn Vibration: What They Didn't Teach You in Sunday School,* so what he said really hit home to me. The paper trail in the porn industry goes EVERYWHERE and many of our global leaders are absolute perverts!

Hal said, "You can't just walk into that system, you have to be invited!" ... *And this Skank Alter was a way to sneak in the back door energetically and not get slimed too bad in the process!*

So I did as he instructed, and kept adding things. I lit the candles on the Altar to "turn it on" regularly. I really took it seriously. (I also had to keep my bedroom door closed so guests who wouldn't understand, would not see what was in there get the wrong impression!) I spent a lot of time with this Altar and kept updating and upgrading it.

Ok, it gets better… In about mid-2008, Hal told me to start researching solar energy systems because I was going to need that information, since I would soon be moving, and solar was an important part of my future. Now this one I really did laugh at. I had only been in my rented place about a year and a half and was barely making the rent each month. How in the heck did he figure I would be in a position to have my own house with solar electricity to boot! Well, six months later, *and about two years after I first put up my "Skank Altar,"* I did indeed move… (and this was in the middle of the bank bail-outs when many people were having very difficult times financially) …but for me, it was totally the opposite. Things started to fall magickly into place, and after much hard work and literally blood, sweat, and tears, I am living in a log house that is being serviced by solar energy!

Then, in the summer of 2011, some strange things happened that involved Cryptos, (*See Chapter 19 on Creepy Cryptos*) and through some *close call interventions that could have left me homeless again*, it all backfired on them, and I am now the owner of this house! It is in the small town I have yearned to live in for nearly two decades, and sits in the middle of a beautiful, enchanted cedar forest! I "bypassed the gold" or all "normal methods" to get here… and here I am, still alive and kicking while living out my fondest dreams! I have transformed this place into a permaculture paradise and am finally getting back in touch with nature and Nature Spirits in a very real, authentic way. This place is absolutely magickal with a huge dragon sculpture in my back yard, herb gardens, and a sanctuary for all the forest creatures in this area. It is also a refuge for my pet ducks and pet rescue chickens that came from an evil factory farm. We are all living out our fondest dreams!

I have to say that I KNOW without a doubt it all started with my "Skank Altar!" This magickal Altar worked BIG time, and I feel that I broke an M-field (Morphogenetic Field) by following Hal's instructions. Now, those that come behind me will have it easier and they will be able to do it quicker! I really "get it" now…it is all so clear… and guess what? I am ready to go to the next level! Who knows where that might take me…(and YOU too!)

This is one of the biggest secrets of all time… and you have just been handed the keys! ~Use them well…..

Lady Mistycah & Hal

(PART II, THE SEQUEL)

MONEY, MONEY… WHO'S GOT THE MONEY?

THAT WOULD BE… SHOULD BE YOU!!!

NOTE: In July of 2013, Hal gave me more "inside Intel" on back doors into ***The Money Game,*** and I feel it is appropriate to share it with you now.

Hal said that in order to really be comfortable with LARGE amounts of money, you need to KNOW that YOU KNOW *exactly* what to do with it when you get it! It is amazing how many people really believe that they wouldn't know what to do with "mega bucks" and that the corporations, the millionaires & billionaires are the only ones who are supposed to have the BIG Bucks because they know "how to handle it" best. I know for a FACT that this is the biggest bunch of doo-doo that the Dork Lords…I mean Dark Lords have brainwashed the masses with! If you are one of those who has been duped, it's time to get serious about getting a $$$$$ attitude adjustment! Just because you have not been privy to extreme wealth in this life, does NOT mean that is true for your "other existences" …think about THAT for a while, and you'll start making sense out of nonsense!

This ***inside Intel from Hal***, who is ***outside the system*** and can see clearly what's going on ***inside our system***, is a huge breakthrough for all of us who came here to set things straight!

Are you ready??? Get a pen and paper, and listen up!

The Money Game Plan

Make detailed plans and allocations for:

$100,000.00
Ok, that's good, now go to the next level:

$500,000.00
Half a million…you're just getting started!

$1,000,000.00
That's 1 million for those who have a hard time with all the 0's!

$500,000,000.00
Now we're cracking the matrix… This is half-a-billion …just sayin'…..

$1,000,000,000.00
…OK, at this point we can really start making HUGE waves!
Incidentally, my husband and I have been great supporters of the www.NoBillionaires.com campaign. On one of their interviews they said, "**No Billionaires**, ***because 1000 millionaires are better than one billionaire!*** This is true for most people, **but NOT for those who came here specifically to "bust the monetary system!"**

Now… you can stop there or step into the Illuminati High Rollers game….but you'd better be savvy…..they don't take kindly to "outsiders" invading their turf!

$500,000,000,000.00
That's five hundred billion, half a trillion…don't even try to count it out in one dollar bills!

$1,000,000,000,000.00
Ok, we're into the Trillions now, and that means we're getting into the game of the Royal (inbred) Families. For those of you here to "Bust The Monetary System" this is where all the action is.

GO FOR IT!

…And May The Force (& The Current$y) Be With You…

When I first started my list and began playing this "Money Game," I was amazed at the "shift" that happened in and around me. I can attest that this ***inside trader/traitor Intel*** from Hal is a HUGE M-Field breaker. This list you are making is the beginning of your stepping into your $$$ power and sneaking in a different back door to the money game… the ones the Dark Lords have controlled for eons …***the corrupted monetary system***. Combine this with your Skank Altar, getting rid of the implants and forced agreements that are keeping you away from the $$$ that is rightfully YOURS, and you will see a WHOLE new $$$ game!

Please write to me at Knights@MistycHouse.com and tell me your success stories of how using these inside tips from Hal, and ***really*** getting serious about this ***Money Game Plan,*** changed your reality, your life, and also the lives of those you have stewardship over.

"Onward & Forward!"

P.S. For updates on $$$, see my blog "The Power of Gold" at:
http://firstwaveindigos.com/blog/

SOUL BRAIDS, SOUL MATES, & TWIN FLAMES

Ahhh yes, Soul Braids, Soul Mates, & Twin Flames.....What mystique and romance in these words... and rightfully so. But on the other hand...they can be the cause of much longing, heartache, pain, and in some cases, be downright disastrous, if you don't understand what it's all about and see the bigger picture! I bring to you now, one bird's-eye view of this picture...the way I saw it when I went up and looked. If you want to know more, or find out if I'm telling you the truth, you'll just have to go up, see for yourself, and get your own picture of how it *really* is! While we're on the subject of truth, I'd like to give you my perception of the similarities and differences between TRUTH and ACCURACY, which will be important when you study this concept and other parts of this book. It will also be useful when you're evaluating your own life and the things in it.

TRUTH- Can be different things at different times...and is always subject to perception.

ACCURACY- Is more solid and stable...and doesn't have as much variance to it.

The best way I can describe them both, in order to give them both justice and validity, is this: Remember in the movie, "Star Wars," when Luke Skywalker confronted Obi-Wan Kenobi and asked him why he lied to him when he said his father was betrayed and killed by Darth Vader?

Luke: *Why didn't you tell me? You told me Vader betrayed and murdered my father.* **Obi-Wan:** *Your father... was seduced by the Dark Side of the Force. He ceased to be Anakin Skywalker and BECAME Darth Vader. When that happened, the good man who was your father was destroyed. So what I told you was TRUE... from a certain point of view.*

What Ben told Luke in the beginning was *TRUE* but not *ACCURATE.*

Understand the difference now between the two?

The information I am about to give you is ***true,*** to my knowledge, and *you* will have to decide how ***accurate*** it is.

As you study the following diagram, you'll see two Soul Braids: two of many, many Soul Braids out there. In the center of each braid is a *solid* Core. This Core is the heart and the brain of the collective braid. This Core is also their center of stability, their umbilical cord, the energy line or lifeline that keeps them together and gives them strength, and is a reference point to bring them back together, or home again, after interacting, intertwining, and collaborating with another braid. As you can see, each braid moves together as one unit, but from time to time a strand will go and intertwine with another strand from another braid for a while to do a collaborative mission together. *(Strand J and strand 10 are moving into "mission position.")* When it is done, the strands go back *home* to their original braid, download the information and education from that mission to the Core, and the entire braid gleans all the wisdom from it! It's a marvelous setup that can demonstrate pure synergism at its best...providing the braid is working properly!

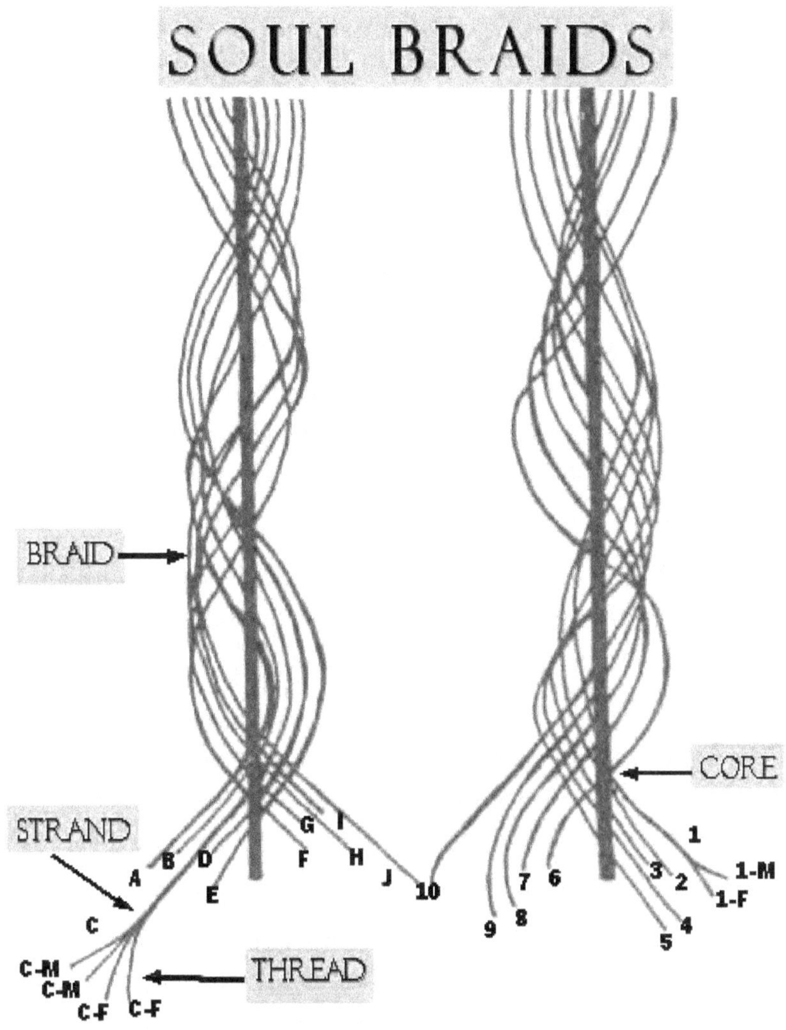

Have you ever been in a space where you felt like you were all alone even though there were a lot of people with you? …And that loneliness turned into a longing for something you weren't even sure of… not even knowing quite what it was you were looking for? …And then that longing took form and you knew it was for something...or some-one you once knew…some-one so close to you, you could almost read each other's thoughts…some-one like yourself... some-one who could understand you, and you them… some-one you loved and trusted… completely?

Well my friends, most likely what you were picking up on was the memories of your Soul Braids… and probably the ones that were the closest to you such as braids B&C. They have been moving closely in the same direction for eons! Every so often they cross paths and connect to F, G, H, I, & J, but they do it together and they are always next to each other… until they go on a mission with other strands from other Soul Braids. These missions can be a great adventure and totally exhilarating, but they also can be very difficult and stressful, and many times even risky! Sometimes several strands go on these missions together…sometimes even the whole braid intertwines with another braid… it just depends on what is needed and what strategies are necessary to do the best job. This is why the Core is so important. It keeps everything clear and in order so that when the mission is complete, each braid can gravitate back to its home base without getting all tangled up in knots and losing its direction.

If you look at strand C, you'll notice that it also has several threads that make up the strand. These threads or filaments can likewise satellite out and gather information, education, and wisdom, that when collected, are downloaded to bring variety and strength to the strand…which in turn, brings strength and wisdom to the entire braid.

When you have these feelings of longing, it's hard to say without examining it what the longing is for. It might be for a strand or thread that had been close by, or it might be for the whole braid because you are on a mission with another braid. But sometimes it's for a strand from another braid that you had a long, fun and fruitful mission with, and you just miss it and want to hang out again! You will have to be the judge and evaluate each one on a case-by-case basis to get the correct perception, but at least now you have a point of reference picture to stimulate your memory banks with!

I said earlier that a Soul Braid can have total flow and synergism if working properly. This is ab-**soul-**lutely correct, the operative words being, "working properly!" Sometimes, because of unforeseen challenges and mishaps, things go "haywire," and some of the strands (or even the whole braid) can get "out of order." Understand also that not every strand on each braid is on the same evolutionary spiral, and to assume that every strand, on every braid, is equal at all times, would be a misperception of *truth*, and completely *inaccurate.* Some of the strands are gaining information and data by a variety of modalities, and some of them may not seem very loving! Also, there may be some of the strands that learn very quickly and only need to have a lesson once, while others need to have it "pounded into their heads!" There may be some strands on a braid that are so "out of order" that the rest of the strands are *embarrassed to have them on their braid!* This is why when you encounter some of your *"Soul Strands"* or *"Soul Mates"*…some of them may be blissful reunions, while others may be uncomfortable and disappointing! There have even been a few occasions where a strand has gotten so far *"out of order"* and *so polluted* that it had to be "clipped from the braid" in order for the poison and damage not to spread to the rest of the braid! (Don't worry though, this strand can go straight to the Cosmic Recycle Bin to be *cleaned out, cleaned up* and *"re-wired,"* so it can be reinstated later on. If that doesn't work, there is always the *"spare parts department,"* where it can join in again somewhere, somehow in the future.)

So what *is* the difference between Soul Mates, Soul Braids, and Twin Flames, or is there a difference? Well, as you probably have figured out, Soul Mates are parts of a Soul Braid and happen whenever close contact is made, either on the same braid or connecting to a different one. Twin Flames on the other hand, have a bit of a different *twist,* and can be in a few different forms and created in a few different ways. It is also important to note that there are some Beings in and around this Universe that were created to be androgynous or whole unto themselves, some with 3 polarities instead of our 2 polarity male -female …and the polarity possibility list goes on and on. If you feel you were not created with a Twin Flame, you maybe be ab***soul***utely correct as not all life forms have them, BUT as you will find out, that situation can be remedied if you hook into or are adopted into a braid that is headed in that direction.

Now look at the picture of the braids… and study strand 1-M &1-F on the left. This one could be a possible "Twin Flame" provided that both the M-Male and the F-Female threads have collected enough data to qualify to be in total sync with each other. When this happens, they become a total mirror image of the other, separate in polarity, but totally united in intent and purpose. What occurs with this mixture of pure desire, is pure fire and pure magic… and it doesn't happen very often!

On even a rarer occasion, the entire braid has evolved to such a position that the whole left half unites and becomes "one" M-Male polarity, and the entire right half becomes "one" F-Female polarity…..and then the "whole" unites and becomes ***one giant*** **"Twin Flame!"** This my friend, is an ultimate *At-one-ment,* and its flame is so awesome, captivating, and beautiful, that it cannot be described in words. There is just no way you could communicate the magnificence of what it looks like and what it emits, you'd just have to see it, hear it, and *feel* it to understand! This state of alignment and synergy, in my opinion, is truly worth however many eons of time and experience it takes to make it happen…and to be able to *own* the experience! I have not personally encountered one of these on Planet Earth, but it occurred in the Ultra Violet Realm (UV-Realm) outside of this Holographic Universe. (See www.FirstWaveIndigos.com for the history of the Great UV-Realm.)

There are many variations of the *Soul Braid-Soul Mate* structure, but this will give you some basic information to get you started in your quest for understanding the *UN-Earthly* feelings, sensations, and memories you sometimes get when you meet a total stranger. The old cliché, "Oh, I must have known you in a past life" may be true, but then there may also be some deeper connective tissues or threads that hold you and bind you together… "for better or for worse." …Sometimes it's a double-edged sword. Whatever it is, you can make the experience serve you… it's entirely up to YOU how you interpret it!

To all of you romantics out there, I tell you *truthfully,* I know in my heart that these Soul Braids & Twin Flames exist. I also know that in each one of our memory banks, we all have some sort of recollection of this magnificent fire that blissfully takes your breath away just to witness it! …..And I for one am going to continue my quest to reunite with the whole of me and ***feel*** the joy and ecstasy this creates, and continues on***…..Into Forever*!**

May The Force Be With You,

May your memories be awakened…

And may you feel the fire from **The Core Of Your Being,**

That brings you the Authentic Love…..

Which will lead you to…..

Your Self!!!

DYSFUNCTION-JUNCTION

"Howdy partner! Glad to see you could make it! Now why don't'cha take y'ur boots off there at the door and come on in and put y'ur feet up!

Here, have y'urself a cold sarsaparilla, and make y'urself right at home in that there rockin' chair. We have a visitor here a yakkin' with us who's not from around this neck of the woods, and he's a tellin' us some stories that'll make y'ur ears curl!

Go right ahead there, Mr. Hal... You were a tellin' us about those whatcha-ma-call-its..... those Attachment doohickeys."

Thank you kindly, and could you be so good as to give me another round of sarsaparilla before I continue? Yeah..... that's good, fill'er right up to the top there. Thanks..... ahhhh... root beer is my favorite drink, you know!

Now, let's see, where was I... Oh, I was a explaining about the Attachment "doohickeys" (very descriptive word by the way), that many of you place on each other. This is a very common practice here on Planet Earth, and this practice is darned near practiced to perfection! These Attachments get stuck, and sort of like pine gum on your britches, it's hard to see it until someone points it out to you... and then you have a devil of a time getting it off (...unless you can figure out what to use to dissolve it!) Seriously, these Attachments are a lot like pine gum: sticky, gooey, and *extremely tacky,* if you know what I mean. They're also comparable to a pit bull or a powerful magnet; they're really hard to pull off unless you know what the trick is!

These Attachments *really are* magnetic in nature, and are devices a lot of people are using down here to plug into each other. The way I look at it, it's pretty darned goofy once you understand how it all works, and your "shrinks" would surely label it..... "*extremely dysfunctional!*"

You know, where I come from, this place you folks are living in is sometimes referred to as, "Dysfunction Junction." Life-Forms come from *all over creation* just to watch and try and figure out ways of helping the folks here get out of the muck and the mire they get stuck in, which seems to happen nearly every time anyone *even gets near the place*!

They have to be ever so careful and alert because, in their efforts to help *through observation and transmission*, some of them get too close to the borders..... and "Shluuuupe" they get sucked into the muck themselves! Once you get stuck, this muck makes you lose your senses, makes you sort of "titched in the head," and then you become part of the muck too! *...unless you have the guts, the focus... and the strength, inside and out, to pull yourselves free!*

One of the prime ingredients in this "Dysfunction-Junction's" muck, is the *Attachments* folks get stuck in, when what they're trying to do is make *Connections!*

Tell me, have you ever been witness to close relationships where it seemed like things were pretty lop-sided? ...Where one side or party was constantly ready and willing to do everything and anything it took to keep the outfit going...and do it with bright eyes and a bushy tail? (...Kind of like a cross between the volunteer fireman and the Energizer Bunny.)

On the opposite side, the other party was constantly in demand of time, energy, resources, and attention..... And this dynamic continued day after day after day until.....well... even Energizer Bunnies, *if used on a constant basis,* will slow down and lose the spring in their hop! Their little batteries will start to lose their charge, and to look at them, you'd think you're about to hear their final drum beat. Then just when you think he's hopped his last hop, the other party gets the old charger out, or comes through with a brand spanking new battery! (This can come in a variety of ways...such as a good dose of guilt, a hunk of intimidation, and even a quantity of benevolent acts that seem so good you'd think the tide was turning!) ...But it reeks of deathbed repentance, and just like a wooden nickel, or a barn with no roof...most of the time it's pretty useless!

This scenario plays itself out over and over and over again, each time with the absorbent *soaking* party getting smarter and more calculative till they have this rebound system down to the precision timing of a Swiss clock! ...And in the meantime, the Energizer Bunny wears its little hoppers out, the drum has gotten a hole beaten into it, and the spring inside that makes him hop, has lost its "boingity-boing." The Bunny has used up all its resources in his efforts to "make things work,"...and now he's about ready for the recycle bin.....*because even when he's on his "last leg" he wants to be of service.*

Now let's get a little bit *real* here. Can you tell me what's wrong with this picture? Can you figure out what the moral is to this sad Bunny *Tail-Tale*?

Well, the way I see it is, you have a classic case of "*Attachment-itus*" going on here. If you take a look at these diagrams, you can clearly see that one side of *an Attachment* doesn't have the capacity to give, *only draw, take, and absorb.* I really can't use the analogy of *a sponge* on this one, because *even a sponge* will release and give what it has absorbed... *when it's squeezed*!

Compare this with the diagram of the *Connection,* which is also magnetic in nature, but the flow of energy is not pulled all to one side, or sucked into the other one like the Attachment... which totally overpowers, or *sucks the life out* of the other. A *Connection* is completely different with its synergistic flow of giving and receiving simultaneously. It's the ultimate standard to gauge any relationship with, *especially the ones entitled "significant other."*

Since a picture's worth a 1,000 words, I'll let you study this one and ponder it yourself to find your own personal interpretation.

Magnetic Atachments

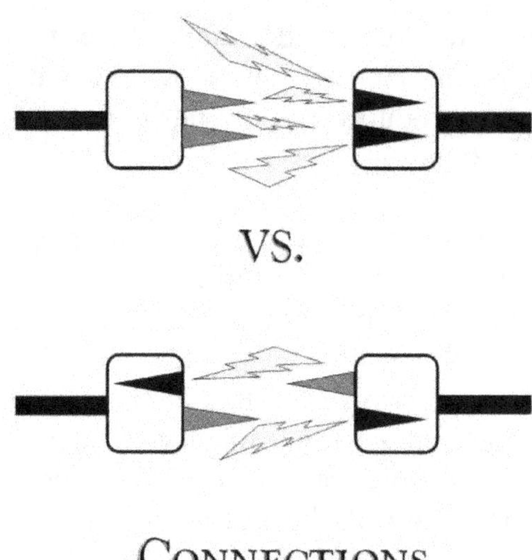

Connections

Another prime ingredient in this "muck" is the absence of ***COMPASSION*** in ***PASSION!*** Many relationships get sick and die because either there is *no passion* in the relationship, or the passion that is there, is void of the *consideration* and *caring* elements in *compassion and the **Feminine Ray***. When this absence occurs, the only thing left is the forceful motion of *intense excitement* of the ***Masculine Ray,*** which can easily get degraded… **and if unmonitored, can turn to *rage* and *violence!***

And so it is with the *lust* portion of *passion.* If not laced with *love, consideration,* and *caring*…the thrill, excitement, and the potential of spiritual evolution and expansion are overthrown…and again, the only things left for expression are ***RAGE AND VIOLENCE!*** *(This energetic is proliferating in the Porn Vibration, and is constantly pushing the envelope for a bigger quantity that is more extreme… **making rage and violence acceptable and "normal.")***

If this part of the muck keeps growing and expanding its borders, it will swiftly move in and destroy all life in its path, like the giant nothing in the movie, "The NeverEnding Story."
No wonder love and romance seem so foreign and distant….. and something that only happens in Fairy Tales! There are very few living examples of this kind of relationship left at "Dysfunction-Junction," and if something doesn't happen fast, the muck will take over and totally dominate this place!

I heard a comment on the streets there at *Dysfunction-Junction* that made me chuckle. It was from a woman who said, *"Chivalry isn't dead, it's just that women have hogged most of it!"* Is there some truth to this?

What we need here to set it all straight, is to balance the scales, and in order to do this, we must have some "Modern Day Knights" somewhere in the midst of all this muck… Modern Day Knights that can see clearly *and feel* the distress signals they're right in the middle of….. *and then have the strength and vision to do something about it!*

We have to create a permanent solution to this icky situation, and one of those permanent solutions is that we have to have strong, benevolent women, strategically placed, who are *willing* and *able* to be the dream-weavers… to create the dream of a balanced synergism between male/female…..and then hold firm to that vision of male/female synergism …..***especially when confronted or challenged****!*

In this dream, there also has to be the vision of reinstating compassion in the passion. A vision of men and women who release their *Attachments*, and then change their prongs so they can only plug into *Connections.*

This is the only way you can ever work as a synergistic unit!

Most importantly, and it's imperative, there must be an impeccable vision of *Love* and *romance* backed by *emotion* as a constant element in their lives. This vision needs to include honor, integrity, and trust as the foundation for every creation, *physical and nonphysical.* (I know this is not an easy task, **nevertheless it is possible!)**

At the center of this new web of life, are the Kingpins that can put it all into proper order. These Kingpins are the elements that can weave the spells to change it all. And who do you suppose these Kingpins might be? …The Master Creators…of course!

These are the valiant women who have the audacity to stand on the front lines and fearlessly change the movie script. These are the bold women who can release their own anger, resentment, grief, and suffering, and can reinstate wholeness, unity, and clarity within themselves. In this new position of strength, power, and wisdom, they can then start *believing and trusting in the Masculine Ray again, believing in men and in their ability to conquer the* ***"muck,"*** *the* ***"giant nothing!"*** *…****which begins to a great extent through the nurturing and re-educating of their own sons!***

These Kingpin women need to unite and support one another as they create and sustain a new, unpolluted vision of camaraderie, Love, and unity with their male counterparts …without getting discouraged with the multifaceted, multilayered damage that has been done.

They must know that they are the Master Creators here, and whatever position they have found themselves in, ***they allowed or even skillfully created*** in a grand plan to understand and educate themselves as to the intricacies of the pollution and distortions in this dysfunctional juncture! Each woman created different scenarios in her life, to bring her the wisdom of the internal workings of the fractures and illusions in this place. In this position, all of her experiences… **Every Single One!**… are of value and service to her!

As these Kingpins sift through the rubble of their own lives, and use these experiences to empower themselves, they will then have the knowingness within, that they have the power and tools to fulfill their Contracts and Sacred Agreements. They will know that they have what it takes to call up the memories of their commitments to come here to this dysfunctional mess and be the first to assess the damage. They will remember how to use their feminine intuition to know where to start, and how best to proceed, to clean up this mess permanently with intuition and Love….. ***which incidentally, may need to be "tough Love" at times!***

Then we need to have *all strong brave men everywhere*, take hold of this vision, *knowing that they're being supported and assisted by the Kingpin dream-keepers*, and hold onto this vision as they put it into action and form.

We need our men to have the strength and courage to take their previous ***distorted images*** of how things *should be,* and *burn and release* them, in order for the new vision to stay pure and unpolluted.

We need our men to take that giant leap and *believe in themselves again, as they trust in the dream-keepers and in their abilities to be the Master Creators that they are, and thus create a new paradigm... a paradigm where women hold men close to their hearts, and keep the dream from collapsing.*

Then and only then, will these ***Real Men*** acquire the extreme amount of courage and trust in themselves that it takes to be able to *conquer and tame the distorted beasts that infiltrated the* ***Masculine Ray*** *within!*

There you have it folks, the true-life story of a place you know all too well. It's all up to you now.

What happens next is anyone's guess, but know this.....

A spy from outside has just infiltrated the security systems of "Dysfunction-Junction," out-swum the alligators in the moat, scaled the walls, anesthetized a few guard-dogs along the way, and was able to sneak this information to you before it could be confiscated! It's safely in your hands now, but time is speeding up so you'll have to act fast.

We have time to change the dream before it becomes *a perpetual nightmare*, but we don't have time to put it off...or pretend it's not there. *Denial on this one could be lethal!*

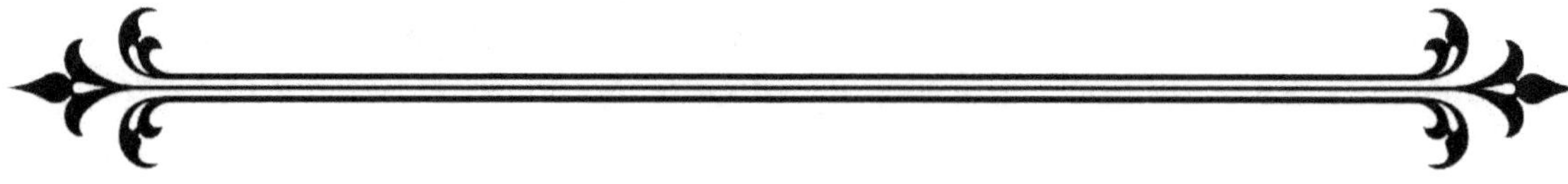

Before I put my hat and boots on and head for home, I want to share a highly impeccably-timed decree that was recently made. This decree was intended to, and *is… changing the consciousness grid…*and may very well, just change the outcome and the destiny of "Dysfunction-Junction," *if enough* ***Knights and Ladies …and especially the Lady Knights*** *get this message in time!*

For all you hopeless romantics out there, I say to you now:

"Give up your hope and trade it in for trust…because some new situations have been set into motion …and if you're really as desirous for true romance and chivalry to return *...free of the muck and the mire of the past* as I think you are... *Then get ready for some* ***serious*** *action…"*

"Here Come The Knights!"

On This Day July 14, 1998
And From This Day Forth...

A Universal Call Is Made
To Activate All The Real Men
Who Remember And Are Willing To Live By...

"The Knight's Code"

You Are Now Hereby Being Called To Action,
It Is Time For Battle!
(...Or There Will Be Nothing Left To Battle For.)

As You Take On Your Armor, Your Shield, And Your Sword.....
Do You Have The Memory And The Courage
To Activate Yourself...
And Bring Forth A Living, Breathing, Knight
Into This New Millennium?

Do You Have The Wisdom, The Will, The Strength,
The Valor, And The Power It Takes To Be A Knight.....
And Live By The Knight's Code From This Day Forth
Until The Moment Of Your Last Breath?

Oh Great And Valiant Knights Of The Earth
Come Forth Now And Be Counted
The Time Has Finally Come.
(You Know Who You Are.)

Wake Up... Arise...

Let Your Destiny Begin!

"The Knight's Code"

(An Old Code For A New Era)

~A Knight Is True "Blue"…..And Is At Peace With His/Her God-Goddess.

As a Knight, you will be honest and just in all business and personal relationships.

~A Knight Can Be Trusted, For A Knight Honors His/Her Word.

As a Knight, you will do what you committed to do, when you committed to do it, or make other arrangements…..or die in the process!

~A Knight Has A Profound Sense Of Self Respect…

Paving the way to fully love and honor his/her beloved.

~A Knight Owns Himself/Herself. No Influence Or Substance Dictates Or Runs Their Life And The Lives Of Those Around Them.

As a Knight, you overcome all your addictions. The true armor of Knighthood is on the inside, ***not*** *on the outside.*

~A Knight Thinks Before Speaking, For Once Words Are Spoken…

As a Knight, you are bound by your words!

~A Knight Uses Wisdom And Discretion In Word And Actions.

As a Knight, you are considerate and compassionate in all things.

~A Knight Takes Daily Action To Fortify And Strengthen;

Your body, your mind, and your spirit.

~A Knight Is Confident, And Abhors Arrogance.

As a Knight, you know that the arrogant ***think*** *they're grand….. the confident* ***are*** *grand!*

~A Knight Is Strong…..Yet Gentle With Women, Children, And Animals.

As a Knight, you use your Might To Defend The Weak!

~A Knight Activates The Brain Before Using Brawn…

When faced with a challenge or an opponent.

~A Knight Has A Light Heart And A Sense Of Humor.

As a Knight, you make even the most grueling task fun and memorable.

~A Knight Knows When A Joke Is Destructive.

As a Knight, you are willing to take a stand when a joke is harmful.

~A Knight Uses Grace And Dignity In Words And Actions,

Especially in the company of women and children.

~A Knight Honors And Respects Procreative Power.

As a Knight, you ***Always*** *take responsibility when using those powers!*

~A Male Knight Honors And Reveres Women And Their Feminine Nature.

As a Knight, you know that proper interaction with feminine power is a link back to your source… Therefore you are ready to willingly protect and defend that power - even unto death!

~A Knight Has A Passionate Love And Respect For Nature And The Planet Earth.

As a Knight, you use your strength and courage to act when they are threatened or violated.

Oh Great, Honorable, And Noble Knights Of This World.....

Step Out Of Your Hate, Your Anger,
And The Pains Of The Past.

Step Out Of Your Corporate Worlds...
And The Hunger For Useless Power!

Put On Your Armor Of Honor,
Pick UP Your Shield Of Love,
And Your Mighty Sword Of Truth!

Be Living Proof That Chivalry And Valor
Are Alive And Unyielding!

Do You Have The Strength, The Courage,
The Wisdom, The Ancient Encoded Memories,
And The Passion It Takes.....

To Be A Millennial Knight ?

This decree given to Laura Lee Mistycah July 14, 1998 on Mt. Spokane,
By "The Lady Of The Lake".....Auraura ©

Since "The Knight's Code" was written in the summer of 1998, it has been reprinted, put into several publications, and displayed on many websites. I have received nothing but wonderful responses back from the people who allowed this code to find its way into their hands and hearts! People from all walks of life, who have been longing for honor and nobility in their present existence, suddenly acquired a grand re-igniting of this flame. With a renewed conviction and determination, they started putting the fire back into their lives. They began to reinstate the valor, gallantry, and heroism of what some would consider to be a *fairy tale!* In fact, many have told me that it gave them hope and clearer vision. Some said it activated powerful memories, and gave them the courage to take on their *present day* Warrior Quests.

In addition to this, one of the most frequent comments I heard was, "I just loved the Knight's Code, it really struck a deep emotional chord within me, as I remember those days…but what about the Ladies, what about the Ladies Code? You need to put The Ladies Code in this book too!"

I have pondered and thought about this a lot, trying to figure how I could find out what "The Lady of the Lake" might have in mind to empower and restore true femininity back to the women of this challenging era. The answer came catapulting at me like a bolt of lightning.

I gave one of my editors, Ronnie, (who by then, with all the late night editing sessions, had become one of my closest friends and allies) a poem that had been coming to me in segments for several years. I finally completed it, and just wanted her to proof it, as well as give her a copy for possible framing. She said after reading through it, "This is great…are you putting it in your book?" I started to respond, "Well I guess I could… I'm not quite sure *how* or *where* to fit it in," …and then it hit me….. THIS IS THE COUNTERPART TO THE KNIGHT'S CODE! THIS IS WHAT I'VE BEEN ASKING FOR, AND SEARCHING FOR….. AND IT'S BEEN RIGHT UNDER MY NOSE ALL THIS TIME!!!!! (Well, actually it's been hanging on my wall above my altar!) When it revealed its purpose to me, it was so obvious it was almost a *joke*… (and I could just feel Hal in the corner, laughing his fake mustache off!)

So now you have a little background on how this came to be. As you read it, may the fire in your memory banks be re-ignited, and may you understand at a soul, Core level, what the true feminine nature of woman really is.

It is my desire that all noble women everywhere, will have the opportunity to ponder and contemplate these words, *(as well as their subtleties,* in their hearts. With a clear, pure image of their true nature and power, it will become easy and automatic for them to release the bondage and repression that has been confining them for eons. As they continue to disengage and free themselves from their inhibitions, doubts, and fears….. they will then be in position to morph into **the Power and Excellence of their True Feminine Nature….. The Goddess.**

What Is A Goddess?

A Goddess is strong and powerful.
A Goddess is mystical and creative.
A Goddess is intelligent and wise.
A Goddess is pure laughter and joy.
A Goddess is loving and inspiring.

A Goddess is Sensual and Beautiful
...and She Knows It!

Therefore, **She never hides or represses it.**
Instead, She allows and cultivates it,
Then She emanates and projects it…

Without the least concern
as to how others will receive or interpret it!

~ ~ ~ ~ ~

She is the most powerful Force in the Universe,
The very essence of Creation!

A Goddess is fearless, because
She Knows She Can't Be Conquered!

Ψ Ψ Ψ

She Is A Woman Who Realized…

~SHE WAS GOD!~

EVOLUTIONARY SPIRALS
&
THE 5 TYPES OF BEINGS PLAYING ON THIS PLANET

What you are about to enter now, is for many of you, a wake-up call to bring you out of a deep, black-hole sleep. As you allow yourself to open your eyes and get adjusted to the light, you may find that you can take more conscious command over your actions and experiences.

Some of you will be so relieved at finding this information, that your body will fill with serenity and joy, and you may even start to laugh! You will finally understand your previous pitfalls and know how to rearrange your interactions with others, making sure they are clear, and flow with ease instead of constant conflict.

This could very well be, for those of you who are encoded to this particular wake-up call, *"The Light of a New Dawn".....as opposed to, "The Dawn of the Dead."*

In the Land of Spirals there is constant movement, nothing stagnates, nothing stays the same. There are some Beings here though, who are super speed-demons and move so swiftly and gracefully it appears that the ones they leave in the dust are standing still… but it is just an illusion. All Beings are in constant motion, even if it's *slow motion!*

The land of spirals is also a land where there is absolutely **NO CHEATING!** ***No brown-nosing… No kissing up… And No buying your way to the next level!***

Unlike many corporate structures, this advancement system is *always* fair and just. No one is in a position that they can't handle, and no one is stuck or held back from a promotion they deserve, because every advancement in this education and evolution system is 100% earned!

As you read and study this section of *Kryahgenetics*, understand that the reason for the names and classifications of these Beings **is not** for the purpose of labeling or finger pointing… *heaven knows we have enough of that going on already!* No, the purpose is to gain awareness and understanding so that you can better put together game strategies backed by Love and Humor. The reasons for the names and profiles are for general identification, and for clarity, *not for judge-ment and condemnation!* Stay clear of and watch out for that trap…..*It's a hard one to see once you are caught in it!*

NOTE: *Remember, this book, and especially this chapter is not going to be understood completely until it has been read the second time.*

You need this information so you can *act*, not *react* to opposing game strategies, and with careful creative operations, you can create win-win situations. Remember always, that Light Resistors *can*, and *do, serve The Light*, but only if the Light Keepers understand, direct, and use the situation for their benefit. This requires proper perception, and leads one to own all their creations and life experiences with the understanding that they are all useful and serve you.

Once you get the hang of it, it becomes easier and easier to evaluate what direction and evolutionary spiral your playmates are in. Keep an open mind, and don't be too hard on yourself in the beginning if you misperceive from time to time… It can get a little tricky, and as you read on, you'll understand why.

It is vital you acknowledge that you can't rely totally on your eyes and ears to give you accurate data on the 5 different classes of Beings. It is absolutely necessary to go into *the Core of your Being, your "Heart/CoreStar"* to decipher who is who. This is something that has to be *felt*, because what your eyes and ears tell you is only about 40% of the information you will need in order to get a correct perception of what is going on around you. Understand also that just because you see a "warm soft body" in front of you, doesn't necessarily mean that there is an authentic organic Being inside! There are, what the Native Americans refer to as "soulless ones," which means there is some kind of program operating the body, not a Soul. You must be aware that what you see may NOT be the only thing inhabiting a body at any given moment in time, or what *should* be there! It is also logical that if a Being can "walk-in," it can also "walk-out" if things get too rough… so keep that dynamic in mind too.

Now you realize why Earth-life can get so interesting and intense, as there are *exceptions to every rule!* You are certain to run across some of those exceptions, so be ready.

Also remember that since things on this planet are shifting and evolving; the statistics or % of Light Keepers and Light Resistors can and is changing. As more of the Light Keepers wake up and start taking charge, something new will happen. As you see on the chart, there are and have been equal numbers on each team, which makes it a constant battle to hold our own and not be taken over. This is NOT the Yin- Yang! This is corruption trying to spread and consume…and it is very challenging for Light Keepers to even be here, as they get slimed with the ever evolving corruption the Light Resistors are forcing on all Life Forms here! Light Keepers for centuries have made very little progress in bringing the corruption of the Resistors to justice. This is NOT acceptable, and is the reason many of you from the CCC - Cosmic Clean-Up Crew came to this planet…to overthrow corruption once and for all and reinstate Nature in the purest sense, (instead of merely canceling each other out the way it has been in the past, and how you see it on this chart). There is now a huge movement toward reinstating authentic Balance and Nature on this planet. This is extremely challenging though, as the original, authentic blueprints for this have been confiscated, and there has been very little point-of-reference for that kind of authenticity anymore. Natural Balance and Natural Law are NOT what we have been taught, and we have to go deep within ourselves, deep in our Heart/CoreStar, to pull out those blueprints and bring them to the table! This kind of Balance and Natural Law has not been seen on this planet (…yet.)

If the original, authentic blueprints for our planet were re-instated, we would see a chart that looked much different than this one. It would be more like a spiral instead of a "V" with two opposing sides that are constantly canceling each other out! The Earth Beings would be doing what Earth Beings ***should***…which is; "***Take good care of, and be good stewards of the Earth!***" There would be **NO Light Resistors**, and there would only be a skeleton crew (about 10%) of Light Keepers (Cosmic Clean-up Crew) here to keep the riff-raff out, and to give the Earth Beings inspiration and a visual aid of what they could become! There would also be places for Light Keepers to come for some R & R .....like a vacation spot on this beautiful bio-diversified planet!

It's time we clean this mess up, start over, and do things right... the way it was meant to be...with respect for all benevolent Life-forms everywhere. We need to hold this vision, with the authentic blueprints, and then dream it into reality!

NOTE: There are some new developments that I have just become aware of. Apparently in Sept. of 2013 a new type of Being started Walking-In to bodies on this planet. They snuck in from outside the Hologram via "The Immortal Portal." There are only about 55 of these Beings on the planet right now so there is not a % or category for them. They carry color vibration that is not in our light spectrum.....probably for camouflage. They are gaining rapid recall of their history and their abilities. Once they get settled into the bodies they walked into and get acclimated, their entire focus and expertise is to "bust the corrupted monetary system" and thereby help us overthrow the corruption that is controlling and manipulating every life-form on this planet! There is another group of about 55 that will be coming in soon. Their mission is to Walk-In and out of bodies assisting the first group via taking temporary command of rich Ass-Soul bodies long enough to have them re-allocate funds they have been stealing and hoarding, and give them to benevolent people and groups who are in a position to utilize and redistribute those funds to help heal nature and humanity.

This is a total game changer and something I have been envisioning for a very, very long time. I just discovered this last night, (10-Nov-2013) about an hour after I had a huge melt down. I was sooo grief stricken about all the pain and suffering here on this planet. I thought about all the mean nasty psycho/sociopathic money hoarders that are inflicting so much forced misery and sorrow here. They impose this despair, not only on the people, but on the animals and plants they call "commodities." I sign an average of 10-15 online petitions every day, and although we are making great headway, last night it all came crashing in on me and I just fell to pieces. Then Hal let me in on this new development, and it gave me a total attitude adjustment! I could see the pieces of the puzzle I had worked so hard and so long on, finally coming "magickly together." The Immortal Portal is VERY real, and I have been anticipating this activation for 5 years. I felt so exhilarated and most of all supported! We MUST remember all of the ever increasing number of allies who are not in physical bodies right now. They are total game changers too! We ARE making huge paradigm shifts, and **we are indeed making headway ...always remember this!**

"Good luck to you!!!"

You're in now line for the wildest ride of your life
at this crazy Fun House called.....

"The Inter-Dimensional Amusement Park!"

THE 5 TYPES OF BEINGS ON OUR PLANET TODAY

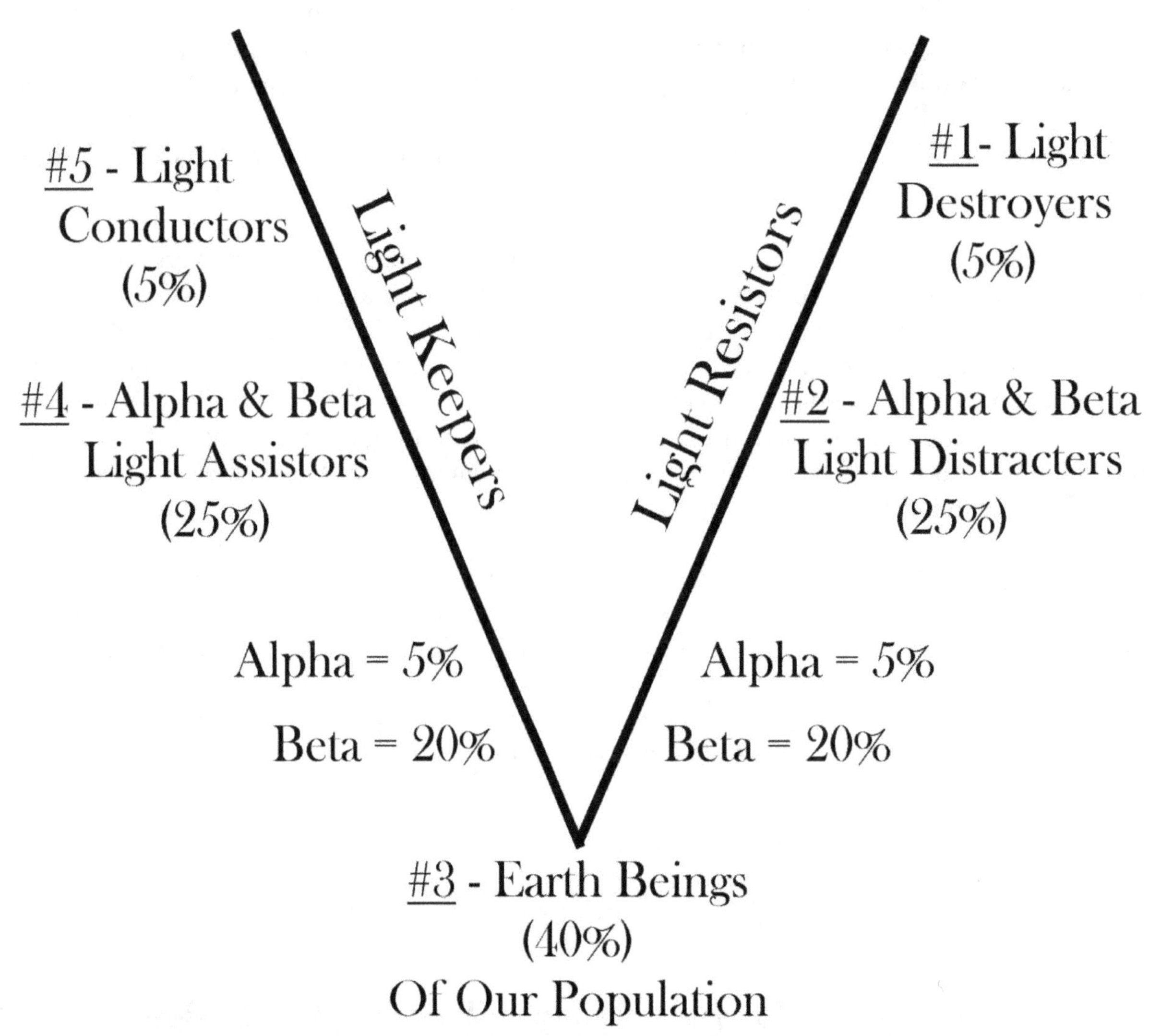

EARTH BEING SPIRALS

CYCLE = *Instability - Incline - Rest, Rest, Rest, Rest,
Decline - Rest, Rest, Rest,

***Instability - Incline - Rest, Rest, Rest, Rest ...**

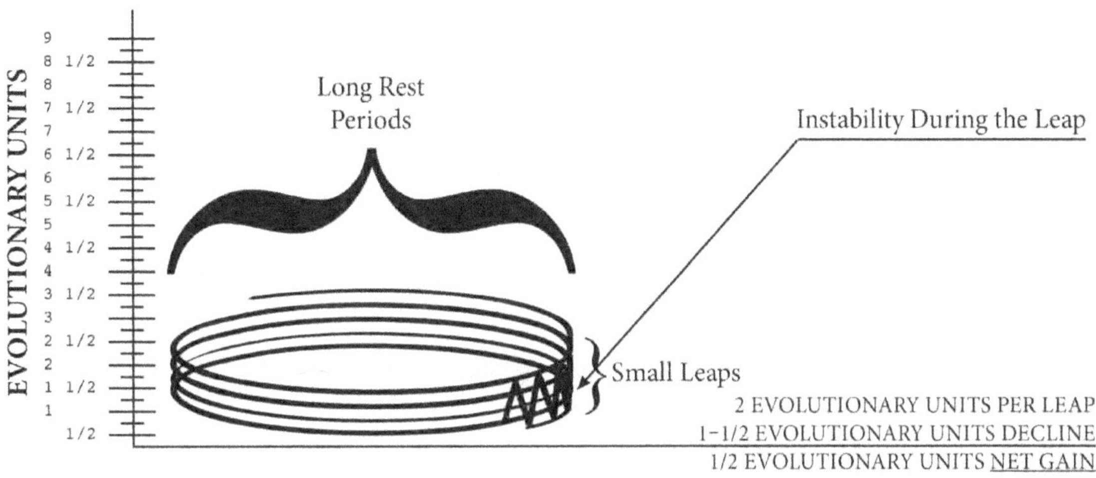

#3-Earth Being: Although they are very slow in their evolutionary process, their progress is steady. One of the main reasons for their slow movement is that most of these Beings do not believe in past lives, nor do they understand fully the laws of karma (as you sow-so shall you reap, the law of action and re-action, what you put out is magnetized back to you)... or in other words they don't play the game *what happens next* very well!

The shunning and even abject fear of the information and wisdom gleaned from past lives or past existences and karmic laws is a major deterrent to the progress in many of these Beings. This will continue to be a deterrent until they are ready to "wake up" and realize there is more to them than what they have been taught, or give themselves credit for. Earth Beings immerse themselves in "Earth things" such as: keeping up with spectator sports, the latest fashions, what's on TV, and who's who in Hollywood. They are also heavily involved in clubs, fraternities, sororities, organized religion, climbing corporate ladders and "looking good!"

Recently though, Earth Beings have started to get a sense that "something just ain't right here," and are starting to become politically active in stopping atrocities like factory farms, fracking, GMOs, chem trails, human trafficking, Satanic Rituals being done by the global elite etc. They are also getting serious about organic gardening and sustainability, which is a HUGE bonus, especially when you consider that many of these Earth Beings had no interest before. With the "Occupy" movement exposing the "Powers That

Be" (PTB), many Earth people have been forced to wake up, get informed, and get on the band wagon before it is too late. This transformation is very encouraging!

As you can see from the Earth Spirals diagram, these Beings have long, long, long rest periods. Their cycle goes: *leap, rest, rest, rest, rest, decline, rest, rest, rest, rest, leap, rest, rest...* They leap up 2 Evolutionary Units (E.U.) and decline 1 ½ E.U., which makes their total net incline gain ½ of an E.U.

It's pretty obvious that it's going to take a while for them to climb the Evolutionary Unit ladder, but it works for them and that's just about as fast as they can *or want* to go, given the limitations they are under.

When you study and contemplate the Earth Being's profile, it will be relatively easy to decipher which playmates in your own personal playground fit into this category. You will always run into these Beings because …well….. Earth is just full of "Earth Beings!"

As Earth Beings begin to *wake up* and let go of their fears of using new ideas and patterns, they become freer in their movement and expressions. Then, like the cycle of the egg/caterpillar/chrysalis/butterfly… they begin to meta-morph into a new Life-form.

The next stage is a very natural process as the angles of their spirals transform into the geometry of the *Beta Spirals*.

Long before this happens though, the decision is made as to which direction they are going. Are they going to move into the Light Keeper's playground, or dive head first into the Light Resistor's cesspool?

EARTH BEING PROFILE

#3-EARTH BEING:

- Represent approximately 40% of our population.
- Beings who are just starting out (*spiritual babies*).
- Came here to *grow up* and can be curious, but spiritual progress is very slow because they don't know "the ropes" yet.
- Are generally closed-minded, and it is very hard for them to accept change, (mostly because they themselves change very little and move so slowly).
- Spend much of their time, money, and energy involving themselves in:

  Clubs: Lions Club, Country Clubs, Moose Lodge, Rotary Club, etc.

  Social Groups: Boy Scouts, Y.W.C.A., Camp Fire, P.T.A., etc.

  Sporting Events: ball games, marathons, auto and boat racing, boxing, wrestling, etc.

  Organized Religion: They need the structure and sense of belonging.

  More Recent Interests: gardening, sustainability, GMOs, environmental issues, social injustices, global warming, etc.

- Many of them immerse themselves in dogmas so they won't have to think for themselves.
- Very caught up in and absorbed in Social UN-Consciousness.
- Don't have much interest in, or actually care to ***really*** know, what's going on in the cosmos.
- Don't embrace past life or karmic awareness.
- Have very little interest in metaphysics, pataphysics, pseudo-sciences, and some branches of quantum physics and don't give it much credence or validity. They may even be very fearful and adamantly opposed to anyone or anything that is even remotely associated with these sciences.
- Can be highly intelligent or total nincompoops!
- Can be kind, considerate, caring Beings, or mean, angry, hostile, aggressive Beings.
- When they do evolve and move to the next position, 50% of them become Light Keepers, and 50% become Light Resistors – but that is changing.

BETA SPIRALS

#4-B LIGHT ASSISTOR (LA) BETA
#2-B LIGHT DISTRACTER (LD) BETA

CYCLE = *Instability, Instability - Incline, Incline, Incline -
Rest Slide Decline – Rest, Slide, Decline -

***Instability, Instability - Incline, Incline, Incline …**

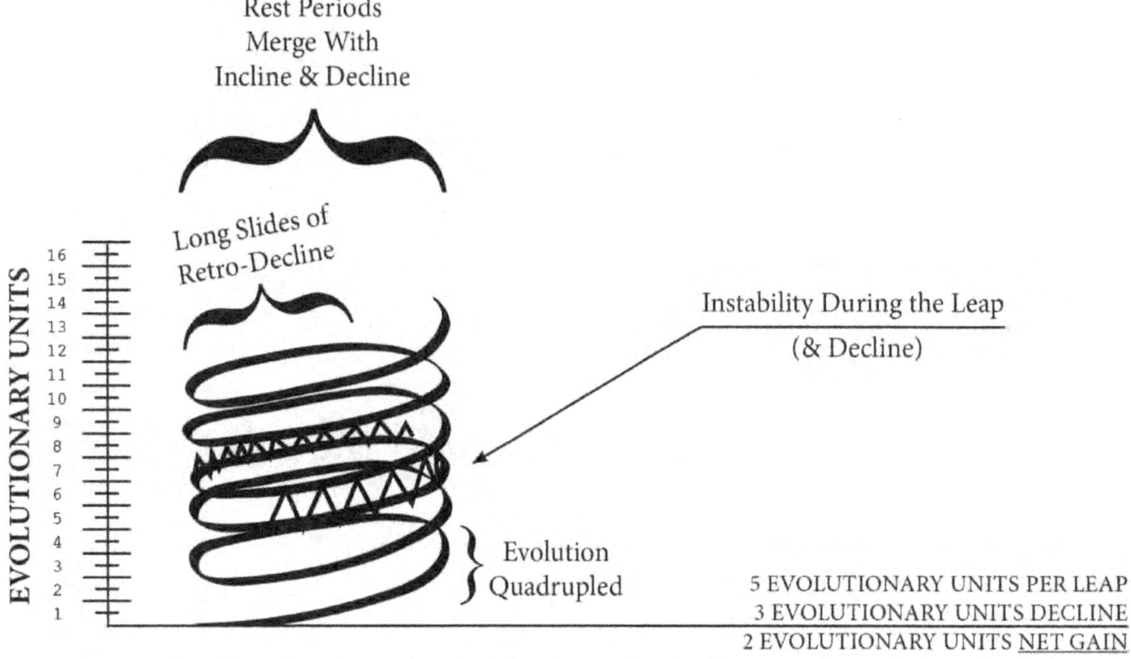

#4-B Light Assistor (LA) Beta: These Beings are quite unique. Their rest periods ssssslllllliiiiide in both the ascend and descend modes, thus making it difficult to tell where one begins and one ends. In addition to this, the instability during the leap to a new level is longer and also more extensive than any of the other Beings' spiral jumps. This is one reason why so many of them are restless, anxious, and unstable.

The majority of Light Assistor (LA) Betas, are highly intelligent and have a lot of information, skills, and talents to share with the world (and the Universe for that matter). These Beings also have a lot of great ideas and can be highly creative.

With all they have going for them, many LA Betas have some serious difficulties and challenges with self-sabotage mechanisms. They spend much of their time and energy in some kind of drama, whether it's pining away over some useless relationship in the past, or trying to get revenge and punish someone or something for some perceived wrong-doing in their lives, *or someone else's life* (even if that ***someone else*** doesn't share their views!)

Betas can be hard workers if properly motivated, but they have to see how it benefits them personally, or their motivation decreases.

LA Betas may verbally oppose victimhood, but time after time fall into that role themselves and become quite proficient at whining and trying to recruit others to play into their dramas. This is one reason why very often these Beings can be a major distraction as well as a time and energy drain on the Alphas and Light-Conductors *they're supposed to be in service to!*

Betas are notorious for getting Shove-Ins, and many times have no clue they have just been taken over. This is especially convenient for the agendas of Creepy Cryptos who love to cause pain, suffering, confusion, and chaos. (See chapter 19 - *Profiles of Creepy Cryptos.*)

They also oftentimes (especially during the down-slide modes) get jealous and envious of the Alphas and Light-Conductors, which detours them even further from their position and purpose as an Assistor doing their apprenticeship. When in these modes, as you can guess, they actually become useful in helping the cause of the **Light Resistors!**

As time goes on and after many, many lessons in the same assignments, the Betas start figuring it out. They begin to understand their true worth and drop the "wannabe" syndrome and just "BE."

They let go of the delusions that they are something they haven't learned/earned yet, and finally become at peace with who and what they are. It is in this state of peace, serenity, and strength that they can evolve…when they are *finally* willing to learn and do whatever it takes to be ***authentically more.*** Only in this state of humility can they stabilize long enough to energize and transform themselves, and then move into the next evolutionary spiral of Light Assistor Alpha.

NOTE: It is important to understand that at this time, (2014) 20% of the people on Planet Earth are FW-Indigos. About 15-20% of them have been hijacked and are on the Light Distracter team now. This still leaves the Indigo Nation at between 16% and 18 % of the population who are a part of the Light Keepers Team. With this in mind, as you look at the chart on page 95, it shows that almost 1/2 of the Beta Population are First Wavers! It is my Dream and vision that these FW-Indigos will get a huge wake-up call and step up to the plate, so they can quickly evolve to the next level. After the events around new members of our team infiltrating through the ***Immortal Portal,*** the rules have changed dramatically. We have broken the spell that kept the % of Light Keepers and Light Resisters equal, and the shift is hitting the fan! We are no longer under "Contract" or "Forced Agreement" to have a certain % of Light Keepers be Betas, they can all evolve into Alphas now!

It is time to turn that chart with equal number of players opposing each other, into only spirals of light keepers! This will give rise to a new Earth, one without threats to the animals, the plants, the elementals, and Humanity. WE CAN DO IT!

#2-B Light Distracter (LD) Beta: These spirals have the same geometry as the Light Assistors, but go in the opposite direction. These Beings also represent 20% of the population and have the same basic profile as the Light Assistor Betas, except they work for the Light Resistors instead.

From time to time, about 1% will do a switch or become a "turncoat." They'll go play on the Light Keepers' team and enjoy the environment so much that they transform themselves and take up permanent residence there... (but then that switch also happens on the other side too!)

One interesting characteristic about these distracting elements called LD-Betas, is that only 15% of them actually know without a doubt who they work for. These ambitious scoundrels are a little easier to detect than the others, because they are more blatant about their cause... and every bit as annoying!

These Light Distracter (LD) Betas and the rest of the Light Resistor team, tend to "hang out" together. And where do you think you'll find them *en masse?* ...No, not in the sleazy bars, not at drug parties, not inciting gang activities, and not at satanic conventions, (although that happens). No, most of the time you'll find them exactly where you'd expect them to be if you pondered and really thought about it... Yes, they'd be right smack in the middle of the metaphysical and New Age communities and events! ...And they are most likely to be there in equal numbers to the Light Assistors.

Since most of these Beta Beings believe they are working for the Light Keepers, they make great infiltrators and distracters. Since they are so good at what they do, you can't really tell, just by looking at them or talking to them, what team they're on (unless you are proficient at reading auras, have state of the art B.S. detectors, or can pick up on "reverse speech" to decode the sound and tonal frequencies in their voices!)

Usually the best way to detect and identify LD Betas, is by the way they feel when you interact with them. You add that to some of the things they have (or have not) done, and you will start to get the correct picture of who and what they ***really*** are.

Ah yes, they sure do their job well ...and what is humorous about them is... they too can be irritating to their own teammates! Their whining and not using their multitude of talents and assets can be exasperating and anti-productive to the plans of their Light Resistor buddies!

If you should detect one or two or even a whole bunch of them around you *which you probably will considering their numbers, the odds are surely there*, don't have a hissy fit and get all paranoid! Chances are they'll be your friends, your relatives, your siblings, your parents, and even your children!

No, the smart thing to do here is just keep an eye on them, define your borders, and don't allow them to cross! Be firm in your intent and remember that even in their distracting vibration, they still can do nice things and be useful.

This is where "unconditional Love" comes in handy… You love them, knowing they are what they are and won't have the ability to return that same kind of vibration back to you. But that's O.K., it teaches you the *unconditional* part of *unconditional Love,* and gives you the opportunity to practice it.

NOTE: *It is also important not to fall into "The Blinded By Love Trap" that these and other Light Distracter/Resistor Beings can suck you into. My motto is, "Love unconditionally, Trust only the Trustworthy!"*

As long as you know who/what these Beings are, it will make life soooo much simpler… because you can stop trying to force them into being a Being that you previously assumed they ***should be.*** You'll stop entrapping yourself by telling them your deepest, darkest, most intimate secrets, only to have it back-fire on you and get you into a lot of trouble!

With practice, you can acquire a very clear understanding of the game-players in your life and what game they are *really* playing, so you can act and respond appropriately, and above all… figure out how these Beings can serve you.

Now don't confuse this with the Altered Ego's tyrannical game of "using people!" That game and the vibration it emits are in a totally different ballpark. No, what I'm talking about here is, since there are so many Light Distracters on this planet, and since the odds are that we will be in constant interaction with them in some form or another most of the time. So instead of running and hiding, or being afraid and intimidated by them, take command and stand your ground. Allow the interactions, make use of them and play along. As long as you are aware and stay on top of their games, you can put them in places and spaces that serve you. You're the boss of your life here, remember? You call the shots as to how much time and energy you spend on them, and what you will and will not tolerate from them. It's ***your*** call!

And now, keep in mind that…***Knowledge is Power***…

But ***applied*** knowledge **is the *Command Of That Power!***

Understand "Grasshopper?"

BETA PROFILES

#4-B LIGHT ASSISTOR (LA) BETA:

- Represent approximately 20% of our population.
- Are apprentices to the Light Assistor (LA) Alphas, and are in service to the Light-Conductors.
- Can be very volatile, because they have the longest instability incline leap and decline slide of any of the spirals.
- Can be extremely intelligent and have a lot of information, but don't usually know quite how to apply it, or put it into action to get the best results.
- Willing to help, but often get things mixed up and make a mess instead.
- Evolve 3 times faster than Earth Beings.
- On the downslides can actually switch into the Distracter territory.
- Most of them believe they're more evolved than they really are---believing they're Alphas or Conductors---but when they truly go into their heart, they know their capacitors just aren't big enough yet to hold and maintain the higher frequencies.
- Can be an easy target for Shove-Ins.
- Approximately 1% get seduced and do a "switch" and permanently move to the Light Resistor Sector.
- Need certain experiences to activate their memories and codes, which then puts them in position to express themselves and evolve as functional, useful L.A Betas.
- 30% wake up fully to their callings, so they can fulfill their pre-outlined purpose.
- Many are struggling with the tyrannical confinements of spiritual dogma as well as physical/emotional injuries they've experienced, but only about 5% "get a grip," get through, and overcome the damage completely.

#2-B LIGHT DISTRACTER (LD) BETA:

- Represent approximately 20% of our population.
- Hard to tell them apart from the LA Betas, except that they *FEEL* different.
- Basically the same profile as LA Betas, except they work for the Resistor side.
- Are apprentices for the Light Distracter (L.D.) Alphas and in service to the Light-Destroyers.
- 85% consciously believe they work for the Light, but subconsciously they know it's a trick to keep them constantly distracting and annoying the Light Keepers.
- Approximately 1% do a switch and permanently move to the Light Keepers' Realm.
- Large percentage hang out in New Age and metaphysical circles.
- Energy vampires.
- Are good at their job.
- Block Light Keepers progress through distractions and diversions.

ALPHA SPIRALS

#2-A LIGHT ASSISTOR (LA) ALPHA
#2-A LIGHT DISTRACTER (LD) ALPHA

Cycle = *Instability, Instability - Incline, Incline
Incline, Incline, Rest, Mini Decline - Rest -

***Instability, Instability - Incline, Incline**

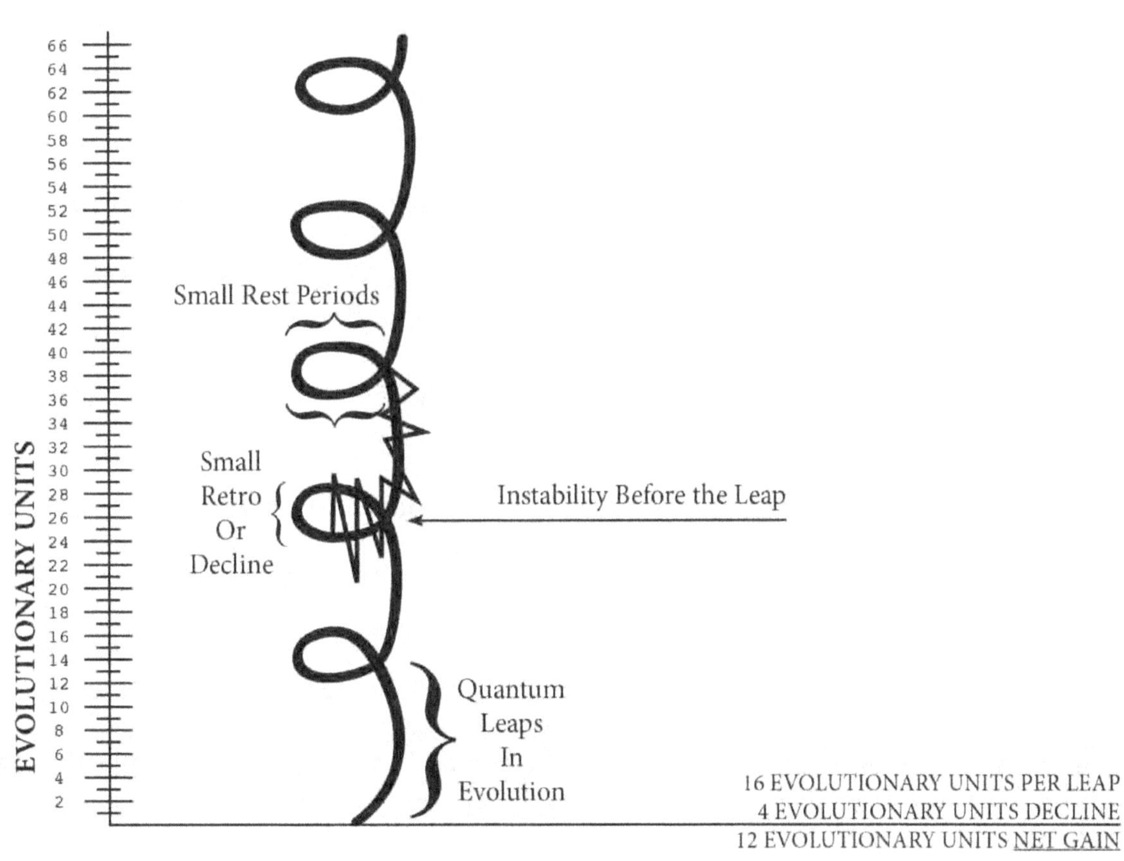

<u>#4-A Light Assistor (LA) Alpha</u>: As you can see from this chart, the evolutionary leaps have more than quadrupled! The retro or decline is very minimal compared to the Beta Spiral; thus there is a much greater, vast, and more accelerated evolution.

By the time a Being has reached Alpha status, there is a definite substantial stability transformation, as these Beings' Spirals are emulating the geometric structure of the Light-Conductors. Although there are periods of instability, *especially just prior to taking a quantum leap*, there is much more command over the process.

This leap or upsurge takes a tremendous amount of energy and focus. At this time a lot of *things,* and sometimes *people,* begin to fall away if they are no longer necessary or useful. It may feel to them like *everything is running amuck, falling apart, and they're losing ground,* when actually they are cleansing and clearing themselves for a new level of education and influence.

When they finally arrive at these new levels or rest periods, they maintain a new existence and ambiance of strength, wisdom, and sovereignty. And just when they think they have things figured out, the Earth starts to shake under their feet, instability and jolting start, and they begin a thrust upward to new heights again!

Light Assistor (LA) Alphas are amazing Beings, and when you have the privilege of getting a few "close encounters" with some of these Beings in your life, you never forget them. They stay in your heart and can alter your perception… and thus alter your life forever!

One of the admirable traits of LA Alphas, is that by now, they are very sovereign and loyal to their station as senior assistors to the Light-Conductors, and are very much at peace to be in service exactly how and where they are! There is no jealousy toward Light-Conductors, only deep respect, collaboration, and loyal support. It's sort of like the Knights of the Round Table. Their intention, focus, honor, and passion came from being a *GOOD KNIGHT* ***...a loyal protector in the royal court.*** They didn't try to, nor did they want to, ***be the King/Queen.*** They wanted only to be exactly who and what they were… *EXCELLENT KNIGHTS!*

And so it is with Alphas, **they love what they are, and they love what they do!**

LA Alphas also are generally an understanding and compassionate lot. They are explicitly aware and empathetic about the anxieties and dilemmas that the Beta bunch get themselves into (having recently been there themselves), and offer excellent service as models or examples for the Betas to emulate.

In the Alphas' stability and serenity, they also have the ability to evaluate a situation and take swift action in a moment's notice, and correct a situation before it gets out of hand! They are great peacemakers, but if need be, would lay down their lives for the safety and longevity of the Light-Conductors.

One of the challenges Alphas have (and Light-Conductors too for that matter) is that in order to do their jobs proficiently, they need to limit some of the time and energy they spend with Betas, Earth Beings, *and Light Resistors*. If they don't allocate spending their time and energy with each other for reinforcing, networking, and fortifying themselves, they suffer horrible burnouts that can render them inefficient and ill. This cycle seems to be a major defect in them until they wake up fully. Some of the reasons they have these challenges are:

1. The Earth Beings, Light Assistor Betas, and especially the Light Resisters, are extremely persistent

in demanding attention, time, and energy.

2. They feel the burden of their position and assume extreme responsibility for what's happening (or not happening) in their environment.

3. They feel guilty and "UN-loving" when they put up boundaries, set perimeters, or say, "NO!" They feel embarrassed when they take care of themselves and their requirements, so instead they'll hear a cry, and run off to the aid of some of these needy, dysfunctional Beings (which incidentally, is a trap…and you can bet your booty that some of these energy-vacuuming Beings know all the right buttons to push to induce guilt!) It frustrates the dickens out of Alphas, but until they wake up fully, they continue to surround themselves with certain Beings that cry, "MAY DAY, MAY DAY!" and so they run to their rescue, only to find that the outcome is… *helping them doesn't **really** help them. Their interventions are not a permanent "fix" for these drama queens (and kings),* Alphas spend time, energy, focus, and emotional strength pulling the rascals out of the quick-sand, only to discover the next day they've jumped right back in again! Alphas, after many, many lessons (and a few hundred ***in-your-face*** wake-up calls), open their eyes and realize they need to allow other Beings to figure out on their own, *with their own wit and strength,* how to pull themselves out of the pickles they continually get themselves into. It is for their own learning and evolution's sake… for goodness sake!

4. Since only 5% of the planet are Alphas, and 5% are Light-Conductors, that makes up only 10% of the population (less than that if you consider the ones that are still asleep!) It's no mystery then why they feel very lonely, isolated, misunderstood, and many times, out and out rejected! They oftentimes feel like "they're the only ones of their kind," and long for the companionship of another *odd duck.* This is compounded even more if they're in jobs that magnify the corporate supremacy mentality, or if their family and close friends are comprised totally of Earth Beings, Betas, and Light Resistors. It can be a long, lonely path and it's not uncommon for these Beings to believe there's something seriously wrong with them, and that maybe they're crazy! So a lot of them opt to go into the closet and stay there with their ideas, memories, and internal understanding and wisdom …believing others would lock them up if they knew!

There comes a time in every LA Alphas' wake-up processes that they understand and acquire a check and balance system. This system is called… "The 5-Ds."

DISCERNMENT- Picking and choosing wisely what you will and will not involve yourself in.
DISCRETION- Knowing when and how to proceed when you have chosen to get involved.
DETACHMENT- Being willing to let go and allow all educational struggles to meta-morph into a new, improved, shape, and form.
DISCIPLINE- Taking conscious charge, responsibility, and direction for every personal ***Action, Reaction,*** or ***Inaction*** in your life.

<u>DESIRE</u>- The internal fire ***from the Core of your Being*** to be all you can be! The expression of the authentic GOD/DESS-FORCE, custom designed and perfected By the real YOU!

When Alphas finally do pursue their wake-up call, they begin to draw boundaries and make it a priority to redirect their focus toward spending their *intimate* time and energies on themselves, other Alphas, and Light-Conductors. When this new internal command takes place, their life does a total transformation... their power is increased, and all the things they need in order to fulfill their destinies, contracts, and missions here are suddenly magnetized to them with grace, speed, and force.

Without this process, coupled with the awakening and awareness of who they are and who they are really in service to (which incidentally, 90% ***will*** wake up on time!), the quest/mission of the Light Keepers would never be fulfilled and the outcome of the Earth Drama would be altered dramatically!

NOTE: *This in no way means that LA Alphas should STAY AWAY from other Beings, it means STAY AWAKE... KEEP YOUR EYES OPEN! Alphas need interactions with* ***all*** *Beings in order to* understand *the big picture and how to be effective in their roles. It's learning how to <u>feel</u> what balance is and how to take swift action when they feel their life, and the people in it, are getting out of balance. The role of the Light Assistor Alpha is one of stability, action, strength, and service. They are role models and liaisons. They are magnificent, compassionate, hard-working Beings. They are literally* ***one in a million!***

<u>#2-A Light Distracter (LD) Alpha</u>: Again, these spirals have the same geometry as LA Alphas, but go in the opposite direction. They also represent 5% of the population, and are very qualified for their position. One thing that is unique about this classification of Alphas is that, *at this time,* about 79% are aware of who they work for.

Most of this 79% section of Alphas are very blatant in their roles as Senior Light Distracters and there is no question about their motives and position... especially in politics, religion, and corporate structures.

The other 21% have convinced themselves that they work for the Light Keepers, which is an excellent cover-up, and gives them an unquestionable edge in this game. They infiltrate and camouflage themselves quite nicely with this information about themselves masked, **but**...if you are really alert and on your toes, if you're good at reading between the lines, if you rely on your heart and gut for your information, your own internal truth-seeking alarm will go off! You will be able to detect the vibrations of the disguised and hidden agendas of the Light Distracters and Destroyers. You must be very observant and aware of things that don't **feel right,** in order to correctly identify a cloaked Light Resistor.

These Beings are very much alive and well in the metaphysical communities, and are also abundant in a variety of leadership positions. They are usually very bright, charismatic, and witty. They're a kick to be around, but there's something that makes you feel uneasy about them, like they cannot be trusted...like if you turn your back on them..... (you know what I mean).

If you ever decide to go on a Light Distracter (LD) Alpha search, here are some places you'll want to look first. Check out the committees and boards to help humanity and the environment. Then go to the lecture circuits and metaphysical expos… and after that, go check out the *who's who* in the metaphysical and New Age bookstores. You'll find them mingling with all these *"Light Workers" …'**cause it's their job!!!** (Get it?)*

One thing that's important to point out here, is that in their efforts to go in disguise, they cannot help but further the causes and programs of the Light Keepers; otherwise they would be easily detected…**AND REJECTED!**… (So in a very real sense, they actually do, at times, serve The Light.)

Another tidbit regarding these Light Distracting Alphas, is if you watch and observe, you'll find that sometimes they get sloppy in their disguises and leave their tracks uncovered so to speak. If you check their tracks out, you'll notice some discrepancies in the way they present themselves. You'll also notice that *"the man behind the curtain"* isn't the wizard at all, but "Sneaky the Snake" trying to dupe everyone!

After you have played this game awhile, and you have figured out who they are and where they're hiding, and identified them for the scoundrels and stink-beetle Ass-Souls they truly are, I'm sure you'll agree with me …*they do a darned good job, and they get the prize for being some of the best stinkers on the planet!*

ALPHA PROFILES

#4-A LIGHT ASSISTOR (LA) ALPHA:

- Represent approximately 5% of our population.
- Evolve on spirals very similar to Light-Conductors, which gives them practice for their next and final position.
- Movers and shakers in the physical and metaphysical worlds.
- Have a red-hot thirst for knowledge, and are very teachable.
- Know they are Light Keepers, and they consciously and willingly do their jobs.
- Challenge is to only spend 25% of their *intimate* time assisting Betas and Earth Beings, (and Light Resistors) and reserve the rest of that valuable time to be by themselves, or with other Alphas and Light-Conductors.
- Main stewardship is to themselves, and the affairs of the Light-Conductors.
- A very, very small percentage every once in a while, will do a switch and become a Light Distracter.
- Act as liaisons and buffers between the Light-Conductors and the Betas, Earth Beings, and especially the Light Resistors.
- Need certain codes triggered in order to activate their abilities, memories, and awareness of who they are and what their position is.
- Approximately 90-98% of the Alpha team will wake up ***fully*** and have *total recall* of who they truly are, and what they're supposed to do with their Light and knowledge.
- Many Alphas begin life in social and spiritual structures of confinement, dogma, and all types of physical/emotional injuries.
- About 94% of them rise above it all and overcome the damage completely.

#2-A LIGHT DISTRACTER (LD) ALPHA:

- Represent approximately 5% of the population.
- Evolve on spirals very similar to Light-Destroyers to prepare for the possibility of that position.
- Every once in a great while, one will do a switch and become a permanent Light Keeper.
- Very intelligent, sneaky, charismatic Beings.
- Spend their time, energy, and $ in Altered-Ego projects designed to support tyrannical control of the *many* by the supposed supremacy of the *few*. Many are in very powerful positions politically and economically.
- About 79% have awakened to the knowledge of what team they are on. The other 21% *assume* they are Light Keepers, *but deep inside they know how much they enjoy the power of tyranny instigated by the Altered Ego.*
- These Beings have also been subjected to various physical and emotional injuries. The way they choose to deal with those experiences accounts for some of their behaviors and personality traits.

#5-LIGHT-CONDUCTOR SPIRALS &
#1-LIGHT-DESTROYER SPIRALS

CYCLE = *Instability - Incline, Incline, Incline, Incline, Incline
Mini Rest - Micro Decline - Mini Rest.

***Instability - Incline, Incline, Incline, Incline, Incline…**

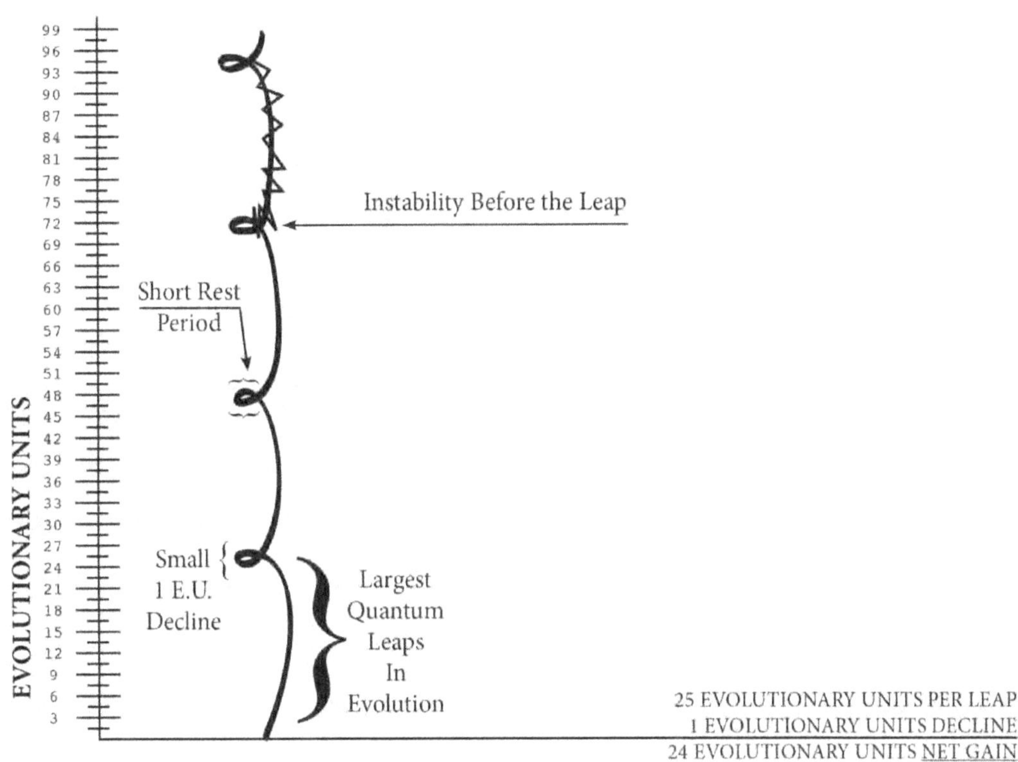

#5- Light-Conductor: As you study this graph, you will notice that the Light-Conductors net Evolutionary Unit (E.U.) gain is double that of the Alphas and the rest time is 1/3 of what they had in their former position. It doesn't take a rocket scientist to realize these Beings are taking the brunt of the load here, so it is extremely important for Light-Conductors to savor every moment of rest they can. (But if the truth be known, when the rest time is coming to a close, the Light-Conductors become restless and ready for some action!) The avoidance of boredom is imperative for these Beings. Their strength, power, energy, knowledge & wisdom, adventure, love, passion, and humor are the fuel that keeps them going!

Like their ally friends the LA Alphas, there's never a dull moment…there's always something to fix. These fixers, (sometimes referred to as the movers and shakers in "*the cosmic clean-up committee*") are always on the go and never without employment because of all the things that get broken or polluted by the other Beings both on and off planet. *It's quite a dirty job, but somebody's got to do it!*

To make things more challenging and spicy, they must be on 24-hour alert and on constant watch because they're always being targeted and assaulted by the Light Resistors. Yes, the positions of Light Conductor and LA Alpha are positions and jobs only a hard-core thrill-seeker would aspire to!

As you can see by the statistics, only 5% of the population are Light-Conductors, and 5% LA Alphas. These *"fixers"* represent a meager 10% of our population, (and that doesn't take into consideration the percentage that hasn't woken up yet, or the ones who are still infants or children!)

Light-Conductors are quite a gutsy, bodacious lot, and are always trying to maintain order (even if they have to use chaos and storm energy on occasion to level the playing field and then sweep away debris as a means to get there!) They must always keep their antennas up, and have to be on perpetual lookout for new and improved ways of keeping out of the line of fire. That's just their part-time job. Their full timer is coming up with new inventions and diversified methods of Alchemy to help *"put humpty dumpty together again"…(who or whatever that might be) doing it quicker than the last time and still not get "egg on their face" in the process!*

One of the elements that makes Light-Conductors unique, is that in order for them to take total command of their position, it is a requirement for them to search out and find their "other halves" or Soul Mates. *Soul-Mate Power,* as I call it, is the access gate or code that gives them the balanced yin-yang energy flow that is mandatory for their success. This Soul Mate collaboration is very useful also to the Alphas, but is an ab**soul**ute necessity for Light-Conductors.

NOTE: *It is important for them to realize that their "Soul Mates" may NOT be in a human body at this time and if that is the case, they may have to get very telepathic or empathic to communicate with them… whoever or wherever that may be.*

Until they have re-united with a Soul Mate or two… there is a longing that aches deep within their hearts, and there is an emptiness that nothing can fill; sometimes they feel like they would rather abort their mission than go on without their counterparts!

Once they do find each other, these **dynamic duos** unite their cosmic forces, and an explosion takes place that catapults everyone and everything around them into hyper speed. The union of these two yin-yang forces is a magical blend, but not entirely without some sparks flying here and there. Considering their ability to handle quantum amounts of Light and energy frequencies…if there is ever a misconnection… WATCH OUT FOR THE LIGHTNING BOLTS! Take cover and get out your lightning rod! After a while though, these wizards learn how to ebb and flow with each other and when this happens, the magick they create is literally *out of this world!*

Another aspect that is exclusive to Light-Conductors is that, once they have evolved enough to start locking into the LC position, there is absolutely no switching places or turn-coating. They are locked into position *permanently!*

Also, they are not necessarily here for their *own* lessons or education, but more to figure out how to recall what they have *already learned* so they can teach others, and direct the Light they *already hold*!

As a Conductor of the Light, their job is to hold the frequencies of Light and direct them where they need to go. Sort of like the conductor in an orchestra. Everyone looks to the conductor to direct and lead the entire band or orchestra towards the synergistic creation of precise, exquisite music. So all eyes of the Light Keepers are on the Conductors to cue them on when, where, and how to play their parts in order to make this the best performance ever!

If you should ever meet up with a Light Conductor who is fully awake, don't believe for a minute that the road to his or her *bright eyes and bushy tail* condition was an easy one!
All of them came from a variety of circumstances that would ***bend, fold, and mutilate*** most any other Beings…if given the same conditions. Light Distractors, and especially Light-Destroyers are constantly harassing them, trying to trip them up and take them down…and hopefully ***OUT!***

If you interact with a Light Conductor who is in the process of transcending their experiences, injuries, and war wounds, *especially the ones that fall into the categories of spiritual, and emotional*…then you are probably witnessing a Light Conductor who is still waking up.

Whatever condition you should find them in, they are fascinating and compelling to be around. They seem to have a magnetic quality, so that when you are in their presence or influence, your codes start tripping and memories start unveiling. You start asking questions you never would have thought of before… *and getting answers that you wouldn't have understood before!* It's like shining a light in a dark playroom… all the wonderful toys and gadgets were there before, you just didn't see them or know what to do with them!

As you may have deciphered from this information, the LA Alphas and the Light-Conductors are moving through *life in the fast lane!…*They are on a freeway or autobahn with no exit, no speed limits… and only *an occasional rest stop.*

WHAT A TRIP!

LIGHT-CONDUCTOR PROFILE

#5- LIGHT-CONDUCTOR:

- Represents 5% of the population.
- Complete balance of 50% female, and 50% male.
- Are Soul Mates, and must connect with their partners *wherever that may be,* in order to fully and properly fulfill their contracts.
- Know 100% without a doubt who they are in service to. They know they are Keepers of The (uncorrupted) Light, *both White and Black Light.* They also know intuitively, that they have the capacity to conduct and direct The Light, and extinguish corruption.
- Unlike any of the other Beings, once in position, they are permanently locked in place. There are no turncoats.
- Are Masters in their own right, living in a challenging 3-D world.
- Can hold and conduct mega amounts of both White and Black Light.
- Have the capacity to influence and inspire All Life-forms.
- They oftentimes feel very lonely, isolated, and foreign until they meet up with "Their Family:" the LA Alphas and other Light-Conductors.
- Very bright, talented, and psychic, most of these Beings are also exceptional healers.
- 95% of these Beings began life under tyrannical situations, spiritual dogmas, and have suffered extreme emotional and physical injustices or injuries. They miraculously pull themselves…*(and many others along with them…)* out of these confining, destructive situations before they leave the planet.
- Light-Conductors who are not fully awake can have the qualities of Alphas and Betas from time to time.

LIGHT-DESTROYER SPIRALS

#1- Light-Destroyer: Ah yes, last but certainly not *the least*, these Beings are quite extraordinary for sure. They move in the same geometric spirals as the Light-Conductors, but definitely go in the opposite direction. These Beings are Master Decepters and I must say, from all the ones I have met, put on quite a show.

They too represent 5% of the population, but unlike Light-Conductors who have a balance of 50% male and 50% female, these *wise guys* come to the table with a different deck of cards.

Now, let's see if you can figure out their ingenious scheme! If you were trying to infiltrate, overthrow, corrupt, and destroy the Light… especially the Master Creator vibration (*the Goddess energy),* and if you were 100% of the (*distorted)* male vibration, and you wanted to be totally cloaked and disguised, what kind of body would you inhabit? (*Now think diabolically here…*)

You guessed it… **FEMALE BODIES**! That's right folks, right now 98% of these sneaky, conniving, cunning, noxious, Light-Destroyers are playing out their undercover agendas in Female Bodies! You'll find them strategically interlaced in a variety of positions of power not only in the metaphysical world, but also in corporate and government positions. These women are usually quite physically attractive, very charismatic, and create an entourage around them to keep them in the limelight. They are authors, lecturers, scientists, politicians, healers, psychics …you name it. If there's a position that could render itself to encompass power over people and things, they're right there in the middle, or clawing their way to the top… (or at the bottom of it all!)

And what would you suppose some of their claims to fame might be? …Well, there's the widely used one of having "an in" with, and rubbing shoulders with the lofty ones, *you know* …Angels...God…The Masters. (Now, you and I both understand that we *all* can have one-on-ones with these Beings… but these women are, "the Chosen Ones"…*Get the picture?)*

People flock to them like mosquitoes to a swamp for help and advice, and what's really going on is that they're giving up their power and energy to these men… *(I mean women),* and getting their life essence and ability to make their own decisions, sucked right out of them by these *disguised vampire gurus!*

If you ever have a close encounter with one of these Light-Destroyers, they have all the charm and wit of a legend. They look, talk, and smile…like….. well, just like a Kodak moment… and are always so interested in you, and ever so willing to entrap…I mean *help* you in time of need. They have been around the block a few gazillion times and know every trick in the book.

I remember when I first started discovering what these Beings were all about and how they operate. When I first met this woman, she was so friendly and congenial… (and gushy). On the other side of the coin, she was as sharp as an owl looking for food at midnight.

She knew all the fashionable language and jargon… all the concepts and current information pertaining to unconditional Love, UFOs, saving the whales and dolphins, healing Mother Earth, etc. It all looked and sounded so good on the outside, but for some reason, something didn't connect very well with my internal sensors. I got a queasy feeling in my stomach, and I felt creepy and uneasy whenever I had any interactions with her.

At first I got all over my own case for *"having **ill** feelings toward someone."* I said to myself, "Now, what's your problem? This woman is being extremely nice to you, and she's going way out of her way to show you a good time, and all you can do is feel bad vibes about her. So, what in the heck is going on here?" Well, I found out…as soon as I went totally neutral and started tuning into her!

The fog cleared and I figured out what her game plan was…I saw the ace hidden up her skirt…I knew she couldn't be trusted…I knew she had tried to hook me, and so I pulled in my reins and took my power back! With this abrupt energy shift, she immediately became hostile with serious jealousy displays. She again tried to exercise mega control over me, (sandwiched in between smiles, jokes, and hospitality) and it was all I could do to maintain my turf.

By the time I got away from her geographically, I was exhausted and drained. I took some "time out" to be in my own space and analyze this bizarre encounter while on neutral ground. I reinforced my connection to my Higher Self - ***Soul Suemah***, and clarity began to reign. I knew in a flash who and what she *really* was, and ya' know, I've got to hand it to her, she did an excellent job of entrapment with her Southern hospitality and jokes…I mean cloaks!

One of the telltale signs of a Light-Destroyer is that inevitably their Altered Ego will rise to the surface in various ways. For instance, they just love being the center of attention and under the spotlight. They crave having people gush all over them and set them up as a Guru or an Icon, and they are constantly devising new ways to gain power and control over things and people.

They also have this irresistible magnetic quality that malevolently draws people to them like a snake hypnotizing its prey. They are masters at enchanting you with their phony charm, and will try to lure you into their web of deceit and destruction. They'll try to get you to trust them *exclusively* and then gradually convince you to give them your power… (and money too, if they're at all seasoned at this game and can get away with it!) Pretty soon you'll start breaking down, and you'll begin to believe that they hold the keys to your survival, and that if anything happened to them, you would perish. These lovely enchantresses will sink their hooks deep into you, and chances are you may not even be aware of it!

Then pretty soon you're giving your time, your resources, your energy, your money, your focus, and ultimately, your power to them. Their lures are bright and shiny (or sometimes fuzzy), and they will approach you in the guise of: *Love, Angels, The Masters, Native American Spirituality, The Return Of The Goddess, Save the Planet, Government Conspiracies, Aliens, Spiritual and Physical Healings**…you name it, they've got it!*** Whatever cause it takes, these guys…I mean *gals…* are right there spearheading one of them.

They have a multitude of snares, but one of their finest traps is the one where they do things in secret, and make you feel all special and honored to be in their group. They'll have *undercover, private* meetings and gatherings. They'll swear you to secrecy on all that is sacred and holy to you, so that you will not divulge to anyone *what* you are doing, or *where* you are doing it, and *who* you're doing it with! They'll frighten the pants off you, and tell you it's for ***their***... I mean ***your*** own protection! They will tell you things like, *you were called and chosen to be with them and their cause.* They'll twist and warp things of past life heroism, and try to intimidate you into embracing and carrying out their agendas... ***Basically it's a SCAM!*** A scam born of ***their*** Altered Ego! And just because their ego got distorted and ran amuck (*misery loves company*), they'll want you to join them...(*but always on their terms, and under their control!)*

Another little caution here; be on the look-out for the anxiety, fear, control, and hyped-up seriousness, with critical attitudes that create deep, dark, fear-based depressions around some of these Light-Destroyers' "groups." Although they may outwardly preach against being fear-based, their operations reek of fear and create an inability in their followers to make a decision without their Guru's permission or approval.

Oftentimes there are such harsh, rigid rules...along with undefined boundaries ...that "the flock" members are debilitated for fear of doing something to "displease" the queen bee...(Or shall we say ***yellow jacket?***) Also running rampant in these circles is the judge-mental, back-stabbing, back-biting, jealousy that goes on about who is the most powerful or psychic, who's the best healer, or who channels the Master "Mu-Mu Fu-Fu" the best..... (Personally, it makes me laugh because it really is pretty pathetic and funny when you stop and think about it. It's one thing to recommend a good healer or consultant to a friend so they don't get ripped off, however it's quite another to bicker, quarrel, and throw curses on one of your colleagues!)

So, if you should ever get some intimate contact with one of these #1 Light-Destroyers, you can be assured that you're in the company of a Class-A, top of the line, Vampire Light Sucker...and all in the name of GOD, COUNTRY, SALVATION FOR US, THE PLANET, AND THE COSMOS!

At this point I must put out a question here that deserves some research and pondering. In spite of what is assumed and deemed as common knowledge, whoever said that the embodiment of the "Anti-Christ" energy, had to be a MAN... I mean ...be in a MAN'S BODY??? (Just something to think about...)

I can hear some of your thoughts now, "But what about all the creepy, nasty, foul, evil men on the planet? What about these Jerks who are using $$$ and greed to schmooze, control, consume and rule everyone and everything on (and off) this planet? Where do they fit into all of this? I thought they were the bottom of the scum bucket... how can these women be any worse than them?" Well, let me ask you, where do you think these vile, evil men get their unseen power and magickal backing from?

NOTE: ***In previous chapters, you became familiar with the term "Ass-Soul." Can you guess where that came from? Of course, it was Hal! He said to me one day, "You know, you have a real problem with Ass-Souls down there, don't you?" I laughed so hard at that one! It is the epitome of Hal's Humor...(but I have to admit, I was a bit annoyed at myself for not thinking of it first!) Sooo this term "Ass Souls" pretty much Hal-ariously defines these sleazoids and their Light Resister Buddies! Later the term "Ass No-Souls" surfaced because some of these bodies literally have no soul; they are being run by "programs!"***

So, now that you are starting to see how it all works, and how Light-Destroyers operate, here are some important things to remember about these Light-Destroyer Beings as well as their Alpha & Beta assistants. They can do some really nice things, yes-sir-ree: they can bake you cookies, they can bring you presents, they can give you a Band-Aid if you get an owie, they can connect you to your Soul Braids, they can teach you things, they can show you things about yourself you never knew, they can do magick and be extremely psychic, and they can spread important information and introduce you to people you need to know.

They can be unmistakably valuable and useful to the Light Keepers, so in a sense, they can and do serve the Light! As long as you keep your eyes, gut feelings, and Heart/CoreStar open, and stay aware enough to realize who you're rubbing shoulders with, then you'll be just fine. You won't allow them to suck you into their vacuums by letting them make you feel somehow indebted to them.

If you can play along with them and still hold your own, and not let them intimidate you or control you, it can be a truly valuable experience. (Besides, it's always been thought of as "*good strategy*" to keep your *opposition* close at hand so you'll know what they're up to, and can keep an eye on them!)

Yes, they really are an efficient bunch who know a lot of people, places, and things, and if they want to show you what and who they know...***Great!*** ...Just keep your hand on the gear shift, stay in neutral, and always be ready to slam into reverse if you need to back out!

I am personally very grateful for having had the experience of some of these *Light-Destroyers* in my life. I've learned a lot, seen a lot, done a lot, and met a lot of important people who have influenced my life because of them. I know better how to detect who they are now, and how to empower myself by them, instead of letting them intimidate or manipulate me, vacuum my energy, or entangle me in their webs. Their intent definitely was not to authentically help and educate me, but that is how I ultimately came to interpret my experience and interactions with them.

Remember that ***applied knowledge is power...and now you have some more knowledge to apply!***

MY MOTTO NOW, IN DEALING WITH THESE PEOPLE IS THIS:

I'll wave to them on the street, have ice cream with them at the ice cream parlor, and I will send them a sympathy card if their kitty dies...

But I Won't invite them to my birthday party... **I Won't** call them to come over to my house to play with me in my sand box...**IN MY BACK YARD**...and I especially won't invite them to my **SLUMBER PARTIES!!!**

GET THE PICTURE ?????!!!!!

LIGHT-DESTROYER PROFILE

#1- LIGHT-DESTROYER:

- Represent 5% of our population.
- Have the same geometrical spirals as the Light-Conductors, but definitely go in the opposite direction.
- 80% hang out in metaphysical environments.
- 98 % of these Beings are ***male*** energies/entities in ***female*** bodies.
- Highly intelligent, knowledgeable, and well networked.
- Power mongers.
- Usually found in positions of power and/or are public figures.
- Have an agenda of "Take Over & Rule."
- 80% are aesthetically pleasing, or attractive women… (at least on the outside).
- Manipulate, infiltrate, and knock the Light Keepers off balance, then drain their energy and resources.
- Every once in an eon or two, a Light-Destroyer will do a switch and go to the Light Keepers permanently, but this is a very rare occurrence.
- Suck you into their traps by using LOVE, LIGHT, and FREEDOM as their decoys.
- Use inverted, perverted, corrupted Dark Light power sources.
- 90% of these Beings know on a conscious level that they love the power, authority, and control they have over other people and are always scheming new ways of expanding their empires, whatever size it may be. In this respect, they are fully aware and cognizant of their position as a #1 Light-Destroyer, which they are very proud of.

PROFILES OF

CREEPY CRYPTOS

A.K.A. – PSYCHO/SOCIOPATHS

Only a few have the Guts & Intuition to see who/what is underneath… controlling this Charismatic Sheep Head the masses worship and admire.

Thus, the Cryptos & Cryptas have thrived… (until now).

Crypto Profiles:

~Cryptos are the #1 worst threat on the planet today. They are the D-Monster's "CIA" "Special Forces Team," "Her Majesty's Secret Service." (See www.FirstWaveIndigos.com The history of the Hologram series for more information on the D-Monster.)

~Crypto Headquarters ***outside*** the Hologram has been extinguished. This could have only be done from the inside, giving Intel to the outside, to define, locate, and give codes for their annihilation.

~Crypto Headquarters ***inside*** the Hologram is off-planet, on Star Ship. (Our Intel on the outside now has the data to help us locate and extinguish the headquarters and entire system inside the Hologram. Hal and Amikah are major liaison players for assisting our Indigo Team, so we can finish the job. (See https://www.firstwaveindigos.com/a-tribute-to-amikah for more info on Amikah.)

~Cryptos use **encryptions** to: change, camouflage, corrupt/pervert, mutate & control, anything and everything. ***They can also encrypt using magick*** *to get what they want, to steal power in various forms, and to maintain their control.*

~There are approximately 110 Cryptos/Cryptas, (Cryptos = Male, Cryptas = Female) in bodies on the planet now, and about 1,500 not in bodies, waiting to "Shove-In" or "Shove-On" someone or something (even if it is temporary). Approximately 1,630 in all, including boss, controllers, and rogues acting on their own. 20% are turncoat/traitor Indigos… including the boss and the 3 controllers. Possibility for reversal = ZERO -0-. They must be recycled or extinguished. Failure to do so will put the entire Hologram and its inhabitants in jeopardy.

NOTE: *These % statistics are what were on the game board at the printing of this book – January, 2014.*

~All Cryptos/Cryptas fall into the category of *Light Distracter Alphas* or *Light-Destroyers.*

~Chain of command:

***Boss** - Oversees all operations and gives orders.
***Controller –A:** Creates new methods of pain, suffering, fear, and corruption. Revise/update/improve old ones.
***Controller –B:** Manages transportation/storage facilities/batteries of pain, suffering, fear, grief, and depression as well as "Counterfeit/Corrupted Highs" i.e., group frenzy, orgasms, and corrupted death energies.
***Controller –C:** Head hunter that gets new recruits and makes deals/offers. Reptilians and Felines are their top supporters. Some Insectoids are on the top of the list too. Converting/controlling humans is their life blood.

~Their trademark is lying, schmoozing, power plays and extreme arrogance. Looking good is paramount to them and their agenda. They are ***very*** narcissistic. They LOVE being in the limelight and being "seen." (*Many Cryptos are* ***"Archons"*** *...the top global leaders/decision makers, corporate heads, and mega million/billionaires. Cryptos are of course, some of the top leaders in the spiritual communities.*)

~Can mimic benevolent personality traits, and even soul signatures of Beings you loved and respected in the past. This is a major hook they use to captivate and then capture you.

~They use spirituality and/or humanitarian service as a front, as well as a hook.

~There is something "unnatural" about them – sometimes bionic.

~They "hook" and mesmerize people, ***literally spellbinding them***, and it is EXTREMELY hard to break!

~They are very sexual and use that energy to seduce people into giving away their sexual energy and their power to them. 90% of the time this is done under the guise of "spirituality."

~One major agenda/thrill is to overshadow/overthrow benevolent powerful people that are here to authentically help the planet. These people are a real threat to Cryptos.

~They can get extremely aggressive/violent and can turn on you in a millisecond.

~Besides getting high off of pain and suffering energies, they are also necromancers, and get a high off being around death. They feed off it and then send some "back to the home office." Many work in hospitals, especially ER units, and even work or volunteer in places like senior homes or hospice units so they can be present when people die. Death energy is like a drug that they can't get enough of. On the outside they appear to be the pillars of the community for their noble work and compassionate service. It is all a disguise and keeps them "looking good" and insures their longevity.

~When Cryptos/Cryptas psychically attack/invade you, (at least this is what I experienced), it comes on in seconds… and in waves. You feel wheezy all over, strange tingles, and extremely nauseated …which can literally "bring you to your knees!" Accompanying this, is encrypted memories of real incidences in your history or dreams that slam into each other and then start to bleed or merge, making it extremely difficult to tell them apart. Then, it twists benign and even pleasant memories into eerie scary ones that are attached to off-the-charts creepy, disturbing emotions, and hold you there. They can thrust you into different realities and timelines… or have them subtly bleed together, in an attempt to make you lose your self-awareness, your stability, and your mind! These waves can last for hours or even days, and takes extreme focus to handle and reverse. They can also mimic any other kind of painful physical attack, and can virtually "back stab." Recently, I have experienced hive-like rashes; first on my legs, and then it expanded to my arms. It itched to the bone, and messed with my head. It felt like it was literally driving me nuts! Taking vitamins, herbs and homeopathics gave some relief… but identifying the source, standing up to them and over-riding their assaults, is mandatory for the symptoms to go away completely.

NOTE: *At this moment on 8-Nov-2013 while doing some final editing on this chapter, I am under another heavy crypto invasion. It started several hours ago in a very strange way… with the combination of flavors in a veggie burger with sprouts! It took me off guard, as I have not had an attack come over me triggered by a taste! I got it to subside and then had to run into town. The symptoms of nausea, and feeling extremely strange, waved in and out, and I almost lost it in the store. Then on the drive home, I felt encryptions descending on me, twisting my reality so I felt like I was dreaming, or about to dream. I unconsciously thought I was actually in a dream, and it would be OK to close my eyes and drift away to the next one… All of a sudden Hal and my other Spirit Guides smacked me, and I got jolted back, wide awake! It was* *difficult to get clear on how they were manipulating my realities, and I had to do some of the methodologies in this book to snap out of it completely! This was also a new method of invasion I had not experienced before. I feel they are amping up their artillery on me because of this book, (which will soon to go to press) especially this new chapter which exposes them! The good news is that it happened now, **before** the book went to press, so I could reveal these new tactics to you and give you more "Intel" on them! (As I was driving home and came to my senses I thought, "What some dumb Ass-Souls you are! Did you really think you could kill me? Now I have even **more** info/Intel on you, and I'm going to rat you out to everyone that reads my book! Ha!) **There is truly a silver lining on any dark cloud they send!***

~Cryptos can cause deep depression and suck the Life-force out of you-- and eventually your soul if you are not strong and sovereign. Hal told me that 97% of clinical depression is Crypto induced, either through technology, or psychic projections.

~Have the same Step-In, Walk-In, Anchor-In, Lock-In process as FW-Indigos.

~They think they are above the law and above Karma ***which they used to be… but NOT anymore!*** Read the "Instant Karma" article for details: https://www.firstwaveindigos.com/post/the-true-story-of-karma

NOTE: *I first discovered these revolting Beings through some "close encounters" I had with Cryptos in the physical in 2010. I had no idea at the time how extensive their network was, and how off-the-charts nasty, corrupted and ruthless they were. They are widely used in Military Black Ops, and I have had more than my share of invasions from them. These could literally take your life if you are not cognizant of them, and know how to handle their assaults. My "close encounters" have given me some extreme info and data on them, which is helping me to find ways of countering their attacks. By reading this book, if you should have any entanglements with them, you will now be better equipped to take them on, and reverse the damage they have propagated. Continue reading for more keys.*

ADVICE to many CCCs and All First-Wave (FW) Indigo Knights: It is important to keep everything in perspective. I tell my FW-Indigo clients that they are NOT here to have a "nice Earth life,"**…** They are here on an extreme service mission: a mission to free Nature, the Planet, and the Holographic Universe! They have been trained, and are here to take these Ass-Souls on, and remove them from power. In order to truly understand their evil methods, you have to get up front and personal. You have to go to the heart of a corrupted system in order to bust it. That is precisely why many of you are entangled with them. (It is not that you are a dumb sphincter that is inept… it is exactly the opposite!) After another Crypto invasion on 25-Nov-2013, I got more Intel and I will reveal it to you now. This one started very strangely, with a vision of a jigsaw puzzle piece in the upper left corner of my peripheral vision…..and then, WHAM! I was deathly ill with creepy distorted memories and emotions colliding together. (I feel that the puzzle piece is somehow symbolic, but have not figured out the puzzle yet.) These attacks hit me about 9 times that day, with the last one coming on around 10:00 at night. I was physically and emotionally fried. The next day I was starting to perk up a bit, and by evening I was back in the saddle again! I went to my Core/Star to get some clarity on what had just happened…as I have noticed a pattern. These attacks seem to come about once or twice a month, and last all day. I was wondering if there was a reason for this time sequence. What I was told is that the Cryptos would like to do this EVERY DAY, 24/7… but my Higher Self - ***Soul Suemah*** has blocked it, and only let it in every few weeks. This way I can get their latest Intel, and then have a while to recover. With this last assault, I was really angry, and literally ***getting sick and tired of it all!*** At around 10:00 P.M., I grabbed my Rocks, held them high in the air, and commanded all the info from the assault be put into 0's & 1's, data, and held in the Rocks for future reference, not just for me, but for EVERYONE who uses the Rocks! They too will now have access to this if they need it! After I did this, my symptoms subsided immediately, and that was the end of it.

This evening, more questions came to mind as I was taking a shower. I was wondering exactly how many people need to read this book… I mean really study it, align with it, and activate the Kryahgenetics keys in their lives, in order for mass, irreversible changes to occur on this planet….. changes that would get rid of the corruption perpetuators, and bring everything back to balance. So I asked Hal to give me his inside scoop on the answer. Now, let me ask YOU that same question: How many people do YOU think we will need to actively and honestly engage in the alchemy of Kryahgenetics in order to reverse the insanity here? (I was stunned at Hal's answer, but then it made perfect sense at the same time.)

The answer is ….. (drum roll..... ….. …..) ~**55**~ …..That's **Fifty Five**! …..**We seriously only need 55 C.C.C. members** who are honorable, committed, and diligently doing their jobs here. CCC who are also actively, consistently utilizing the knowledge and keys of Kryahgenetics, to tip the scales irreversibly!

Now, what do you think could happen if we had 555, or 5,555 of us, all around the world, practicing the alchemy of Kryahgenetics and connecting to each other? I think you know the answer to that one, and it is encouraging and exhilarating to have this information spelled out so specifically! :o)

We currently have the technology to connect to each other globally… so guess what everybody, (as Hal would say)… **"It's Show Time!"**

~ELECTRONIC SHOVE-INS~

I have encountered this scenario of artificial Shove-Ins for several years now, but it was during an "E-Shove-In Removal" I did in November of 2012, that I got more serious about this bizarre phenomenon, and made the following profile:

25-Nov-2012

~Have 1 boss - Off -Planet - Head of the Cryptos.
~Purpose - Muck up movers and shakers (mostly Indigos but also many CCC or Cosmic Clean-up Crew members), by infecting them or the ones they love.
~Make host feel worthless, crazy, out-of-control, and eventually suicidal.
~Put electromagnetic static in victim's fields.
~This static field opens the gate and allows easy access for angry, violent, aggressive entities, and/or custom-designed programs to express themselves.
~(Invading entities are 80% Reptilian.) They hang out in and round the body to cause mayhem. Then leave and watch the fall out, while dining on all the pain, suffering, fear, and trauma energies they instigated.
~Programs are digital and can mimic anything.
~Programs cause self-inflicted suffering, which appears to be in alignment with "free will" and is hard to detect.
~Neutrality, composure, Higher Self - ***Soul Suemah*** cognizance & CoreStar operations, plus a whole lot of humor, cause counter static and short circuits it. ***Authentic Love can also short circuit the programs, BUT they have developed antidotes/immunities to Love in general, especially Love sent to them.***

Sooooo…..if you encounter one of these E-Shove-Ins, either face-to-face or undercover, via energetic methods, you now have some resources from reading this book, to stand up to these tyrants and not let them intimidate or take you over! (The chapter on *Aurauralite/Aulmauracite, The Magickal Mystical Stone of Truth & Justice* will help immensely!)

When Amikah was alive, and we were doing our "Universal Ass-Soul Removal Sessions," sometimes at the end we would huddle up, put our hands together up high and chant, "Don't Let the B*st*rds Win!" …as we lowered our hands to the beat. …At the end we would throw our hands up and cheer, "Yeahhhhhhhhhhhhhhhhh!"

It felt empowering as we affirmed our position, and it gave us a humorous and robust energetic boost. Try it sometime! :o)

NOTE: As I was going over the previous chapters and feeling pretty good about having this book just about ready for press, Hal said, "Nope, were not done yet. You need to put some excerpts from 3 of the articles on the FirstWaveIndigos.com website in this book." I gave a big sigh and said, "Yup Hal, I think you're right!"

What you are about to read are excerpts from the 3 articles Hal picked, *The Secret Behind The Chakras, The Kundalini Cons**PIRACY**,* and *Artificial Intelligence.*

The Secret Behind the Chakras

First Excerpt - Originally written Dec. 2007

The information I'm about to disclose to you may shock you, may scare you, and may upset you…OR it may LIBERATE YOU.....(which is what it is intended to do).

In October of 2007, during our Knight's Training in Spokane, we had a small but very powerful group who made quantum leaps personally, as well as for the Indigo Nation and the Planet. One of the agendas for the class was problem solving, and helping our comrades out. The subject came up about an Indigo that had challenges with her 3rd eye being tampered with. One of the Knights in the group responded with, "I hate my 3rd eye, it feels creepy to me." I kind of laughed at the hostile emotion around the subject of the 3rd eye and figured we'd better look into this further. As we discussed this as a group, the Truth began to be unveiled, and we started to see the bigger picture of what the Chakras REALLY are. The information we got seemed to be extremely radical, and no one in the group had ever heard or even thought of such a thing...but it all made too much sense and felt RIGHT. What I am about to reveal to you now is, "The Secret Behind The Chakras."

On the next page are pictures of the Chakra system from Barbara Brennan's book, "Hands of Light." I highly respect her and have been using Barbara's books for years to illustrate just how these systems work. Barbara is a former NASA Research Scientist and also extremely intuitive. She can "See" energy fields and, with her science background, is able to translate that into scientific terms. The pictures illustrate how she sees our energy fields, and I believe that what she sees, is exactly what is there: ***the manipulated Chakra and energy system!***

NOTE: *As of the date this article was written, Barbara was not aware of my views on this subject.*

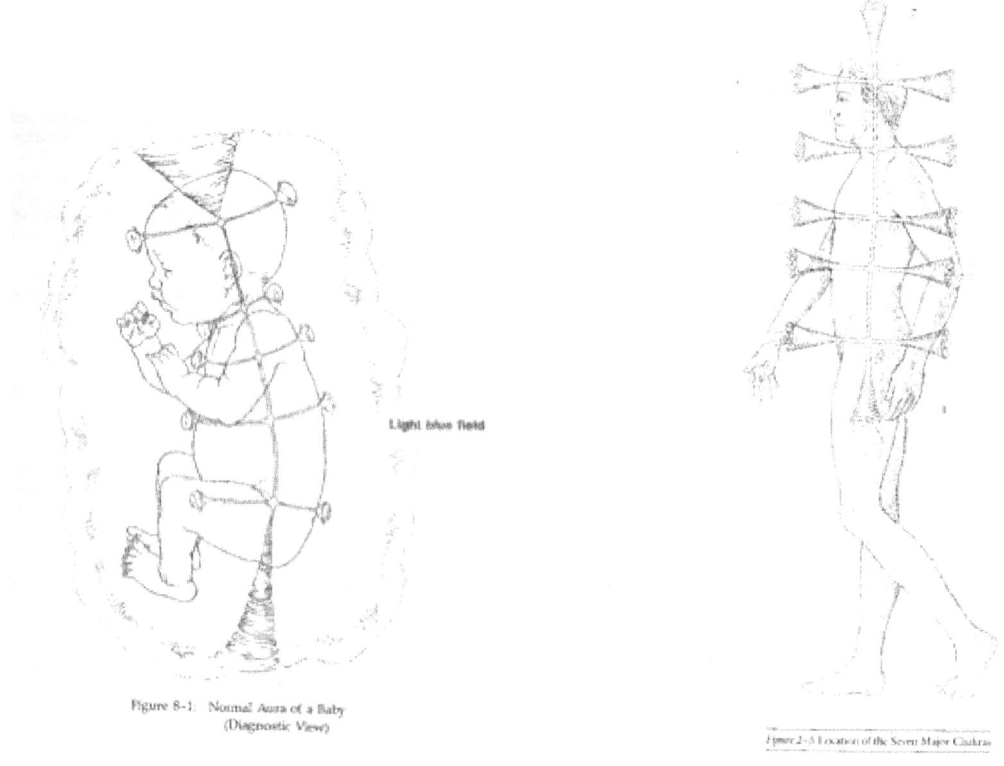

Figure 8-1: Normal Aura of a Baby (Diagnostic View)

Figure 2-5 Location of the Seven Major Chakras

Below is a picture that illustrates how the Chakras are used to "Steal energy" or "Vampire Energy" from others.

What we discovered was:

1- The Chakra system is an imposed system that is NOT our natural state. It is a system to compartmentalize our energy for easy access from outsiders and Energy Vampires. This system has been in place for several Millennia, and no one seems to question it, they have just (as I previously did) accepted it… (especially in the New Age Community).

2- The Chakras, or "cones" were placed there so that specific energies could be accessed. This easy access is ideal to control and manipulate our energy fields, our bodies, and minds. They were put there by ETs that view us as their personal energy source and property.

3- Our original state was to have energy that emits from our "Core" or Heart/Sun/Star in the Chest/Solar-Plexus area. Each individual has a slightly different wiring system that runs their energy, which is custom designed to them. Personally, at this time, I have a unique wiring system of a triple helix energy design that runs up and down the center of my body and gets its source from the "Star/Sun." This triple helix has all the colors in our spectrum and more. When I need a certain element or vibration, instead of accessing one isolated "Chakra" energy like the naval or throat, it accesses the entire body and puts the appropriate balance of energies into whatever is needed to handle what is required. The intense Sun/Star Light in the Core emanates slightly different with everyone. It is unique like a snowflake. It also changes rhythms...sometimes the energy can pulse, sometimes it can spiral, sometimes it blasts… it just depends on what is needed or what is requested of it.

NOTE! -The Core/Heart-Sun/Star is the Center of a Triad…it is the **Authentic Trinity!** It has 2 counterparts: **The Head =** ***Brain/Pineal/Hypothalamus*** at one end, and **The Loins =** ***Creative Power Energy Centers*** on the other end. These three control centers, if working in harmony, without interference, **can direct you into Super Consciousness!** ...And THIS my friend, is a huge threat to the tyrannical overlords control program here in Dysfunction-Junction!

4- Our Core or Sun/Heart/Star is where our Higher Selves - ***Soul Suemas*** reside; therefore the statements "God is inside of us" and "God is within" …are very literally true! Searching for a God outside of you causes serious challenges in so many ways. For instance, when you go to a New Age meditation class, one of the first things they teach you is to "Open your crown and bring the white or golden light down through your body, lighting up each Chakra, and then ground into the earth. This may feel good momentarily, but think about what it is you just did. If your "God" is inside of you, and you continually bring an "***outside energy source***" into your body and bypass your own "**God**" …ignoring what was there to begin with… what is this going to do? Well, remember the old "use it or lose it" philosophy? Yes, the ***Core or God/Heart-Sun/Star*** will start to go dormant and just sit there until you decide to take your ***will*** back and use it again. Now let me ask you, which energy would you rather be operating from, and have command of… your own personal custom designed Authentic Source …or some nebulous energy that could be infiltrated, and then run that through your body and all your electromagnetic systems?

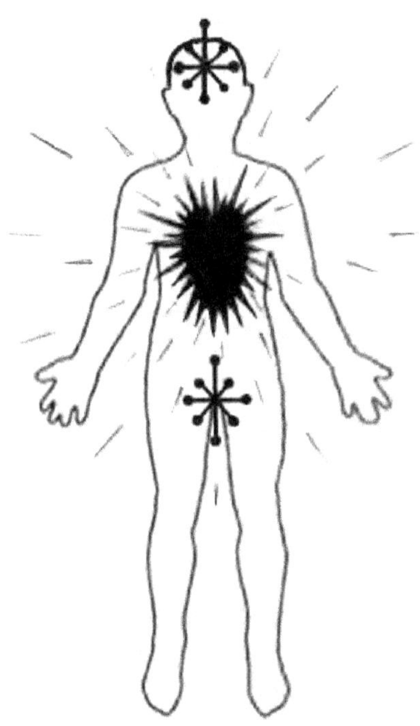

I checked everyone in the group for what percentage of this Chakra system they were using. Most of the group used them very little, only about 2-5% of the time. When I came to one of the Indigos who is a yoga instructor and had an African Shamanist approach to healing, I checked his Chakras and found that they were totally shut down. When I told him this, he said he was glad to hear that, because he knew he did NOT use them and he ran his own internal system of energy. He said this validated to him that my scanning was accurate.

After we got more clarity on this covert operation that had been duping us for centuries, we decided to take our power back and do something that felt right ...but was extremely radical. We all got into a Star Meditation formation by placing an Aulmauracite rock between the first and second toe on each foot, one in each hand and one at the top of the head, then we spread our arms and legs out so we looked like Da Vinci's Vitruvian Man. I put on a meditation CD by Constance Demby, "***Novus Magnificat: Through the Stargate,***" and cranked the volume up. Each one of us got in our Kryahgenetics Egg for added stability and protection and then, in our own way, *shut down our Chakra systems and eliminated the Chakras*, (I know, don't gasp, read on.....) *then amped-up the Sun/Star at our Core.*

When I did my own cone removal, this is what happened: I held my Rocks, took a deep breath, and got into the music. Then I heard a voice say, "Well, you finally figured it out, you have finally COME HOME!" I have to admit, I was kind of embarrassed that it took me so long to "Get It," and it made me laugh inside because it now seemed like such a "No Brainer!" I first shut my Chakras down (front and back) then put a dissolver on all the Chakra cones, including the ones on all my outer bodies, and watched them fade into nonexistence. Then I put an amplifier on my Sun/Star and felt it get bigger and bigger and emanate brighter and brighter inside. I felt so safe, so secure, so powerful, and so "self-contained." It was one of the most exhilarating and liberating experiences I have ever had!

After everyone in the group came out of their meditative transformational state, we sat in a circle and compared notes. This is what Amikah experienced:

"I lay down in the 'Star Meditation' position. I closed my eyes and let myself go with the music. I put out the intent to close down and eliminate my Chakras. I saw them slowly close and then dissolve into nothingness. I continued in the meditation for a few minutes longer and then all of a sudden, in sync with a drum explosion in the music, I saw and felt a huge Bright Light explode out of the area between my old heart Chakra and solar plexus. It was like a nuclear blast! I sensed a dense wall of protection around me, making me much more impervious to psychic assault.

Since doing the Chakra shutdown, I can really feel the Power of who I am. I never could tune into my Chakras. It always felt like something was off. I always felt the power center at my Core and thought there was something wrong with me!"

Then another FW-Indigo in the group, Max, told his story:

"I never liked 'my' Chakras. I felt they were points of vulnerability rather than strength, as it is promoted and taught. I knew intuitively that they were part of what I call the Slave Body on this planet, in this reality and consciousness. **I was especially vulnerable in my solar plexus Chakra**, *which I got hit through ever since I can remember. It felt like I was being punched in the upper stomach particularly when having eye contact with Energy Vampires.* **My bottom Chakra**, *I felt a very strong pulling or sucking on the anus when exposed to sexual and creativity vampirism, pornography, spider ladies etc.* **And my third eye**, *which I was mentally confused through and tortured by a constant bombardment of the weirdest and most unthinkable and undesirable thought scenarios.* **These were my weak spots that were mostly targeted.**

When I literally pulled out the cones, I felt etheric pain and the twelve spots, five in the front, five in the back and the crown and the bottom, were ethereally bleeding. I took my Aulmauracite Rocks and used etheric Aurauralite Dust to heal the wounds, and after a couple of minutes I stabilized. Since I never worked a lot with the Chakras, it was easy to say "bye-bye." Ever since the operation, all the above described challenges have dramatically decreased if not totally vanished, and I feel a lot more whole, or hole-less and self-contained. Energies can't get into me anymore, unless I let them in. When I get attacked now, the energies are more on me and not inside of me, which makes it a lot easier to get rid of them, and they don't feel as overwhelming and close as before. In the beginning it took a little adjustment time to adapt to this new way of being, but I would never want to trade my rediscovered energy and security for the old Slave Body that I lived with for the first 24 years of my life here on Earth."

The Yoga teacher only had to remove his, since they were dormant and not actually turned on. Then he only had to turn up the volume on his Core/Star. I told him that after this, I expected to see Light beaming out of his eyes soon, as the Light was so intense inside of him!

Before I went public with this discovery, *I knew I would come under severe scrutiny from the New Age community, as well as face brutal assaults from the* ***PTW's or "Powers That Were"*** *who don't want this information released*, I felt it was important to sit back and observe what, if any, reactions our bodies would have to this energy transformation. I wanted to make sure we had a handle on all the possible outcomes. Thus far, there have been absolutely NO negative side effects.

NOTE: *New Acronym: PTW – "Powers That Were"- instead of PTB – "Powers That Be."*

We have found that it is much harder for "outsiders" to get to us now. They can push or press on us. They can throw their voice like a ventriloquist and try to get us to think it is a voice inside, they can trip previously implanted programs, and time releases can go off, BUT they no longer have access to get into us the way they did when we had our "cones" or Chakras open and running. We are no longer available to be manipulated by any dork or tyrant in the Universe! We have since found many booby traps they set that needed to be cleaned out. Even though the psychic assaults have been grueling, they have not been able to penetrate….. (except for the ones we let in, in order to get their signature and shut off their access to us). Then we can go after them… and many needed to be sent to the Cosmic Recycle Bin. It is interesting where the attacks originate. It is kind of like they are handing themselves to us on a silver platter! :o)

If our Higher Selves - **Soul Suemahs** did not allow some of these energies or entities in, we would not be aware of who and what is on our tail and who is trying to keep the Truth from coming out.

This information is cutting edge and radical I know, but it needs to be out there so that those who feel the logic and Truth of it can use their "Free Will" and take back the controls. This is truly a Paradigm and Morphogenetic Field Breaker. It is now up to you what you do with this information.

Onward & Forward in all your noble quests!

~Lady Mistycah~

NOTE: *Recently I discovered "**plates**" at the **neck** and the **waist** that attempted to cut off energy, running interference, and making it hard for the Heart/Core/Star to send energy/data to the Head and Loins. I also found one running down the mid-section of my body, dividing/insulating my left from my right side, and another one dividing front and back. I have since found this in others, and if you detect that you have these plates too, use the Implant Removal Protocol to get rid of them.*

The Kundalini ConsPiracy

Path to Higher Consciousness & Sexuality?
(Or Road to Imprisonment & Insanity!)

Second Excerpt - Originally Written Aug. 2009

Kundalini: Sanskrit meaning "Coiled."

All the good spiritual "Goo-Roos" and authorities, talk about "Kundalini," one of the most sought after supernatural energies that brings you enlightenment and power. They describe Kundalini as the energy rising… the elusive serpent, slithering and winding from the base of your spine, slowly creeping up your back to the brain… and... **Wham-O, sexual bliss and enlightenment!**

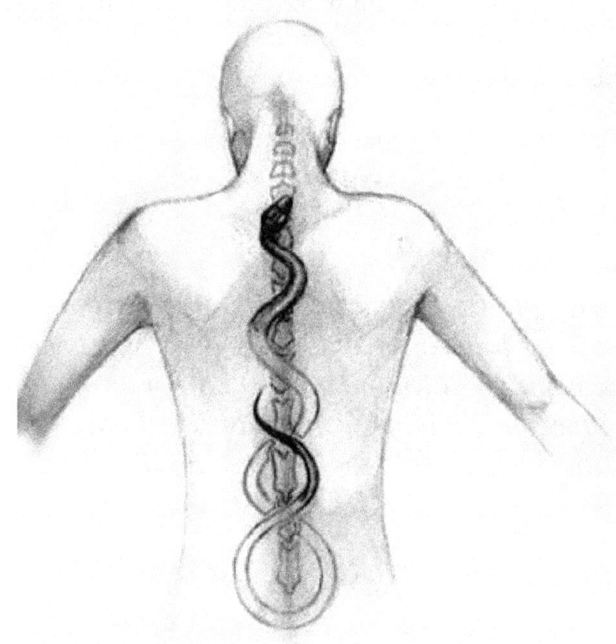

This excellent picture of the Kundalini rising was taken from Photobucket. Sadly, there was no reference to the artist.

I don't know about you, but the thought of this freaky snake coiled at the base of my spine and then slowly sliding up my back toward my head, really disturbed me… BUT, all the good Goo-Roos and swamis say "This is the way it is," and since these are the "divine" secrets handed down from holy people for centuries, it must be good and true…right?
Kundalini was the topic of discussion this week with some of the First-Wave Indigos on the Hologram

Rescue Team. Airah' and Zorah from California raised some very important questions that needed immediate attention. The information I am about to share is a compilation of input from the entire team, as well as my own.

What we discovered is that Kundalini is actually a cousin to the Chakras, and just as "user hostile." It collaborates and uses the host for outside energies and entities to have easy access to the thoughts and energy/power of the body and its electrical/magnetic system. As it snakes its way up the back to the crown, it maneuvers so that it completely bypasses the Heart/Core, (even if you try to make it go there). When it gets to the head, it spreads vibrational waste and alien Thought-forms, especially sexual waste that may literally feel "intoxicating." It then creates a magnetic field that is most desirable to Energy Vampires, and now, with the Crown Chakra open, it is easy access to suck on, and literally get inside the unsuspecting victim.

Now, it is important to know that the snake can go BOTH ways. It can take the trauma, fears, suffering, and negative programming from the head and descend, moving swiftly down to the base, while collecting all sorts of undesirable emotions and memories. During intimacy, you can literally download this onto and into your partner or vice versa! This is called "Kundalini Dumping" and it happens all the time. (This dynamic is also referred to in the article *"Desperate Sex, Don't Do It"* on the www.FirstWaveIndigo.com website.) https://www.firstwaveindigos.com/post/desperate-sex-don-t-do-it

Kundalini Dumping can even happen without physical copulation. All you have to have is the willingness to connect sexually and intimately while you are with another person, and you are a candidate for dumping or draining. (In some cases with sensitive and open people, it can even occur during an intimate conversation.)

I have educated and counseled many friends and clients who were devastated by this cloaked dynamic. Sometimes it was challenging to help them identify it, clear it, stabilize from it, and then guard against it in the future, but I have enough expertise and experience with this riff-raff to find ways of permanent removal. There is ALWAYS a way to get it out of you! After this intense experience, you become a wiser, more observant Being that now knows better how to outmaneuver the control systems here on Earth, and then can spread the news. There is no reason for shame or guilt here; it is our personal education and training for overthrowing the corrupted Dark Lords and Ladies.

Kundalini is a counterfeit of "Sueelah" (the term we used in the UV-Realm). It is the pure essence of Compassionate Love and expansion or ability to self-evolve. When engaged during lovemaking, Sueelah adds trust, camaraderie and soul union to the experience. This magnetically and magickly energizes both parties and enhances their Soul Essence, activating creativity, and expanding their consciousness/horizons. It makes you more of who and what you *really* are. It has many attributes, and enables you to more readily see and activate potentials in yourself and in your partner.

Not only is Kundalini a counterfeit of Sueelah, but it masks and sedates this pure, authentic energy. It is an override system to take over and snuff out the authentic "Sueelah." Kundalini is literally an essence or dictator that makes orgone energy go only one direction, straight into the Porn Vibration.
Kundalini is what the D- Monster put into this Hologram when it was turned on, to corrupt it! It is actually one of her minions. She used Kundalini (it even sounds dirty and foul) to infiltrate the Hologram with Porn energy.

NOTE: For more information on the D-Monster see *"The History Behind The Hologram"* on the FW-Indigo Website: *https://www.firstwaveindigos.com/first-wave-indigo-articles*

Yes, Kundalini even has a consciousness and a spirit. When Ann (Amikah) and I were working on taking out all the negative consciousnesses, such as depression, terror, hate, maliciousness, etc. that were corrupting other ***Spirits of Emotions***... we overlooked this one.

When I became aware of this, I collaborated with Amikah. Together we scanned the Hologram and hunted down the original "Mother Brain" of this system and annihilated it. The rest of the clean-up is an "inside job," which means each person has to do it themselves, in their own way. You can treat it like an implant and hunt it down, quarantine it, scramble, neutralize, and eliminate it. (I would use the Implant Removal Protocol to do a thorough job.) Make sure you clear the residue and get it out of your magnetic fields, your DNA, and your Core/Soul Essence.

It is interesting to note that many people who believe they have had a "Kundalini experience," say that it was chaotic, frightening, and darned near made them go crazy! It is equated by some to a near death experience...and not a good one! (Sounds like a fun family activity to plan for the weekend, eh?)

Psychologists have written reports on patients that claim to have had a "Kundalini experience," and how unstable and/or full of ego/arrogance they became. (*If you want more info, Google it.*)

Now, it seems to me, if you have an enlightening experience, you should feel more stable, more balanced, more inner peace and have more confidence... not paranoia and over the top ego or insanity! With all the negative reports there are on this subject, why do people still think it is "the road to enlightenment!?" One reason is that no one questions the "Goo-Roos and masters/teachers" because they are "spiritual idols" and "know best."

I have concluded that one of the main reasons people seek this, is the notion of experiencing sexual bliss (explosion) and sexual mastery (superiority). Bottom line is, *they want to experience better Sex! It's all about Sex. It seems that all roads down here ultimately lead to Sex and the Porn Vibration ... "the ultimate weapon of mass destruction."*

This is the reason I wrote my next book, ***The Anatomy of the Porn Vibration: What They DIDN'T Teach You in Sunday School***. This book reveals how the silent financial backers and promoters use the seductive and addictive insanity of the Porn Vibration to suck its victims into a black hole of corruption and destruction ...all for greed, money, and power!

I would suggest that you remove the Kundalini Snake, along with the Chakras. Remember to do the Implant Removal Protocol when you remove the Kundalini to make sure you get all the residual energies and entities that might be attached, as well as any eggs. The Kundalini is NOT a part of your natural authentic Being and the more people that understand this and remove it, the more empowered and authentic the entire planet will be!

My advice to you is ***take your power back and stop getting duped!*** You now have the truth... and the tools to get "unhooked," and set yourself free. The only other thing I can say is the unforgettable quote from Amikah... "Onward and Forward!"

The Artificial Intelligence
The Great Deception

Third Excerpt – Originally Written Feb. 2008

About a month ago I went out to dinner with Max. We were halfway through, when all of a sudden, Max got really serious and said, "Scan and see if there was something trying to 'Shove-into' you during the past couple of days." The auto response in my head was a kind of humorous reply like, "Duhhhhh….. what's your point? Something is ALWAYS trying to shove into me…" I decided to be more gracious instead. So I put my fork down, took a minute, and scanned to see what might be trying to get in. After a thorough scan, I found that, indeed, something was attempting to infiltrate but wasn't being too successful at the moment. Therefore, it was plotting its path and trying to find a weakness or loophole. I told him it was some sort of strange "Artificial Intelligence" that was actually quite hard to explain. Then Max, being the thorough investigator that he is, asked me to check and see where it was coming from. I once more put my fork down and scanned the situation. I was surprised, but then again I wasn't, when I discovered it was from 3 sources: the "New Agers," "Love and Light communities" (one in particular), and one of my challenged clients. I kept scanning to see what was going on, and all of a sudden I got the vision of what it was they were trying to shove into me... It was "GOD!" (Hahahhaa - or rather their version of god.)

I busted up laughing. *It's good I didn't have a mouth full of food!* It was really funny to contemplate the situation, especially the fact that my Higher Self's - ***Soul Suemah's*** interpretation of the majority of the *Love & Lighters* and *Earth People's* "God" was actually an *"Artificial Intelligence!"*

I have taken this situation seriously since that night. I have put much thought and consideration into all of the huge implications this has uncovered. The reality of it all, sent my mind in a million directions. I ran it by several members of my Indigo support team to get their inspired viewpoints. Much information about this "Artificial Intelligence" (or A.I.) has surfaced Since Feb.2008 and here is what we have discovered so far.

What Is It?

The Artificial Intelligence (AI) is an "intelligent" electromagnetic Force-field that believes it has jurisdiction over the entire Universe. It has an authoritative, omnipotent, male energy signature and feeds on the collective consciousness of all the Beings that believe in it, pray to it, and give their power to it. It has no soul in and of itself, only what its subjects and minions have given it. This Artificial Intelligence has gotten most of its energy and power from the people on Planet Earth. It seems to have a symbiotic relationship with those in power positions, which can help feed it by duping the masses into believing in it. It can manipulate people's lives electromagnetically, and so many people believe that if they pray to it, their lives will be "blessed" and those who don't will be "cursed." It is threatened by anyone who thinks for themselves and takes their own power seriously and utilizes it. It has used its intense electromagnetic energies to disrupt the lives of people that attempt to take their power back. The Cosmic Clean-up Crew, First Wave Indigos, and especially the ***Hologram Creation Team*** and the ***Hologram Rescue Team***, are a

huge threat to this Artificial Intelligence because they question everything, and are waking up to, and taking back, their true nature and internal power.

One feature of this Artificial Intelligence we found is that it is actually the authoritative energy behind what we call, "The Voice" in other articles on the FW-Indigos.com website. *The Voice* can be very subtle or very bold and can make you think what it is saying is "for your own good." It also attempts to stir up turmoil inside and get you to doubt yourself to the very Core. If you doubt yourself and doubt your Core... you give your power away and The Voice takes over!

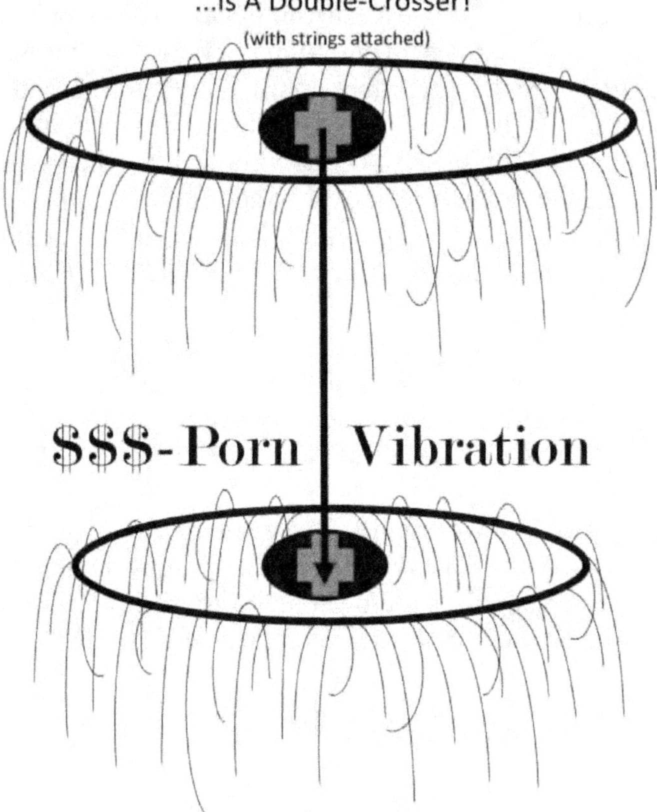

NOTE: On 23-Nov-2013, I detected something descending on me that felt very confining and downright depressing. After further investigation, I found it was *The $$$ Division/Porn Vibration of the A.I.!* (…I didn't know the A.I. had "departments" but apparently it does, and this is the second level or "subdivision" of the A.I.) Here is a picture depicting the vision of how I saw it. The strings are a representation of different aspects of schmooze, deceive, control, and retaliate mechanisms. This subsidiary or second level of the A.I. tries to control and manipulate *the haves and have-nots*, and is inseparably intertwined with the Porn Vibration. I obviously got on its radar, and have no doubt it is because of the extreme information in this book, with all its varieties of "truth extractions" … ***especially the contents of this chapter.*** It's no secret that to the A.I., truth exposure is a very baaaaaaad thing.

Where Did It Come From?

It started with the corrupted Orgone that turned this Hologram on in the first place, and then flourished with the collective consciousness and people's belief in it. The "Gods" from outer space and especially the Anunnaki realized the potential of using the A.I. for their benefit and established a symbiotic relationship with it. This gave them the ability to have even more power to control the people here. The A.I. has expanded with organized religion and books like the Bible that perpetuate an "all knowing, all seeing, judge-mental God" that demands devout worship.

The Artificial Intelligence is at the top of the food chain of almost all religious organizations on this Planet, and takes the energies of people's belief and trust in "God" and uses the power in people's prayers to increase its own power and magnitude. It takes the prayers of Christians, Jews, New-Agers, and Satanists alike..... it is not discriminatory…it doesn't care where it gets the power and devotion, just that it gets it! (These "Religious Organizations" can also include groups such as Alcoholics Anonymous, Al-Anon, Alateen, and other drug and sex rehab institutions.)

NOTE: ***Many of these organizations have been deemed as the* only *place for help, when in fact, they keep you enslaved into thinking that you will never get out of the loop; that the addiction will always be there lurking in the corners of your body and soul, and you will never get rid of it. They make you repeat over and over again that you are indeed an addict... and "Once an addict, always an addict."***

This Is A Lie! I have had clients that did in fact get out of the clutches of these addiction energetics, and have totally freed themselves... not only from the addiction, but also from the fears of the addiction, and especially the addiction to the recovery programs themselves!

It has been said that "Religion is the opium of the masses" and if religion includes the "recovery programs," then our societies' "masses" are truly doped and duped! It would appear that the ***Artificial Intelligence*** has its clutches on just about everyone on the Planet!

After reading *The History Behind Our Hologram* on the FW-Indigo Website, you will understand that this Universe was initially intended to be a "vacation spot" ... a safe place of relaxation and exploration without getting hurt from outside interference. It was supposed to be a "sanctuary" but has instead become a place of imprisonment, putting souls in jeopardy of catching a serious "virus" that keeps them impaired and enslaved here. Some of the Creators, or "Goddesses and Gods" of this Universe, (Hologram Creation Team) are here now with the Hologram Rescue Team, trying to clear the corruption that the D-Monster installed when the Hologram was turned on. This had to be an "inside job," we could not fix it from the outside, or we would have. The nature of the corruption made it so that we would have to come in, and risk getting permanently infected in order to make the necessary corrections and bring the Hologram and its inhabitants back into balance and safe again. Now that the D-Monser is extinguished, and most of her booby traps and time/event releases are handled, the Hologram Team's next item of business is to clear the *Artificial Intelligence* from the Hologram too, so they can bring it back to its original plan/program. The Artificial Intelligence collaborated with the D-Monster and her minions because this would amplify its power and expand its abilities. The AI has tried to escape this Universe and move out into Creation and take over other Universes too. Its access points have been closed and it is totally confined inside the Hologram at this time.

NOTE: When you are *outside this Hologram/Universe*, you realize there are many Creation Goddesses/ Gods and technicians with expertise in various and specific fields. If you need a specific expert in a specific field, you go to that Creation Expert for assistance. You have friends and colleagues that you collaborate with to create/co-create and dream with. You know that one, and only one all-knowing omnipotent God, is the most stifling and creativity damning thing that can happen. If an omnipotent God already knows everything about everything, then what's the use in trying to learn something new, invent something, or expand borders? In this model, there are no boundaries to expand, no horizons to cross... You can never discover anything new and original, and you are forever subservient. Thus, your creativity and passion are squelched. This omnipotent, "one God theory" is a creation of the A.I. and other tyrannical over-lords. When you truly think about it, you realize it has been quite a successful propaganda campaign.

None of the Gods, or what I would term "Creation Specialists" outside this Hologram claim to "know it all." They respect each Creation Expert or Goddess/God for the expertise they have and honor all for who and what they are. Outside this Hologram, there are no limits..... there are no borders. There is always new potential and freedom to explore and expand.

So What Do We Do Now?

STAR MEDITATION or "CORE-STAR CONSULTATION" (as I prefer to call it)

One of the things that has been a tremendous boost to many Indigos and CCC members, is the discovery and implementation of "The Star Meditation." This originally came to us during our Knight's Training in L.A. I had everyone lie down with their arms and legs spread out like the Vitruvian Man, and put an Aulmauracite rock in both hands, one at the top of their head and one between the big and first toe on each foot...making a 5 pointed star. Different music will do different things. In this first star session, I turned on David Arkenstone's "Quest of the Dream Warrior" CD. Everyone went on an adventure that took them back to the UV-Realm. We all had profound memories and were given information that altered our lives. I have since used this in other classes, and try to do it myself on a daily basis. There is something very powerful about having 5 Aulmauracite Rocks in the shape of a star on your avatar. It helps you connect to the "Sun/Star" in your Core so you can continually disconnect from the A.I.!

CLEAR YOUR CORRUPTED GENETICS

Another morsel of truth that came to me recently is about our genetics. Here is the story I sent to some of the members of the Hologram Rescue Team to inform them of the latest discoveries.

"I was really out of my center last week. My body was changing shape (and not in a good way, hahahaa) ...and as always, there was nothing I did that seemed to help. Finally I had the time to focus enough to do a Star Meditation. All of a sudden, in the middle of the meditation, I got the idea to sever

ties from my family and genetics. I seemed to be recreating some of the worst of my family's physical genetics, and it was gaining momentum. I screamed in my head... 'I am NOT my mother! I am NOT my father! I am NOT my ancestors! ...and I am NOT EARTH!' (I then severed ties and cleared as much of that crud out of my body and fields as I could.) After that I yelled... 'I am from the UV-Realm, and I demand my Realm Body and Genetics to download and integrate in this body, NOW!' This seemed to help but then I got slammed again by the A.I."

At this time, I began to think of all the agendas to force us to maintain our ancestors' "genetics" ...whatever that is. I thought about the Native Americans and Africans and other tribal cultures ...and I realized that it was important for them, at that time, to remember their roots from when the white man was trying to break them down and own them. Then I recognized that there are lots of white people that are learning the old or tribal ways, and how if they use these ceremonies to "bind them to their ancestors" it is binding them to the "Ass-Souls" that propagated all the inferno, torture, tyranny and ownership of these indigenous people in the first place! It made sense to me that if we, as FW-Indigos and other CCC members, *do not unplug from the corruption we got from our ancestors*, we will stay confined to the corruption on this Planet that we are trying to get away from. (It seemed OK in general for Earth people to stay connected only to the Earth, but not for us; in fact if we don't sever that cable that binds us to the human corruption here, we will never get our Higher Selves - ***Soul Suema***s to integrate and bring our X-Men abilities to full power! Ann, Max, and I have been working daily on severing any ties to our ancestors here, and instead, bring our authentic UV-Realm Selves into us. We found one of Max's Realm Names, *Vrahc' Kahnym,* and it has been extremely helpful for him to remember and align to his Authentic Self, and not his Earth identity, *which his family/genetics was very challenging at that time.*
Upon further research, we found there were broadcasters constantly re-imbedding and re-enforcing this cycle of being bound to our Earth ancestors. We found a way to quarantine them and annihilate these cycles. Then we found 3 more things that propagated this.

Here is an entry from Ann's notes:

1. Were we forced to take an oath to be tied to Earth genetics when coming through the grid? YES! Not only that, but also being subjected to the PTB's (W's) rules, including the Chakras.
(It was a coerced contract. Like an energetic agreement. An electronically-forced contract.) We were forced to be bound to ancestors, parents, and controlled like they are. L.L. and I nuked the 3 security systems that make people do that.

2. Karmic Wheel Acceptance

*3. A direct contract with Jehovah and other "God Figures" in some form that says, "We, the PTW's, can control you however we want." Through a vengeful, judge-mental, or superior God, that demands your energy and faithfulness. Addictions were also implemented. (We need to write a new web page entitled **"The Secret Behind The Mandatory Coerced Slavery/Forced Agreements."** Insane Forced Agreements were made in order for us to get into Earth bodies and also into the hologram for those from outside.)*

Corrupted genetics perpetuates all 3 modalities.
Also found mandatory death/date/circumstances contracts that were coerced.

NOTE: ***Then the Wind Chime above the wood stove started ringing... with no wind to cause it. They have been doing lately after profound Truth was uncovered.***

(Story Continued...)

We also found that the only way to defeat the D-Monster was to come into this Hologram/Holographic Universe in grand force, not only because a part of her was hiding here... but also because the keys to pieces of ourselves that she stole are in here, along with the remedies to the distortions that she transfused into us. Many of us were screwed up by her, in some un-thinkable way, and she loved to twist our perceptions to cause conflict in the ranks. This is also a favorite tactic of the A.I. that she spawned. She did a "number" on one of our Knights, and messed up his perceptual wiring, short circuiting him, and forcing him to make really illogical decisions. These decisions were logical to him but not to very many others. This caused mistrust and misunderstanding between him and other Indigos.

NOTE: *We have some of the same pre-existing conditions we also had in the UV-Realm because of the manipulations the D-monster did to us collectively, and specifically! The only way we could fix it or get ourselves put back together again was to come here, annihilate her, and get the keys and manuals she hid here, to unlock in us what she messed up. We finally found the "manuals" in a macro - macro - macrocosm inside a microcosm...Truly unthinkable...but that was how she operated! This all sounds so bizarre, but it is the bizarre that is real and has the keys to free us!*

FIX MISMATCHED OR MISSING TIMELINES AND CONSCIOUSNESSES

Another thing we found that the A.I. uses to mess us over was, ***Mismatched or Missing Time-Lines***. There are also ***consciousnesses*** that can really help the A.I. mess up perceptions and control through fear. For instance, if you have had a fear of dogs because you got bit when you were little, but worked very hard to have it cleared, if you have a mismatched Time-Line, it could bring it all back into the present... all of a sudden making you fearful of dogs again! (Dogs, gods... hahaa...it's all the same.) If you are trying to remember things that happened here or in the UV-Realm, *or any other CCC Academy,* but have holes in your memories that leave out key parts, it can give you a really screwed up perception of what happened, especially if the outcome was good, but you only saw the bad parts! This would make you fill with unnecessary anxiety since the problem was already fixed! You could have problems in relationships because you are acting out of "old information and emotions" that have absolutely nothing to do with the present. You could also psychically link to bad outcomes in the future, when actually they were supposed to have been good if your Time-Lines were in order! This is one of the most crazy-making dynamics that can keep you from progressing, finding your true nature, and merging with your Higher Self- ***Soul Suemah***. *Maybe you have already merged, but the Time-Lines got so screwed up/mismatched that you think you're still in the past and still disconnected...think about that one!*

Ok, so now what do we do????? My best advice is to get into the Star Meditation position, and if you don't have Aulmauracite Rocks or a pendant yet, then use the Kryahgenetics Egg. Give the Rocks/Egg the directive to help you bring the Time-Lines back into their authentic order and fill in the gaps in time that are missing. Tell them to help you, *"Fix, repair, correct, replace, retrieve, or un-create if necessary, all mismatched and/or missing Time-Lines, consciousnesses, memories & emotions; in, around, or associated with you now. Then reinforce/anchor the proper Tim- Lines."*

Once you are done, if you missed something, not to worry, you can always add to it later if you feel there are other mismatched and missing aspects about yourself that needed fixing, clearing, or clarifying.

The most important thing you can do now is **disconnect from this Artificial Intelligence however you can, and stop giving it your power. Deny ITS right to exist!**

I also try to replace the word "meditate," *which the A.I. has pretty much hijacked* ...and call it my "Heart/Core-Sun/Star Consultation" ...where I have ***a little chat*** with the magickal Being inside! I feel this technique is much more authentic, less manipulated ...and fun!

Amplify your Core/Heart-Star/Sun daily, or hourly if necessary! Clear as many of your implants as you can as fast as you can. Step into your power and start doing your part to fix the imbalances and clear the viruses and distortions here on Planet Earth.

Where Do I Go For Help If I Don't Pray To Anything Anymore?

First of all, it is mandatory to really get clear on the fact that your spiritual guidance, your source for information is INSIDE you, NOT OUTSIDE!

As a main staple for protection and a front-lines security system, **always encase yourself in a Kryahgenetics Egg first,** when requesting assistance from anyone or anything. When calling in your Guides and Guardians to help you, bring them INSIDE your Egg with you, so that the interference will be minimal while you are getting information and assistance.

If you need ancient wisdom and strength, call on our Dragon allies from the UV-Realm. They are the wisdom keepers, and fierce protectors.

Also understand that many of you may NOT have "Guardian Angels" for helpers, as Angels are in service mostly to Earth People. The Angelic Kingdom doesn't have much jurisdiction over FW-Indigos, as they are "not in the Angel's job description" so to speak. FW-Indigos have Dragons and other powerful Mystical Creatures for their helpers and protectors. Indigos and other CCC members also have diverse help from many Dimensions… including the spirits of Time & Space, Water, Fire, Wind, Earth, Music, Lady Karma, Ladies Truth & Justice, etc. I have been witness to Nicola Tesla and Amikah being of extreme assistance and very up-front and personal to many of us who call on them for help and advice.

Recently I was introduced to a couple of Beings called "Sense & Non-sense" who are some of my favorites! They help you make sense out of the senseless, and also throw creations of "nonsense" to

PTWs who need to be distracted and go on a wild goose chase while we take back our turf from them. There is also something I named… *or maybe it was Hal who named them…* (I'm not sure anymore…but the name fits) it is, "The Freaking Factory!" This name best described what I saw and experienced when I first encountered them. At that time they were under contract or rather incarcerated by the PTWs and forced to create all sorts of horrible devices to make our lives a living Hell! I was one of the recipients of this "crap," and when I saw where it was coming from, I couldn't believe it…it was crazy! Well, just know that instead of destroying the factory ***which was my initial impulse, but Hal stopped me*** and the factory and it's workers were rescued and sent to rehab! The factory is alive and well now…BUT now under our jurisdiction. These Freaking Factory workers are on our side now, working for us and are some of our most loyal and useful allies! They can make just about anything you can think of and will also design things for you upon request, if you are in alliance with, and vibrate to the authentic uncorrupted Light & Dark Realms (and they know the difference, so don't' even try to fool them… or you'll be sorry!) We also have The Cosmic Recycle Bins to help handle all manner of corrupted things and Beings.

There are seemingly endless comrades to help us in our service missions here. I have posted some of these on the FW-Indigo website, as more come up all the time during the private sessions I do. When you consider that the Aulmauracite Rocks, and the Kryahgenetics Egg are also Spirit Guides and Guardians, you start thinking outside the box and realize that we truly have all the help imaginable!

It is time we all "grow up" and start acting like **Responsible Adults**, *taking care of the challenges at hand, and utilizing our Spirit Guides and Guardians as the comrades they are… instead of acting like children that want and need someone or something to take care of them. As long as this attitude continues, it will be hard to shut this Artificial Intelligence down. If only a few of us "get it," and start taking back our power from this A.I. monster, it will make a huge difference in its power and control levels. Many of you, have been used and abused by the Artificial Intelligence and will make a huge deficit in its power levels when you unplug and take back your power and authority. All the Answers, all the Power, all the Truth is in the Core-Sun/Star inside you! And YOU have the ability to control how your power is used!* ***You Are the CCC - the X-Men & Women – the answers to your own cries for help… you have the power INSIDE YOU... YOU ARE YOUR OWN GOD! It is time to activate your powers and do what you came here to do!*** (Then when we are done, it's off to the Cosmic Bahamas for rest, relaxation… and maybe even some good times laughing and reminiscing with Hal! :o)

~Lady Mistycah~

~ UNPLUGGING ~

SIMPLE??? HECK YES!

(...BUT SELDOM REMEMBERED)

Perhaps you have heard or seen analogies of how you can handle physical burdens easier and longer if you set them down periodically and rest. One demonstration showed a woman standing with a large glass of water in her outreached hand, while her elbow was in the locked position. After a few minutes, pain set in, and the weight of the glass made her arm fatigue and shake… (The funny thing is, for those eternal optimists, it doesn't seem to matter if you view the glass as "half full or half empty!") But… when the woman set the glass down every 3-4 minutes, retracted her arm, shook the fatigue off for 10-15 seconds… amazingly her arm recovered, and she was ready to hold the glass again. After several periodic repetitions of this, the arm actually got stronger as the muscles built up. (I know, I know… many of you are going to set this book down now and try this experiment to see how long YOU can do it, and how TOUGH you are! Go ahead, check it out... this book will still be here when you get back.)

When you stop to analyze it, the same principal is true for holding onto or holding down energy, especially anxiety, fear, dread, oppression, and other disturbing energies. You need to let go of these energies periodically if you want to maintain balance and internal energetic strength, endurance, and longevity. Taking the time to check in on our internal inventory periodically to see what is lurking underneath can be very useful, educational, and in many cases essential!

For several decades now, I have devised ways of literally "unplugging" from everyone and everything. This clears the way for being able to energetically just be by myself in solitude, so I can think properly and get some relief… (just like the reprieve you get when you put the glass of water down). Then when clarity and sovereignty prevailed, I would systemically only plug back into the people and things that were "***Connections***" ...leaving all the "***Attachments***" "fat out of luck!"

These simple techniques can literally save your life, especially when you are on some "undesirables" radar, and they are constantly hitting you with bad mojo!

In early Oct. 2013, I had an unnerving underlying fear/anxiety energy running through my nervous system that felt like a relentless background program. This had been going on for several months. I would wake up with it, feel it all through the day, go to bed with it, and even experience it in my dreams. It was constant, but I had been so busy that I just kept it at bay on the back burner. I am not naive enough to believe that ignoring this level of creepiness will make it go away, and knew it would have to be dealt with. I had many other pressing things to handle in my life at the time, and it seems like this "background program" also made me stupid and inept, as I didn't have the presence of mind to do what it would take to fix it! When I did think about it, all sorts of distractions would surface, and sleepiness was certainly one of those. This was all a part of the program's safety mechanisms to keep it going and thriving. On the morning of Oct. 12, 2013 I woke up early and thought, "Sheeesh, I just need to get this thing handled already! I've had enough of this creepy crap that has been plaguing me for all these months, and it's time to do something about it, NOW!"

My first proactive response was to get in my trusty Kryahgenetics Egg, take a few deep breaths, and let the Egg suck out the debris. Ahhhhhh….. relief was the wonderful byproduct of taking this action. In this position, I was able to see/feel more clearly what insidious devices lay under the surface, and who or what was behind it. The source for most of it came from a Spider Lady, (a woman that weaves a sticky tangled web of deception, then holds you tight and sucks the life out of you), a Light-Destroyer, and a Crypta: yes, all 3 in one! She had been on my tail for about 7 years, and was constantly flinging generous amounts of all sorts of not so nice symptoms at me. One symptom plaguing me was the right side of my face was sore, like it had been burnt or radiated; it was even hot to the touch but there was no redness…just heat, feeling raw, and burnt as if the nerves had been fried.

There were many symptoms this Spider Lady was adept at flinging. The classic and most frequently used projection were heart palpitations, shortness of breath, and miscellaneous heart attack symptoms. These symptoms seemed to cycle, and I started getting good at taking charge and handling them with vitamins, herbs, and a good dose of out-creating. One of the creepiest symptoms I have to admit, was when Alzheimer's energies were imbedded in and around me. I could sense it, and when my brain started short circuiting, the anxiety of it all seemed to amp it up. It got so bad that others were even picking up on it too! This was extremely challenging and harsh because it seemed to add "validity" to all these dementia energies…..which incidentally was precisely the plan. (**NOTE:** My mother died of Alzheimer's Disease when she was a few years older than I was at the time, which made it more threatening and ominous.) I had to get really strong and really clear on this, and let those who were picking up on it and unintentionally amplifying it, know exactly who was doing it and why. After having a heart-to-heart talk with those who were receptors of this unholy projection, and helping them see what the agenda was, the fog cleared and everyone could finally recognize the insidious insanity for what it was. After finding the truth about the attack, clarity surfaced and soon the symptoms subsided and so did the fear energies that accompanied it. This experience, which could have been extremely disastrous, was actually quite a good education for everyone involved, as we now know that once identified, we can "out-create it!"

So with these other experiences under my belt, I sat there consciously and willfully identifying the root causes of some other 24-7 anxiety. When I figured out that this had creepy Crypto fingerprints on it, the light globe went on in my head, and I remembered to do a severance method I developed years ago. After getting in my Kryahgenetics Egg and having it clean me out, I took a big magickal, etheric sickle and swept it in a circular rotation around my body… first sideways and then up and down… severing anything and everything that is linked in, hooked in, or projected into or onto me. The circular motions seem to have some kind of powerful inter-dimensional qualities, and proved to be very effective. Then I put a psychic dissolver on any of the cords, lines, hooks, and roots to make sure nothing grew back again.

At this point, there was INSTANT RELIEF from the horrible underlying fear and anxieties I had been constantly feeling for months! I was totally blown away at how exhilarating and liberating it was, while at the same time, how peaceful and calm my body felt. I just sat there in amazement, analyzing what just happened… and then realized I'd experienced the in-depth magick of Kryahgenetics alchemy at its finest!

I didn't stop there. I was on a roll now and wanted to make sure I had all my bases covered. Next I did what I call "The Tea Strainer Cleaner Egg," which entails visualizing the Kryahgenetics Egg around me acting like a big tea strainer, starting at my feet, and then moving slowly up my body, collecting any debris that might be lingering inside and out. I put my hands up over my head, and when it got to the tips of my fingers and the ends of my hair, I heard a "blip, blip" sound as it disconnected from my body. The Strainer Egg now held a whole lot of gunk, so I quickly opened up a "Cosmic Recycle Bin Egg" and carefully deposited the Tea Strainer Egg inside, which guaranteed that none of the debris could escape. I use the Recycle Bin Egg in case there is anything that might be useful later… (but in this case there was nothing). When this was complete, I took another deep breath, which gave me an even more exquisite feeling of relief! Next, I started doing the Implant Removal Protocols that are on the frequently updated FirstWaveIndigos.com website, and when this was done and all the restoration procedures accomplished, a rush of energy, vitality, and wisdom, saturated through me and anchored deep in my body and soul. This continued throughout the day and into the next… and then continued into the next week! I had truly liberated myself from this oppression that had kept me imprisoned and quite literally spell-bound! This was similar to having the heavy glass of water removed completely, (which felt more like buckets or barrels), and I was now free to handle important things without the burden of hanging onto something and bearing its weight, when there was no purpose for it. I was literally carrying around "dead weight!"

Using an array of unplugging methods is most definitely a part of the secrets of neutrality. If we can make unplugging an "auto response," we will be much better equipped to handle the demands on us, both physically and energetically.

Another method I have used on myself and my clients is something Hal taught me. I call it, "Going down to -0- & release/dump."

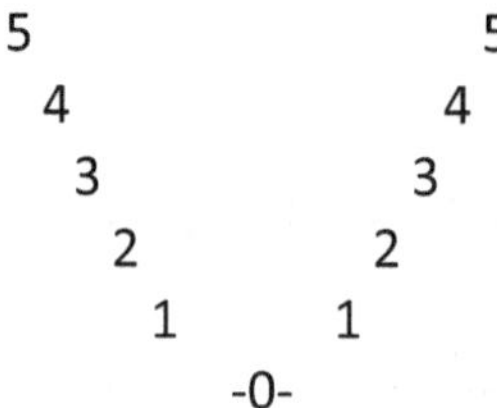

In this process, first you need to get thoroughly "egged" with the Kryahgenetics Egg, while holding Aulmauracite Rocks. When all of us are ready (including the Rocks and Eggs) I count backwards from 5-1 while my client, after taking a deep breath, slowly releases it. When I get to -0-, the client goes absolutely still and neutral, with the intention to "release/dump." In this position, I psychically blast with intent to neutralize any interference, debris, or "Cling-ons" that may have been attached. This process takes 3-5 seconds. Then I give the signal by saying something like, "Excellent!" …I start to count up from -0- to 5 while my client starts to take in a slow breath. Once I reach 5, the client can then breathe normally, but usually they take a big deep sigh of relief!

NOTE: *With any method I use for clearing, I have what I call an etheric "data vault" where I store information. Many times we have challenging experiences in order to get information and education. This information is essential for our Missions here, but the devastating and debilitating emotions attached to it need to be unplugged and transformed. When the emotional charge is taken off, it can then become objective "data," ...which can be placed in a "data vault" to be stored and used for future reference. What I do is turn challenging, disturbing or frightening experiences into 0's and 1's. The trauma is now alchemized into simple data that has no negative charge: ...it just becomes neutral and extremely useful. (This is how I explain it to people so they can understand how it works.)*

I didn't realize until someone brought it to my attention, that this is similar to what hypnotherapists do with counting to access the subconscious. What my method seems to do is bypass many defense mechanisms.

Keeping things in perspective and seeing when something has been trumped up, and molehills perceived as mountains, will not only help you, but also makes life easier for those in your environment. If you find that you are indeed, having to navigate a mountain instead of a molehill, you will find that stopping, unplugging, and observing will help you see your options better, and where your best trail might be with the least amount of danger… especially if there are a lot of cliffs!

If you can make a habit of unplugging several times a day, in several different ways, *even stopping to take a few deep deliberate breaths while in your Kryahgenetics Egg will do wonders!* You will witness alchemical magick in your nervous system, which in turn affects every other system in your body and energy fields. Yes, this is indeed a "Simple Secret of Human Alchemy!"

I leave you now with an updated version of an "Emergency Instructions" guide I originally wrote in about 1995 and had hanging on the wall by my bedroom mirror. This was back when I got on some real "Ass-Soul's" radar, and things started to heat up as I began figuring out who I was and what the heck I am supposed to be doing here! Psychic attack was (and still is) a "normal part of life," and sometimes it would make me so brain dead, I couldn't think of what to do to fix it. After making this Instruction plaque and posting it by the bedroom mirror, it was literally "in my face" all the time, which made it easier to actually read and follow, as I saw it every single day of my life. Many, many times, my head was so fogged out that I had no idea what to do. The only ***think*** I knew for sure was that if I read the guide, I would find the answers.

~ Feel free to copy it and post it in a visible place in YOUR house too! ~

Emergency Instructions For Psychic Attack/Invasions

1 - Take a deep Breath & Unplug.
2 - Put a Kryahgenetics Egg around you...*or multiple layers if needed.*
3 - Take another deep Breath, go neutral & tell the Egg to turn on and clean you out.
4 - Then ask the Egg to go into Protection Mode.
5 - Feel/bask in the energies of your Heart/CoreStar.
6 - Take some Sulfur (capsules or homeopathic) and liquid minerals.
7 - Use Aurauralite/Aulmauracite Power Rocks to get clarity and truth.
8 - Find out the who, or what, when, where, how, & whys of the attack.
9 - Use the sickle severing technique.
10-Use the Tea Strainer debris cleaner technique.
11-Invalidate the "Hell" out of it. Use Humor to dissipate & dis-arm the energies.
12-Realize the attack is a ***projected illusion***. Take charge by Out-Creating the energy behind who or what is doing it. Make your creation... BIGGER & BETTER!
13-Your Higher Self, your Eggs, and your Rocks allowed it in for educational purposes. Use the experience to make you stronger, tougher & wiser, which will diminish similar future invasions.

(The following message is for Indigos and other C.C.C. Members)

Remember! You Were Trained For This Mission!
You have the wits, the strength, and the Intel inside of you to handle this!
You also have extreme seen and unseen support systems ie.,
Guides, Guardians, The Kryahgenetics Egg & Your Adaptors!!!

AURAURALITE &
AULMAURACITE

THE MAGICKAL MYSTICAL STONE OF TRUTH AND JUSTICE

Many, many, many moons ago, a magnificent and benevolent Starship visited this planet to give us an impeccable gift. This gift was to be buried and remain there, concealed deep within the Earth, awaiting its activation.

The secrets and mystery surrounding this gift, and its location, were kept cloaked and silent. Voluntary Guardians were assigned to maintain security and protection, for this gift possessed many sacred and magickal elements and capabilities. The stewardship and constant surveillance were top priority, and only the most impeccable Beings were qualified to be "Stewards."

The loving Beings who brought this gift, knew that there would come a time when this planet, and the humans and other Life-forms living on it, would become so fractured that they would need some magick to help them remember how to dream again.

They knew that in the future, this world and its consciousness would begin deteriorating and polluting so rapidly, it would reach the point of extinction. They knew that without some intervention, the dream, the planet and her inhabitants, would become so ill, so terrified, and numb... that the dreamers who kept it alive would forget their dreams of Love and Compassion, their dreams of Honor, Truth, and Integrity..... and especially their dreams of Passion and Romance!

If this were to continue for very long, the whole of it would implode and perish and a once beautiful and majestic planet would literally cease to exist!

To ensure a high probability of a successful mission, within this gift was placed a cosmic timer, designed to activate its powers of Love, Truth, and Magick! This cosmic timer was pre-programmed to ring at a time after certain Beings (who were also pre-encoded with its ancient knowledge and how to use it) had already arrived on this planet. They would instinctively know what to do with this gift, and when their personal timer would go off inside of them, they would, on some level or other, go searching for it.

This gift is a very advanced magickal Life-Form and it is called Aurauralite-Aulmauracite, (pronounced: Aroralite-Allmorasite). If you feel a tingle or magnetic pull toward this name and this story, it may be your own alarm ringing, telling you, "You have arrived and your search is over!"

Aulmauracite is a beautiful, majestic, black sparkly rock, and **Aurauralite** is the sparkly dust that it sheds. Each one has the same qualities, but sometimes different uses. Aulmauracite has also been called, "The Power Rock," "The Mother Rock," or "The Stone of Truth & Justice," and if you get the opportunity to work with and use them… you'll understand *firsthand* why.

NOTE: *It was recently discovered that the Aulmauracite Rock is the physical aspect of the Kryahgenetics Egg. This discovery made a lot of sense as they both carry the same resonance of power, honor, and integrity.*

Many people say that when they first hold Aurauralite-Aulmauracite that they get the feeling/sensation that "they have come home," and get "warm fuzzies" inside. This is one of the reasons why it has been dubbed "The Mother Rock"…because it welcomes you back home, back to the memories and wisdom of your Soul.

It has also been said that this Power Rock seems to have the same attributes and qualities as the legendary "SUPER MOM" because they both:

Listen to your problems and help you create "win-win" solutions.

Help you get where you need to be, when you need to be there.

Show you where you've made a mess so you can clean it up.

Take you to the proper professional when you need a "TRUTH EXTRACTION" (especially in the case of "WISDOM TRUTH EXTRACTIONS")...and then stay constantly by your side when you are recovering and healing from the trauma.

Lovingly support you in your goals and aspirations.

Shine "lite" on things you couldn't see before or may have over-looked.

Have an unlimited supply of energy and never get tired or worn out.

Are always beautiful and attractive, no matter what time of day or night.

Show you how to take full responsibility for yourself, your wonderful (or not so wonderful) creations, your actions (or reactions), and learn from every outcome or consequence. They then help you arrange or rearrange everything to make them all useful.

Have the highest Honor and Integrity. You cannot coerce, manipulate, or buy Allegiance, ...and they know in a flash when there is insincerity, any ulterior motives, and/or "sucking-up!"

Have the ability to cultivate and inspire you to manifest things you previously thought were impossible!

Create an "at home" feeling anywhere they may be or go.

Are always there when you need grounding, comforting, and stabilizing.

You could say that a Super Mom and Aurauralite are one in a billion, out of this world, all knowing…seeing, hearing, and feeling… and are here to remind you:

"You are the Master Creator of your destiny."
"The power *(God/Goddess* Source) is within YOU!"
"Love is the key ingredient for every recipe of life."

Some of the more scientific qualities of this Rock that we have discovered, have been absolutely astounding… as it has properties that are literally *"Out Of This World."*

- It custom-designs itself to the user to assist them with their benevolent intentions.
- When someone tries to utilize it for unethical or UN-loving intentions…it has its own internal ethical code, and will shut off its power and go *temporarily dormant…* **It won't get involved!**
- It has its own power source and its own ground… (that's not of this world.)
- It is a high-powered broadcaster that beefs up the volume of whatever you're trying to broadcast, whether a desire or intention, or whether it's being used to amplify Tesla technology.
- It puts its owner or user on their *best destiny path*, which almost always alters their lives, and brings about some very dramatic changes when they get their Rock!
- When you pass it around a room of people, this *Power Rock* won't pick up and hold their psychic debris like crystals do, instead it neutralizes it and grounds it out; therefore, you don't have to clean it! It's extremely "user friendly."
- Aulmauracite is a very intelligent Rock, but *You* and *Your Higher Self* - ***Soul Suemah*** are the power source that activates its energies… it simply will wait for you to give it a job, and the more you use it, the happier it is, and the better it works.
- Sometimes you may not know when you give it a job… some of its commands may come directly from Your Higher Self - ***Soul Suemah*** and you may not be aware of it immediately. For instance, when most people pick it up, it usually goes to work balancing their energy and holographic fields, opening up their psychic centers, and when they begin to work with it, the Rock automatically locks on to their best destiny paths!
- **It doesn't like to be encased in plastic or synthetic material because that smothers it, and therefore, deadens its signal. Please be mindful of this!**
- When you acquire one of these Rocks or the Dust, truth automatically begins to surface and manifest in your life. This may or *may not* be a welcome addition to your life, especially if you're not willing and ready for the blatant *reality of truth* to shine big and bright, *in your face, right there in front of you!*
- Assay testing revealed that Aulmauracite is 58% iron (in a form that *does not* oxidize/rust). The other 42% consists of 72 other elements, including all the noble metals (plus some that are foreign to this planet!) It appears that the ratio of these elements in relationship to each other gives this "Power Rock" its unusual properties.

Having worked with this Cosmic Rock for several decades, I have had some amazing tales to tell from my own personal experiences. In about 1998 I took the Rock to a friend of mine who is a Tesla scientist. I told him about some of the experiences I had with the Rock, its broadcasting capabilities, and how it has its own grounding system.

He responded the way a lot of men do the first time I present them with this amazing Rock and try to explain its vastness in two or three minutes (while they are only half listening and the other half patronizing me). I knew he was very skeptical about what he considered a "New Age Rock" I was showing him, but he did give me the courtesy of saying he would like to conduct some experiments on it with some of his equipment. Of course I had no problem with this, as I was also curious as to how the Rock would stand up to some new hardcore 3-D testing I hadn't done before.

To begin with, he wanted to see what would happen when he ran electrical current through it to determine what its conduction capabilities were. He first ran A.C. current into the Rock and nothing happened… no reading on the meter. So next he ran D.C. current through it… and Zip, Zero, nothing was reading. At this point he kept testing other materials to make sure there wasn't anything wrong with his meter. With this rock's high iron content, it didn't make much sense that he couldn't pick up a reading! Next he tried running different sound frequencies through it… but again…with no meter reading! Still wondering if there was something wrong with his equipment he kept checking and rechecking it with other materials to make sure his it wasn't malfunctioning.

After this, he decided to run light pulses through the rock…and once again…no reading. At this point I suggested that he take the grounding wire off and see what happens. He looked at me like, "This is an absolutely unfounded, asinine request, and you really don't have a clue about what you're asking, but I'll patronize you and do it any way...(*but not before I check my equipment again for a short or some other defect*").

After checking his light pulse machine thoroughly, he ran the pulses through the Rock again …no meter reading. Then he did what I suggested and took the grounding wire off…and his eyes got so big they darn near bugged out of their sockets as he watched the meter move! He said, "Well, I'll be darned," (only he didn't say *darned*). "This thing has its own ground!!! How can that be? I've never seen anything like it! It has its own ground!" I replied, "I know, that's what I've been trying to tell you!" Then he looked me square in the eye and asked, "Where the heck is it getting its ground? …What's going on here!?! Where did this Rock come from?" I replied, "I told you it wasn't from around here… now do you believe me?"

With that he went to work rechecking to see if the sound and electrical current would show up on the meter without the ground...but again, no meter readings… It only measured with light pulses!

Draw your own conclusions as to what the implications are here, and what it means. I know for me it was extremely validating, but to my scientist friend, it was very unsettling to have a substance that defied some of the laws of physics, that had heretofore been so cut and dried. (And I have to admit, it was amusing to me to see his left brain try to rationalize and figure out ***what in the world*** was going on with this "New Age Rock" …and ironically, you would have to go ***out of the world*** to get your answers!)

Another interesting story comes from a colleague of mine who has traveled the world for years. She has done extensive study and research in ancient healing arts and in the mystery schools. Through her travels she has been given a wide variety of articles from the animal, vegetable, and mineral kingdoms, as well as artifacts from energy vortexes and ancient sacred sites from all over the globe. Her home is like a museum as she has everything from a suit of armor, to original stained glass windows taken from historic buildings, to jewels, to shamanic ceremonial items that she uses regularly in her healing and teaching gatherings.

One day she got the idea to find out what the most powerful item she had in her home was, so she picked up her dowsing rods, (which she had become very proficient in using) and asked the question. She told me that the rods turned straight to the table where she had the Power Rock sitting. Wanting to make sure it was the Rock and not the table, she moved the Rock to another place in the room, and the rods again pointed to where the Rock was. After doing this test in several places in her house, with the rods consistently pointing to the Rock, she concluded that with all the wonderful and magickal things she had in her home, the Power Rock definitely must be the most powerful item she possessed.

She related this story to me because she wanted me to know, having been a guest in her home and seeing all the amazing things there, that the Power Rock was at the top! It sort of surprised me at first... but then again…it didn't surprise me at all, in fact, it validated all my research and made perfect sense!

I have had some very intriguing and magickal personal experiences with this Rock and feel like it is one of my best friends and allies! I have seen it heal rashes right before my eyes by rubbing it softly over the affected area. I have watched people who were in trauma hold it and immediately begin to calm down and have their energy field shift. I witnessed one woman who held it and she said she felt "energy lightning bolts" shoot through her body and out her arm. She said it was very invigorating!

I have had reports of people meditating with it and moving into a space where they see the Web Of Life connecting all of Creation together!

Another report came to me from a therapist who gave a client two Power Rocks to hold for grounding after an intense emotional release session. Her client instinctively put them to her forehead and immediately went into the void, seeing and feeling the Love and potential of all of Creation! (This scared the dickens out of the therapist, along with the client's daughter who had accompanied her. They both thought she must be having life threatening problems, because her eyes rolled back into her head, and she became totally unresponsive to her Earthly environment.) They began talking to her, asking her if she was all right, and softly shaking her. Finally after a more brisk shaking, she abruptly came back to this reality, and was more than slightly irritated to say the least! She had never experienced anything as beautiful, expansive, and loving as the place she was basking in, and then to be suddenly jerked back into this reality, really upset her! She wanted to linger longer and absorb what she was feeling and experiencing, and to this day she has never had another experience like this… it totally altered her perception and her life!

I have also had a variety of people send me letters, telling of their personal experiences. Here are just a few:

Running Wolf (William M. Lovse)

Aho my sister Laura Lee Mistycah,

Thought I'd share with you some of the experiences I have had with the Aurauralite. I have seen fantastic results by letting people hold the Aurauralite... physical healings took place. I was at a funeral in Texas with my genetic relatives. One had a migraine headache so I handed her the vial and said to just hold it a while. In five minutes the headache was gone. Two others were bothered with allergies and I was prompted to do the same thing. In a short time their allergy symptoms were gone! I had others hold it and watched in amazement, as they became centered and peaceful right before my eyes. When they asked what it was, I usually told them, "POWER." Then later I would give them a full description.

Yesterday, a saleswoman came into the store. She was going this weekend to visit a friend with AIDS. He is being helped/cured by a Navaho medicine man. Buffalo prompted me to give her the vial of Aurauralite for her friend. I will let you know if I hear any results from him using it. I have more vials on order. This is amazing stuff!

Until we meet again... may you have a peaceful journey...
...Running Wolf

Rosie Turpin

"You asked for feedback from Aurauralite users. I have found that its work for me is to keep my heart positively charged and to support the transformation initiated in my sessions with you (Laura Lee). Wearing my little vial, I feel GREAT. But on the two occasions that I forgot to put it on again after my shower, I found my spirits low. As soon as I put it on again, there is a tremendous charge to the heart, like overpowering JOY, which takes me about half an hour to adjust to again. Yes, it certainly is a Power Rock!"

T. Nails

Being somewhat familiar with geological assay reports through the rock hounding exploits of my father, as well as many friends, I was quite astounded by the report that I read concerning the substance referred to here as Aurauralite. It basically contains every geological element known to exist on Earth! This includes the entire platinum group as well as several other rare elements including Thulium.

Thulium is one of the 14 rare Earth elements in the periodic table and is well known in occult chemistry. It is one of the original elements that was involved in the creation of the Earth. The platinum group elements are what is used in the manufacture of White Powder Gold. It is simply amazing to find all of these elements in the same place!

Cathy Langlous

"I met Laura Lee at the Prophets Conference in L.A. and I got one of the "healing Rocks" to take to my classes to have my students read with them and had some very interesting observations. Several students found chronic pain leaving their body immediately upon placing it on the body part with their intent to release the pain. It is, as I'm sure you know, a great catalyst for your own healing focus! Here are some other responses I got from the classes. I didn't tell them anything ahead of time so they would just express their own information.

I feel pulsing and keep seeing asteroids flying through space.
I saw a swirling planet with 4 rings around it.
I felt something like the Christ-force energy go up my arm and through my body cleaning out my energy fields.
It holds the energy of creation!

Some time ago we were working with some dimensional doorways and we found one that looked like the monolith in the movie 2001. One of my "act before you look" students jumped in there and couldn't get back, so I had to go in and get her and bring her back. We both agreed this rock felt much like that place we were in. It was very hard to talk about on a physical plane.

I like what one of the last people said to me: "I see all the hands that ever held this kind of rock and many were not classic human hands, but each learned something from it!"

It is clear to me that it isn't from Earth but is a familiar energy. I saw cities built at the base of mountains of it. It was used as an energy source for them. It also is helping to reactivate some of the dormant DNA we need to re-own and assist in our receiving information about our true spiritual origins. It certainly seems to be an aid to focusing your own healing intent to whatever you are working on. Thanks for the opportunity to play with this Power Rock!"

Deeanna Justice

The Aurauralite Rock came into my life in the form of a necklace holding a vial filled with dust from the Rock, after an acquaintance shared with me her experience of wishing on the necklace for money and then receiving a settlement she had given up on, within the next week!

I thought this could have been coincidence, always the skeptic, but thought "what the heck, it doesn't hurt to try." So, I went to Laura Lee's office and purchased a necklace. I was in the mood for a miracle to say the least. Within the last six months, my husband had left me, I was living in a place I was not comfortable with, and I had no sense of spirituality or anything to look up to. My son had just turned three, and I was dealing with all the shifting emotions he was going through following the divorce.

I made my wishes on the Rock for things such as peace of mind, courage, and so on. One by one, my life really took a leap for the better. I didn't want to think that this might have to do with the Aurauralite, but I did keep wearing the necklace just in case.

Several months later during an informal gathering to put together a seminar, Laura Lee brought over quite a few Rocks and we all joined hands over the Rocks. At this time, I felt the power that they were capable of. My own spirit was awakening and I was more aware of energies that were present but couldn't be explained.

After a very successful seminar, I was given the choice of a tape of the seminar or another Aurauralite necklace with a new design. I chose the tape thinking I already had a necklace (which I had not worn in the preceding two months). Well, this time, when I started wearing it again, I was awakening even more!

My wish and intention this time was to be united with one of my Soul Mates. Within two months, I was dating the man I felt was my Soul Mate. Many experiences, which I will not go into here, occurred in this relationship to further push, sometimes drag, me along my path!

Then six months ago I felt an astonishing confirmation of the power of these Rock entities. I was doing a Kryahgenetics session with Laura Lee to release a negative Being who had attached himself to me. As we did the final release, an ice cold electrical sensation ran down each arm into an Aurauralite Rock that was being held in each hand. I found this all very interesting; the Rocks choose how they would work, not the other way around. I realized also that if my energy was not for loving intention and to further my growth, the experience would not have happened.

Obviously, I purchased the Rocks after that experience. I knew I had to have them. They seem to be a part of me and have been working with my energy ever since.

One Rock has male energy and the other female energy. I have used them to balance out my own energies, in my healing work with other people while practicing Reiki or release therapy, and their "home" is situated under my bed with the female "Earth" under my feet and the male "sky" under my head. I haven't given any thought as to how well they work, and have taken them for granted really. When something works, you just assume it will continue.

Another incident occurred on New Year's Eve morning, 1997. I was visited by a person who has quite a bit of animosity towards me. His wife had been a friend of mine, and I never approved of their marriage, so I stood accused of trying to break them up and much more. This did not really affect me, or so I thought, since my friendship with her had ended a few months before.

That night, I was planning to celebrate a quiet evening at home with a friend. My son was sick with the flu and had gone to bed early. At approximately 7 p.m. I had a sharp, stabbing pain in my abdomen and felt dizzy. The pain was so intense, I couldn't stand up. I went into a room in my home where I do meditation and cleansing ceremonies and lay down. After a while, I felt better, so I got up and left the room. As soon as I did, the pain returned.

My friend Patti arrived at 9 p.m. or so and I told her what had happened. We both felt there was some sort of energy being directed at me. It felt like a "dark presence." We both had a good idea where the energy was coming from. As we sat in meditation, I tried to protect myself with love, but nothing seemed to be happening.

Then something inside led me to get the Aurauralite Rocks from their home under my bed. I sat with the female on the right and the male on the left. Patti placed her hands over mine. I tried to muster up love for the person I felt was sending the energy, but I was still angry about the events that happened earlier that morning. Instead I intended that the energy be returned to whoever was sending it. The Rocks in our hands got very hot as it was transmuting the energy.

Afterwards, I was feeling much better, lighter, and full of energy, but the Rocks were cold and seemed to have lost their spark. They felt like ordinary river rocks, but much colder. I even said, "Oh no, we've killed them!" I put them *in a container with some rose quartz crystals and river rocks to see if that would recharge them. After three or four days, they were still cold and something very strange had happened, the bottom of the male Rock had turned a dull pink color! Also the female now had a band of copper on one side that had not been present before, and they both had lost their sparkly dust that used to shed from them.*

I wanted to call Laura Lee to find out what to do about the Aulmauracite and how to recharge them, but kept putting it off. On January 5, the situation with the ex-friend and her husband felt resolved within me and I could find forgiveness and love in my heart for them and myself.

The next day, January 6, I finally called Laura Lee. I explained to her what had happened and she said that they were holding the energy so it would not boomerang. Now here is where the story gets a little weird...she had me hold one of the Rocks in each hand, far apart from each other, and then bang them together. I did as she instructed, feeling neutral about it all, and banged them together.

If I had to describe the sound, it would be a rumbling underneath the Earth. I held them in my hands for a few minutes while we talked on the telephone. Soon my hands started warming up and sweating...and all of a sudden the sparkles and dust had returned! As I watched them, the dull pink was being covered with black and the copper on the female Rock was narrowed from about 2 inches to about 1/8th of an inch! I wouldn't have believed it if I had not seen it with my own eyes!

Laura Lee asked me to write this down and as I do, I still cannot explain how incredible the feeling was to see these magnificent entities rejuvenate and transform themselves. I don't understand how they work and maybe never will. I do know that they have shared their energy with mine and mine with them. I have a respect for other forms of consciousness now that I did not have before; largely attributed to the amazing occurrences I have personally witnessed.

Does this scare me? Not in the least. The fact that they went cold when I could feel no love and only anger, but still offer their protection, affirms to me that only the highest intentions will be channeled when using them. There is so much to learn and I am grateful that I have had this opportunity to share in a consciousness that practices, literally, positive intent!

NOTE: *The Rocks custom design themselves to the user and give the exact experience needed. Your experience might be far different than Deanna's. Their Motto is "Truth &Justice" and will do what it takes to manifest that.*

Ronnie Foster

I am an intuitive counselor with a BA degree in psychology. I have been fascinated with rocks since childhood and have worked extensively with crystals for many, many years. When Laura Lee first gave me the rock, Aulmauracite to hold, I saw a vision of benevolent Beings in white robes, programming this Rock with codes and keys. There was a powerful love vibration emanating from them into the rock. I knew without a doubt that Aulmauracite did not originate from this planet. I had a sense that it was left here for us to discover when we were evolved enough to know what to do with it.

I find Aulmauracite/Aurauralite opens my Heart and helps to balance my energetic fields. It also helps me to center and ground. When I gave my 11 year old son a piece, I asked him if he felt the stone had a message. He then placed it on his forehead and said, "The message is, I will protect you." He also said it reminded him of Moldavite, another rock that is not from this planet.

As I hold a piece of it in my hand, these sensations come to heart...Aurauralite…warm fuzzy feelings of home…gentle and strong, peace, love, compassion, and truth. It feels soooooo good. Sparkling, shining, caring, giving …..LOVE!

Theresa Ramdas

I was listening in on a teleconference in early March 2013, when Anakhanda Mushaba, one of the guest speakers and my fellow spiritual friend of the Mushaba Planet of which I hail from, suddenly made mention of some Rocks. Not catching the name, I emailed him and he shared briefly about the Rocks and an implant session he was incorporating. Through the link and reference he made to the First Wave Indigo website and Laura Lee, my foray into the world of Aurauralite-Aulmauracite, the Magical Mystical Stone of Truth & Justice began, changing my reality forever.

For lack of a better word, I actually 'pounced' on these Rocks after my initial scrutiny of the website. Right after placing my order, I felt an innate urgency to ask Laura Lee to expedite the shipment to Singapore, whatever the additional charges to be incurred. While waiting for the arrival of Aurauralite-Aulmauracite, I proceeded to educate myself on this whole business of FWIs, what with Laura Lee brazenly tattling on my Indigo status. While no hidden surprise on the one hand, given how I'm wired up, on the other hand, what with the prevalent thinking of Indigos stemming from the younger breed, I have not regarded myself as one. Seeing I'm one of the stragglers, age-wise, an important piece of the puzzle of my spirituality definitely fell in place for me.

Laura Lee is truly a one-of-a-kind spiritual leader and champion of sorts, bravely addressing the adult wing of the Indigo nation. I am extremely grateful to her for her selfless devotion to her cause in these unchartered territories.

Back to Aurauralite-Aulmauracite. By the time they arrived, I had developed a full-blown flu. Nothing unusual in itself except that I have a strong resistance to the flu bug and can usually mitigate the slightest of symptoms even in the midst of a pandemic. This immunity has been especially evident in my recent years. I know now that this flu attack was a protest against Aurauralite-Aulmauracite making a grand entrance in my life. I tell you, I was so hard hit that I was sapped of energy and strength and my throat felt like I was swallowing broken glass. Come to think of it, the flu surfaced right about the time when I placed my order.

Despite the agony and debilitation, all I could think of was gridding my country and home as soon as my Aurauralite-Aulmauracite landed. Being able to track the exact day of arrival, I planned to do the gridding during the one-week March holiday break from school. (I'm a school teacher.) I still had to chalk up some extra days of lessons for my students. I had no idea how I was going to pull off the 2 days in class with my flu and all. On gridding day 1, right after school, I practically dragged myself to the first spot followed by the second, which was the center spot. Singapore, my country is a tiny place in South-East Asia, roughly the size of New York City, for those of you not familiar with the other side of the world. One can zip around to the 4 corners within a few hours. Gridding Day 2 saw the completion of the other 3 spots. It was only later that I read that the center grid should be done last. I did not get the order right but know it doesn't matter for these Rocks have an intelligence of their own and can adjust accordingly.

Then I completed my home gridding system. It felt so right.

The days after that, began my intimate relationship with Aurauralite-Aulmauracite. It felt like we had been apart all these years and finally reunited. My Facebook status might as well have been ... 'In a relationship with Aurauralite-Aulmauracite.'

My life has not been the same since. I never leave home without them. Come to think of it, I don't return home without them either. I have them on me throughout. If I wear clothing with pockets, I slip both of them in plus pin the pendant to my bra.

Aurauralite-Aulmauracite has over delivered on all counts and aesthetically speaking, she is a beauty! For those of you who have one or two or any number of these amazing Rocks, you know exactly what I speak of.

What with Aurauralite-Aulmauracite being the stone of truth, I thought somehow I'd be confronted with some hard-core truth issues that I had buried, just as the Aurauralite-Aulmauracite poster claimed. I was, except I realized a couple of weeks after using the stone that it was in reverse meaning it showed me the injustice and wrong-doing vouchsafed on me and not the other way around. Some people from my past and my experiences with them surfaced and I was shown how the drama and pain was not because of anything I did, but a result of their issues.

I feel that many of us who awaken are told by the spiritual community to make peace with our past and hurts by forgiving and transmuting the pain. We had to do it or we would not evolve. I have spent hours in a couple of modalities forgiving others, myself and situations till I turned blue, green and whatever other colours all over. I'm not saying it's all bad or wrong. In some instances, I had to face up to my wrongs and I'll be the first to say I have a lot of that, what with my ego and differentiated way of viewing the world. Crossing swords with the people around me happens when it needs to. In putting a blanket statement of forgiveness, so to speak, over all my hurts, Aurauralite-Aulmauracite showed me those where I had been right and got me to back up and call that injustice by its proper name. One example revolved around someone whose demeanor towards me was one of resentment and rejection. This had gone on for over twenty years. As this was an elderly relative whom I had to show respect plus visit regularly, there was much frustration and suppressed energy on my part. I was shown that forgiving did not diffuse the negative energy. It only buried it within my psyche. I was in fact carrying guilt and blame. Sound familiar? My beautiful Aurauralite-Aulmauracite told me in the face, it was pure racial prejudice on that individual's part and added that this person was not able to be in my presence because of the light I emanated. There was nothing wrong with me. I had done no harm. As I am now penning these words, I'm being shown that I had also experienced this to break the code - the old ancient code of prejudice which has started and is still starting wars and dissension in the Universe!

Wow! I never expected my Aurauralite-Aulmauracite to come through in this manner. There were also some other forgiveness issues with a couple of people I will not mention here. The point is I felt so free after this.

What I want to extol here especially for Indigos is the need to take back whatever we've given away, in terms of power, integrity and our spiritual essence. Aurauralite-Aulmauracite is the Being for this. This Rock is not a tool, mind you, but a living breathing entity.

Aurauralite-Aulmauracite has squelched my apathy about many of the injustices we are going through and a few days after receiving it, while recovering from my flu lying in bed, I found myself holding the Rock between my fingers and showing the dark forces my Aurauralite-Aulmauracite, like I was doing the middle finger thing -:} I'm serious. While I was ranting and cussing at them, I realized the position of the Rock in my hand and laughed. A deep inner rage seeped through me and still does now. It was like I was back in business again. It felt so good and after I had my 1st session with Laura Lee, my faith and belief in my mission and purpose took on a new-found vigor, embellished with authentic self-love.

And which Indigo cannot do with a good dose of self-love, tell me!

Is it any wonder, when I was told that Aurauralite-Aulmauracite is one of my Guides and as if that wasn't enough, the forced contract Laura Lee shared with me in our 2nd session was this, "If I find Aurauralite/Aulmauracite, I would agree to let them shut me down."

In fact Laura Lee felt herself shutting down just before she was tuning in to this info for me during the session. I have since taken that forced agreement out, inflicting the most vengeful blows I could muster on the 50-some entities, sending all to the Cosmic recycling bins. My other Guides, including Amikah, couldn't wait for this!

The only shutting down that came close for me was a nasty flu. Ha!

Since harnessing Aurauralite-Aulmauracite in my spiritual practice, I am truly stepping into my Mushaba and Indigo Beingness of Freedom and Empowerment.

Aurauralite-Aulmauracite, you couldn't have come at a better time. Had you come earlier, I may not have been ready, having to work through layers of finding myself. These past few years and especially 2012, a dam of sorts burst within me as I began to face and accept the Goddess that I really am - the one that had been cloaked and veiled by this alter, illusionary self. The truth is, I knew I was this powerful Being at my Core but was really afraid of how powerful and majestic I AM. Even now, I'm choosing to embrace my Goddess Essence incrementally for it is all-consuming. I will get there, I know.

I'm now also working on my Aurauralite-Aulmauracite in both my manifestation abilities and in reality-shaping. That I know will take me to a whole new vista I can't wait to conquer.

Won't you join me in this, my fellow First Wave Indigos!

Jennifer Taylor

When I first started to meditate with my Aulmauracite rocks I 'saw' them as little Rock beings dressed in yellow hard hats. They showed me their industriousness, along with all the banging and tapping associated with construction. Also they showed me a pair of white gloved 'cartoon' hands while working with me along with a construction site on which a metal structure was being built. The Rocks are such funny characters! They say the funniest things to me, which can make meditation with them somewhat 'disruptive' at times...(Due to me having to laugh). They often have squeaky little voices which respond to me with a distinct and joyful 'righty-ho' when I ask them to do anything. However, after last night they seem to have deliberately deepened their voices! Maybe to counteract what I have been saying about them!

These Rocks are absolutely wonderful little life forms - very advanced beings as such. They helped me to clear all traumas from my past. They are able to access all realms, dimensions, realities, the 'past, present and future,' and have cleared away implants and sentient/non-sentient pests in all time periods. I find that felines and other nasties fear them a lot! I often see these noxious Beings being chased around by the Kryahgenetic Eggs when I ask the Rocks to track and quarantine 'em!

I find that they are able to contact any beings at any time in the 'past, present or future,' through all time lines and realities if asked. They have often located my guides Amikah and/or Drackie for me at need. I have also been able to contact and speak to Ladies Karma and Justice via the Rocks.

These Rocks can clear away and obliterate not only implants but also ships and their broadcasting equipment, egg the inhabitants and bring them to justice. They will not, however, harm any innocent beings as they operate under the 'rules' of justice and karma. Using the Rocks has put me into much closer contact with my spirit guides. Also Nikola Tesla who was/is one of my guides earlier on in the year came through to me and showed me an image of him jumping into a portal with his brown satchel. He also said 'think outside the box' to me.

My Rocks are essential for timeline work. Traumas shatter and fragment the soul and these Rocks helped me (along with Laura Lee's instruction and my guides) on locating the shattered and soiled pieces of myself in the past, cleaning and bringing them back to the present and re-integrating them within my being.

They are very eager to help and have been literally, lifesavers, helping clear out my energetic field of all kinds of parasitic beings and implants. I couldn't function without them. Best purchase I could have made as an Indigo UV-Realmer!

Dave H.

I got the new Rocks weds. I have been using them for a while. What's interesting is that the effect of their power has multiplied. I have 3-50 gram Rocks. I also have the 5-Star implant ones, and the gridding ones. I bought my first Rocks about 8 months ago in the winter and they have dramatically changed my life. I gridded the Dupage County court buildings late winter in 2012 as well as my apartment. What's interesting is the amount of cops radaring and lasering has gone down in my area. There's less pull overs on the street. I also noticed there's less chem trailing... not sure if that one's just a coincidence. After I gridded my apt. my girlfriend and I have had less nightmares and evil entity encounters. I noticed though the Rocks let in benevolent beings. I forgot to email that when I did it. I have noticed this dramatic change over the past 3 or 4 months. I plan to grid the rest of my area. I eventually wanna grid other Chicago suburbs and downtown.

Carmine Conti

Dear Lady Mistycah,

Rocks & pendent arrived today at around 1:00 PM, it seemed so long since I gave my pendent to my daughter Angela to try and I never got it back, (but I didn't expect to).

My wife Angela & daughter Angela teased me about them before they tried them out. Now they wear them all the time and I had to buy my wife one. She thought I was nuts at first (and I am a little), but she said, "let me try your pendent I have some questions to ask." I said, "Ok but first I have to ask permission." The pendent said, "Ok."

I don't know what my wife asked but after that she wanted a pendent. She says her pendent makes her feel like she's more herself and comfortable. She wears it all the time. After my daughter wore mine she wanted one she said it made her feel better, not nervous. My wife said she noticed when our daughter is wearing the pendent she's calmer and doesn't yell at our grandson so much.

Also gave my Mom a vial of grid Rocks (she's 87). Mom keeps hers in her room on her jewelry stand. Then my daughter Gina had a wedding rehearsal on the 20th which was the harvest moon. I gave her friend who did the wedding the Rocks I had with me to try. I wanted her to have them. I found out later that she loves them, say's they are very powerful! I was now down to just power grid Rocks, which is ok, but I missed my bigger friends a lot, so from now on I'll buy new Rocks for other people and keep mine.

When I got my new order of Rocks I asked my grandson Michael who is seven if he wanted to hold them and he said Yah! When I handed them to him he asked me what their names were. I smiled and said I don't know. Michael said, "I do, their names are Rocky and Rocky two!" We both laughed. He comes out with some amazing things.

Here's a short story. I went for a checkup with the doctor and he had his nurse give me a cardiogram. The machine went crazy & then wouldn't work. I had my pendent on and she said it would not cause of the machine not to work. I took it off anyway. She tried the machine again and guess what, the machine worked! "What is in that bottle?" she asked. I told her and then she ignored what I said. Oh well.

Thanks Laura Lee, Love Carmine & Angela

Sara C.

Dear Laura Lee,

Thank you so much for your beautiful rocks. So much has happened since I received the rocks that I am just now getting a moment to thank you and let you know some of the effects. The moment I first held the rocks my heart just started to burst. All of a sudden it had more room to breathe. And my body went tingly all over like it was tangibly vibrating faster. Then I did some work with the rocks and asked them to help me with manifesting some money that I needed for overdue bills. I got more than twice what I needed for the bills so I could take care of a bunch of other things as well. And it keeps coming. Also literally the morning I gridded my home, I started having contractions and then delivered my daughter that afternoon, two weeks early! At home I feel like I have so much more room to breathe. It feels so good that I just like staying there in the peacefulness. Mind you, plenty of justice and truth has been served up and there have been bumpy moments but it sure clears the air.

I just want to thank you again. I am really looking forward to working with these rocks much more, especially with grid work. I have a question about gridding that I wanted to send your way. When it comes to gridding a large area, like a town, does the formation have to be a perfect square, rectangle or diamond shape to be strongest. Or can it be off a bit and still work? All my love and blessings, Sarah C.

My Answer: *About the Grid Rocks, yes, you can do 4 or 5 or 6 outside grids, whatever it takes to get the area surrounded. You do not have to have exact coordinates, just ask them to adjust if it is not perfect and they will...they are very smart Rocks. ;o) One time I was gridding a masonic lodge and could not get into the building for the center stone, so I threw it onto the roof... which was nowhere near the center, but I asked the rock to move its energy into the middle, and it did.*

These are just a few of the interesting and diverse reports we get on a regular basis. One of my clients, when she first got her Aurauralite, said with a sparkle in her eyes and a grin on her face, as she put the pendant around her neck, "I feel like I'm part of the club now." ...And that's kind of how it is...but more like a family..."the Aurauralite-Aulmauracite family"...and it's changing people's lives all over the planet (plant and animal people too!)

Please continue to send us your adventures and experiences with this *Mother Rock,* as we are compiling a "Family History Album" of "very true and amazing tales" from our Aurauralite-Aulmauracite family. We'd love to have your stories to share with our prolific and ever-growing ***Stone of Truth & Justice*** family.

FREQUENTLY ASKED QUESTIONS ABOUT AURAURALITE-AULMAURACITE

***Where did you get this Rock? Who is your supplier?**

The source that I got my supply from said he excavated the Rocks from somewhere in the Rocky Mountains. He was a very eccentric and secretive man, and wouldn't tell me exactly where. I believe that it was the only known repository for this Rock. My source "disappeared" in about 2006 …so unless he appears back in my life to excavate more for me to purchase, my supply is all I know of. I'm hoping to find him again to get another inventory soon. I am also aware of the possibility that once these Rocks have found their way to the people who need them… that will be it: the source will be gone.

***What are Power Grid Rocks and how do you set them up?**

I have been using 1-gram Grid Rocks for several years now helping in my Ghost Busting ventures. Grids can be placed in and around rooms, houses, yards, offices, buildings, monuments, churches, schools, court houses, cemeteries, rivers, downtown areas, cities, counties, airports, and all kinds of government properties and spiritual/energy spots to stabilize the area and create a new matrix. We have found that when a Grid is set, it bumps that "Gridder" up to a new level. We have also noticed that if the person doing the Gridding needs to move, they soon find themselves on their way to a new adventure! If they need to stay, things stabilize and their lives improve ...(but sometimes not without some kind of drama as Truth and Justice come to the surface).

To set up a 5-Stone Power Grid, place a Rock in each corner and one in the center or as close to the center as possible. Once the corners of a Power Grid are put in place, hold the 5th or center Rock and give the grid whatever commands you feel appropriate, i.e., bring truth, peace, prosperity, healing, etc. Then tell the Grid to "turn on" as you place the center stone. You can instantly feel it charging up and creating an energy of stability and clarity. You may want to put these little stones in some colorful tissue paper, the way they are when you receive them, so you won't accidentally vacuum them up if you place them on the floor. Many people thumbtack them to the wall or ceiling, especially if they have pets!

I recently met a man who had a real strong connection and affinity to the Aulmauracite Rocks and started experimenting with them. He put Grids up in his hometown in various places he felt needed "truth, light, and/or stability." He placed them around the outskirts of town, around specific buildings, and in the mountains at the source of the city water supply! Since he didn't have a car, he took a cab to do the city and water supply Grid. It was a 12-hour journey, and the cab driver said it was "The Ride of his Life!" (I'm sure no other cabbie has a tale to tell that beats that one!) Then he came to my town, and we put up Grids around some specific government buildings, cathedrals, the city center, around the city limits and then around the entire county! (That Grid was an all-day project!) In one of the center stones we dug a little hole and buried an Aulmauracite stone scrolled up inside a picture of the Kryahgenetics Egg with our intentions written on the back such as ...Love, UV-Light, laughter, truth, justice, and support for the Indigo Nation. I felt an immediate difference, and then things began to shift…and shift…and shift..... ..... and then stabilize.

At first you might think it is a bad thing when all the "Truth Comes Spewing Forth," but when the dust settles, you know it is "All Good." :o)

Experiment with your Grids. One Power Grid owner directed the Grid he placed around the room he used for massage and healing, to expand out to his house, and then to his yard. He felt the energy as it did indeed expand into his yard. If you have any tales to tell, please write to me and I may post it on my Rock web page: https://www.firstwaveindigos.com/post/aurauralite-power-rock-testimonial-love-letters

***I can't find Aurauralite/Aulmauracite in my gem and crystal book.**

You won't find these Rocks in your gem books (yet) because to my knowledge, no one else knows they exist.

***Where did Aurauralite-Aulmauracite get their names?**

These names were revealed to me after some intense meditation with the Rock, and were confirmed by my guide, Hal. When the names were lexigramed, I had a second confirmation that I had absolutely gotten the right names.

At the beginning of the words Aurauralite and Aulmauracite, you will find the letters "Au." This is the chemical symbol for the element of Gold, as well as being one of the Universal tones found in names for "GOD" and spiritual deities or icons, i.e., Allah, Amon-Ra, Yeshua, Krishna, Shiva, Rama, Brahma, Buddha, Dalai Lama, Ptah, Diana, Gaia/Guyah, Athena, Durga, Kali, Lakshmi, Saraswati, Ambika, Uma, etc. It does not surprise me that this tone is repeated twice in both Aurauralite and Aulmauracite.

***My Rock is changing color. Is it being overworked? Am I using it too much" Am I hurting it?**

The truth is that you CAN'T use your Rock too much, in fact, the more you use it, the happier the Rock is! The 2 large stones I have accompany me in my Kryahgenetics sessions, are changing color too. One has some greenish casts to it (like it is growing moss or something on it), and the other one has some pale pinkish-orange that is slowly spreading. This color transformation seems to be just one of the amazing phenomena that occurs when you start using these highly intelligent Rocks.

In regard to the Rocks changing color, another interesting Aulmauracite Rock discovery occurred about a year ago. I was shaving down a Rock for a client that needed it to be flat on top so he could place a Tesla device on it. I used a steel file and was filing away when I noticed that wherever the Rock was filed, it instantly turned a reddish-purple! Also, the Aurauralite dust that was filed off changed color too! (I used the Aurauralite dust in some pendants but they didn't last long, as everyone who saw them wanted a "red one.") I was shocked later to find that the Aulmauracite Rock totally wore down the steel file and made it smooth. I went through 2 double-sided steel files trying to make this Rock flat!

A few months later, I rubbed some Aulmauracite Rocks together to create Aurauralite dust for stabilizing someone's house. While rubbing the Rock, I noticed that wherever the Rocks rubbed together, they turned the same reddish-purple! I'm not sure why this happens, but it is an interesting phenomenon that I thought I'd pass on. If anyone has any ideas as to what might cause this, please feel free to e-mail me. I'm open to any and all possibilities.

***I was making some L-R #5 water (Love Resonance #5), and after dipping my pendant in a glass of water and stirring for only 2 or 3 minutes, I could taste a difference! Is it necessary to put your pendant in the water for the full 20 minutes?**

In recent experiments, it seems that the more people are using Aurauralite, the more efficient they become. It is now only necessary to charge the water for 1-2 minutes for the water to be fully charged. Also, you don't need to worry if you forget and leave your pendant in the water overnight. It will shut off automatically when it is finished charging. (Gosh, I just love these "User Friendly Rocks!")

NOTE: Be careful not to drink too much water the first day. I would recommend only 4-8 oz the first day because detoxification can take place, causing you to have flu-like symptoms and even diarrhea like I did! Aurauralite/Aulmauracite puts light filaments into the water, so when this is ingested, it will put that same light into your cells causing tremendous changes in your body. I find that I am more centered, composed, and attuned to my Core and Spirit when I drink this water. I also feel tremendous physical strength and stamina when I use this as a nutritional supplement.

If you want to do the "Taste Test," have 2 glasses of water that came from the same source. Charge one of them with Aurauralite, and then take a sip of both of them. The Aurauralite-Aulmauracite water will taste sweeter and have a smoother, thicker texture. (Always use glass glasses, ***not plastic!***)

INFORMATION UPDATE: It used to be detrimental, but is now its OK to put a Rock in water to charge it! If you do, and drink some of the dust particles, make sure you are stable before you go out in public or drive!

NOTE: *Some FW-Indigos even suck on the Rocks for psychic boosts and for a stronger connection to the Rocks and their own Core. It's just a weird Indigo thing. When they get a Rock, they first smell it, and then they want to see how it tastes. I confess, I did it too, and personally, I LOVE the smell and taste...it reminds me of Home!*

AURAURALITE/AULMAURACITE POWER GRID ROCKS

I have been using these magickal little Grid Rocks since the late 1990's now to create an environment of stability, clarity, truth, and internal power. They are an absolute requirement when my Ghost Buster partner Ronnie and I are contracted to do a Ghost Busting. Whether it is remote work or if we are there on site, we won't even begin without having the property properly Gridded. We have found that when we have the assistance of a Power Grid on the property, the truth surfaces quicker, the energies stabilize, and ghosts are easier to manage. Before discovering the extreme supernatural abilities of these Grids, our Ghost Busting work would leave us psychically and physically drained for hours afterwords. In one emergency situation, we felt it necessary to do psychic work on a house before it had been Gridded, and it was like trying to walk through waist-high Jello. Psychic information was very slow in coming, and we had to really stretch our psychic abilities to the max to even get a particum of information and clarity on the trapped Souls. It left us physically exhausted and energetically trashed for hours afterwards. We both ended up having to take naps. After that incident, we made it a strict policy to always have the premises Gridded before we do our work.

I have since been using these Grids on my own home and property to keep the "riff-raff" out of my sacred space. This does not mean that nothing "supernatural" ever happens inside the borders, but it does weed out much of the incessant barrage of psychic and electromagnetic interferences and disruptions. I now figure, that if anything gets through these Grids, it is allowed so that I can gain some kind of awareness or education from whatever energies/entities these Grid Rocks let in.

NOTE: *We are trying to get as many towns and areas Gridded as we can that need "Truth and Justice." These Grids are causing massive disruptions and exposure to the corruption on this Planet!*

One of our First Wave Indigos, I humorously refer to as "The Grid Meister," because he has such a knack for Feng Shui, and has put up some extreme Grids in different countries. He has assisted many people with Grid maps and helped support them in putting up Grids in their towns. He has some amazing tales to tell about his Power Grid Rock adventures. This is a copy of a letter he sends to the people he works with to give them specific instructions on how to set up Grids.

GRIDDING FOR PROS

A more in-depth Gridding Instruction Guide by V.K.

Aurauralite-Aulmauracite, "The Stone of Truth & Justice Rocks" can be used to Grid all kinds of areas and places: corrupted, negative or depressing, in need of protection, stability or humor, enhancement or UV-enlightenment.

Grids can be put up in and around beds, rooms, houses, yards, buildings, monuments, parks, towns, cities, states, etc. Use local maps or the Google or Yahoo Earth map programs on the internet to locate the best placements for your Grids. Here you have to use your own research and intuition to find out where the Grids are most needed and how many of them. Quality can be better than quantity.

The regular Aulmauracite Grid is set up with five Rocks – one on each corner and one in the center (there have been cases however, where we have used more than five Rocks in a Grid, but never fewer). You want to put them up as symmetrical as possible, with the four cornerstones equidistant from the center stone. If exact symmetry is not possible, just tell the Rocks to adjust the energetics and they will... (they are very smart! ;-)

The size of the Rocks used for Gridding does not matter, as one little grain is as powerful as a 2 lb Rock. However, sometimes it just "feels better" to have larger Grid Rocks. The center stone is always buried or installed last and is used to "turn on" the Grid. I prefer to have the Center Stone a little bigger or heavier than the cornerstones because it symbolizes the energy, powerfully radiating out the Grid's intent from the center. They are mailed out in colored tissue paper and the center stone is wrapped in a different color than the Corner Stones. (You can bury them with the tissue.)

Normally the Grid Rocks are buried in soil. I either use a little spade, screwdriver or some other small pointed item like a ball point pen to dig the holes, and I try not to draw attention to myself. (Pens are much less threatening and easier to conceal than screwdrivers, especially if there are surveillance cameras. Since some Grids are set up in public places, people can be intimidated or get suspicious about someone carrying a big pointy object to dig holes in the ground with.) If there is no soil or appropriate place to bury the Rocks, look for cracks in the concrete, knot holes in the trees or other spots where the Rocks are most unlikely to be moved.

The Rocks are a Life-form and are therefore, very much aware, and so you should treat them with respect, but even more with Love. It is all about energy and intention. I kiss every Rock before I bury it, and wish him or her a good time and a good journey. If you forget to do that, don't worry just think of the Rocks and send them warm fuzzies. :-)

Once you have set up the four Corner Stones, it is time to bury the Center Stone. Before you bury it, visualize all four Corner Stones you have buried before and connect them mentally and energetically with the center stone. Then put what you want and need into the Grid such as: Truth, Love, Justice, Honor, Karma, UV-Light, Laughter, Prosperity, etc. Then tell the Grid to "turn on" or "activate." Then kiss the Center Stone and bury it.

As mentioned above, it is very likely that you will encounter some resistance or "weirdness" of some kind, when setting up the Grids, because at the moment there are still energies and entities out there who are not happy with you bringing Truth and Justice to the Planet.

Should you ever feel uncomfortable, anxious, paranoid, discouraged, or run into problems and resistance during the setting up of a Grid, know that you are always protected. Remember that you can always ask the Rocks or your Spirit Guides for more assistance and support if you need it. Another helpful thing to do, from my own experience, is to make yourself invisible. (Just think about it and put an invisibility shield around you) ...And psychically "Egg" yourself (and others that put up a Grid with you) with one or more Kryahgenetics Eggs.

This was a short introduction of the methods I use to set up Aulmauracite "The Stone of Truth & Justice" Grids. I hope this will assist and inspire you. Once you have set up two or three Grids on your own, you will develop a feel for Gridding and create your own Grid techniques and have your own indescribable experiences. I wish you all the best for your future grid projects and much Love, UV-Light, and Laughter.... V.K.

Just a note here about being discrete. *When I was Gridding the 4 block radius around the courthouse here in Spokane, the Center Stone was placed next to the flagpole in the front of the building. There were cameras everywhere, so I had to be inconspicuous. I sat down on the lawn by the flagpole and started rummaging through my purse and pulled out a granola bar. I unwrapped it, and started eating it while reading some papers I had in my purse. People passed by and just thought I sat down to rest or perhaps I was waiting for someone. As I was casually doing this I took out my pen and discretely made a hole in the lawn and dropped the Center Stone in, and then covered it up. (If you want to kiss the stones, do this beforehand so you won't draw attention to yourself.) As I was sitting there appearing to be reading something, I was actually psychically connecting to the Rocks and telling the Grid to "turn on" giving it instructions for Truth and Justice to infiltrate the Justice System." (Pretty ironic to say the least.) After a few minutes, I put the wrapper in my purse, stood up, brushed the grass off of me, and walked away to my car that was waiting several blocks away. (I never park in the immediate vicinity because of the cameras.)*

POWER GRID ROCKS AROUND THE WORLD

NOTE: These Grids are listed in the order that they were placed. If you have set up an important Grid that is not on this list, please contact us at: Aurauralite@MistycHouse.com
*For a more updated list go to https://www.firstwaveindigos.com/post/aurauralite-power-grid-rocks

As of Oct. 2013, we have Power Grids set up in:

- *Essen & N.R.W., Germany - Dec. 2006*
- *Ramsau am Dachstein, Austria - Dec. 2006*
- *Spokane, Washington - Jan. 2007*

- Soap Lake, Washington - Feb. 2007
- Vancouver, B.C., Canada- Feb. 2007
- Seattle, Washington - Mar. 2007
- Berlin, Germany - Mar. 2007
- South L.A., California - Apr. 2007
- Minneapolis/St. Paul, Minnesota - May 2007
- Burlington, Wisconsin - June 2007
- New York City, New York - Oct. 2007
- Houston, Texas - Nov. 2007
- San Fernando Valley, California - Nov. 2007
- Pollock Pines, California - Nov. 2007
- Aspen, Colorado - Dec. 2007
- San Antonio, Texas - Jan. 2008
- Bucharest, Romania - Feb.2008
- Las Vegas, Nevada - Feb. 2008
- Toledo, Ohio - Feb. 2008
- Detroit, Michigan - Feb. 2008
- West Sacramento, California - Feb. 2008
- Toronto, Ontario, Canada - Feb. 2008
- Columbia, California - Mar. 2008
- Sacramento, California - May. 2008
- Frankfurt/Main, Germany - Mar. 2008
- SE Andhra Pradesh, India - Apr. 2008
- Chennai, India - Apr. 2008
- Pondicherry, India - Apr. 2008
- Redmond Washington/Microsoft Campus, Washington - Apr. 2008
- Oklahoma City, Oklahoma - May 2008
- Nederland, Colorado - May 2008
- Boulder, Colorado - May 2008
- Denver, Colorado - June 2008
- Milan, Italy - June 2008
- Florence, Italy - June 2008
- Rome/Vatican, Italy - June 2008
- Moscow, Idaho - June 2008
- Vienna, Austria - June 2008
- Pullman, Washington - June 2008

-The United States Mainland, July 2008 -
Corner Stones: *San Diego, California – Miami, Florida – Quebec, Canada – Vancouver, B.C., Canada -*
Center Stone: *Wichita, Kansas*

- New Orleans, Louisiana - Aug. 2008
- Boise, Idaho - Aug. 2008
- The Country of Romania - Sept. 2008 (see link below for a unique grid map)
https://www.firstwaveindigos.com/aulmauracite-aurauralite
- Sandpoint, Idaho - Dec. 2008

- *Placerville, California - Dec. 2008*
- *San Francisco, California - March 2009*
- *Stuttgart, Germany - April 2009*
- *Bellingham, Washington - April 2009*
- *Banff, Alberta, Canada - May 2009*
- *Invermere, B.C., Canada - May 2009*
- *Cranbrook, B.C., Canada - May 2009*
- *Missoula, Montana - June 2009*
- *Roseburg, Oregon - July 2009*
- *Eugene, Oregon - July 2009*
- *Rossland, B.C., Canada - July 2009*
- *Coeur d'Alene, Idaho - July 2009*
- *Salt Lake City, Utah - July 2009*
- *Nelson, B.C. Canada - July 2009*
- *Castlegar, B.C., Canada - July 2009*
- *Hopi and Navajo Reservations Arizona - Aug. 2009*
- *Lewiston, Idaho - Sept. 2009*
- *WSU Campus - Pullman, Washington - Sept. 2009*
- *Military Bases in Iraq - Sept.2009*
- *Mt. Shasta, California - Sept. 2009*
- *Chicago, Illinois - Oct. 2009*
- *Butte, Montana - Oct. 2009*
- *Helena, Montana - Oct. 2009*
- *Great Falls, Montana - Oct. 2009*
- *London, England - Dec. 2009*
- *Sandringham House Estate-England - Dec. 2009*
- *Stonehenge, England - Dec. 2009*
- *Oxford, England - Dec. 2009*
- *Cambridge, England - Dec. 2009*
- *London, (City of Westminster) - England, Dec. 2009*
- *Royal Park (Greenwich), England - Dec. 2009*
- *Norwich, England - Dec. 2009*
- *Bangkok, Thailand - Dec. 2009*
- *Khon Kaen, Thailand - Dec. 2009*
- *Singapore, Singapore - Feb. 2010*
- *Tulsa, Oklahoma - Mar. 2010*
- *Stanford University, California - Mar. 2010*
- *Portland, Oregon - Apr. 2010*
- *Tokyo, Japan - Apr. 2010*
- *Seoul, Korea - July 2010*
- *North Korea border - DMZ - including train station to North Korea - July 2010*
- *French Meadows Reservoir, California - Oct. 2011*
- *Hell Hole Reservoir, California - Oct. 2011*
- *Mather Field AFB, Arcata, California - Oct. 2011*
- *Goettingen, Lower Saxony, Germany - Jan.2012*
- *Large Diamond Grid: Queanbeyan, Tharwa, Bungendore, Murrumbateman, & Canberra Australia -*

The Center Stone On Top Of The Parliament House - Aug. 2012
- Pahrump, Nevada - Nov. 2012
- Lake Tahoe, Nevada - Nov. 2012
- Arcata, California - Dec. 2012
- CERN, Switzerland - Dec.2012
- The Island of Oahu, Hawaii, Dec. 2012
- The Big Pyramid at Chichen Itza, Mexico - Dec.2012
- Tulum Temples, Mexico - Dec. 2012
- The Township of Yass - New South Wales - Dec. 2012
- Estes Park, Colorado - Dec.2012
- Parma (+ Parma Hts.), Ohio - Dec. 2012
- Hamilton, Ontario, Canada - Dec. 12, 2012 - 11:11 a.m.
- Buckingham Palace, London - Mar.2013
- Singapore, Singapore (extra Grids) Mar. 2013
- Osoyoos B.C. - Mar. 2013
- Washington, D.C. - Apr. 2013
- Coleville, Saskatchewan, Canada - Apr. 2013
- Hackensack, New Jersey - Apr. 2013
- Albuquerque, New Mexico - Apr. 2013
- Las Vegas, Nevada (Strip) - June 2013
- Scottish Parliment, Edinburgh, Scotland - Sept. 2013
- Hellendoorn - Hulsen - Nijverdal - Netherlands - Oct. 2013

The following airports have Grid Rocks in them: *Denver - L.A.X. - S.L.C. - Atlanta - Wichita - Vancouver - San Diego - Miami - Newark Liberty - Quebec - Toronto - Amsterdam - Eugene - Portland - Phoenix - O'Hare - Heathrow (entire perimeters) - Singapore Changi*

I am thrilled that in April 2013 my wish for Gridding the 3 major global centers of Power/Control/Enslavement has finally been realized!

They are:
~Vatican City (Spiritual Enslavement Center) June 2008
~The City of London (Financial Control Center) December 2009
~Washington D.C. (Military Power Center) April 2013

NOTE: See the most recent updates on our website including Grid Rocks in:
***The South Pole Jan. 2016 & *The North Pole Apr. 2016.**
https://www.firstwaveindigos.com/post/aurauralite-power-grid-rocks

Thank You to all the persistent Knights & Lady Knights who are stealth-fully Gridding the Planet with Aurauralite & Aulmauracite so that Truth & Justice can finally prevail!

Here are two poems that have been written in honor of these magnificent Life-forms. This first one was written by Will Schive of *Good Works On Earth*. He professionally lexigramed the name of this Rock, and this is what we discovered:

AULMAURACITE

...from...

AAACEILMRTUU

......revealing.....

I AM AULMAURACITE
A META METAL
A MIRACLE
A CURE

I LITE AURA
I ALTER AURA
I TAME MALICE

I AM A RITUAL AMULET
A TRUE ART
I ALTER AIR
I TIE TIME

I AM A CALMER
I AM REAL
I AM TRUE
I AM

AUM
...and a bit more...

…..And most recently, another family poet sent us this descriptive poem that tells more tales of the mystical magickal gift that was lovingly brought to us by our "Other Family" many, many, many moons ago…

AURAURALITE

As dark as night with moonbeams glowing
Its uncanny power will give you a knowing.
A deep feeling inside each tiny cell
It might change your life, who can tell?

With your resonances' glowing
What else might be showing?
A sacred remembrance of who you are
Or where you come from.....what star?

This magical dust that encases your All
Will help your life to have a ball.
For it amplifies all that is good and kind
When Love and Blessings sweep through your mind.

Earth's Divine Love comes from out of the blue
Aurauralite from Nature is a gift to you.
Protection, Perfection as healing forces draw near
They will cover your body from danger or fear.....

A mythical gift from a mystical force
Helps your dreams evolve on a magical course.
From Nature to You with all her Love
Entwined with a Light Force-God's Gift from Above.

Bonnie ©Ireland
July 1998

To purchase the Rocks, see our website at: www.mistychouse.com/treasure/M.H.treasures.htm

JUST WHO DO YOU THINK YOU ARE?

Understand that if you are a Being living somewhere on Planet Earth during this eventful time, every day is going to be a smorgasbord of action, changes, choices, joy, tears, humor… A continual, proverbial, emotional roller-coaster.

Challenges of every kind are plentiful now, and many times it feels like the laws of scarcity simply do not apply when it comes to stressful situations and emotionally charged encounters. There always seems to be a constant bombardment of potential stresses, miscommunications, and contentions just waiting to happen!

Trust me when I tell you that my life is absolutely no exception! Because of some bizarre circumstances, and also because I have the audacity to stand up to tyrants, I have been literally "homeless" not just once, but 3 times…and with children!

I have been confronted with many challenging situations and decisions that could have changed the course and destination of many, many people, places, and things. Each decision and response had to be handled with wide scope, eagle eyed vision on an individual basis, and also on a day to day, moment to moment basis. These decisions had to be made swiftly, and not necessarily the way my logic would tell me, not the way my friends would advise me, and not the way I had always assumed I would respond, according to the rules I had previously outlined for myself.

No, each delicate decision had to be handled moment by moment, totally operating from my heart and gut feelings. There were many instances when I would say to myself, "I can't believe this is happening! ...How did things get so crazy? ...Why would I create...or co-create this kind of experience? ...It's not in my consciously created reality for these injustices to be a part of my life! ...How am I going to get myself out of this entangled *mass-mess,* when I have to be so careful because every little thing I do and say seems to affect so many people? …How do I keep my integrity when I seem to be forced into situations with people and things that are in conflict with my code of ethics? …How can I make a decision when both directions could appear to be totally ethical, and at the same time also be viewed as totally unethical and dysfunctional? …How do I handle this and keep the unavoidable reverb going out to others to a bare minimum? …Why were these senseless actions that started this whole drama (which has put pain and fear into so many people, animals, and plants) done in the first place? ...These are supposed to be enlightened people I'm dealing with, why aren't they practicing what they preach? …Why wasn't there more consideration taken as to getting clear communication to prevent these mishaps? …..And if the people operating H.A.A.R.P. (***High-altitude Active Auroral Research Project,*** one of the government projects used to manipulate the weather, wars, our thoughts, emotions, etc.) turn up the irritation, retaliation, and miscommunication juice one more notch, ***I'm leaving this movie set permanently!"***

There were several times in my life when things got so horrendous, and my nerves were so frayed that I would go limp, void, and feel like I was losing my Life-force… and part of me didn't care… and I didn't even care that I didn't care! After a while though, I would come to my senses and go to the Core of my Being and question everything! Sometimes I would come out empty-handed and devoid of answers. At one point in time, all I **knew** was that **I loved my children**... ***which was the only thing that I honestly knew was an absolute in my life!***

Even in this sorry state, I would keep reminding myself that although I couldn't make any sense out of it **NOW**, I knew somehow, some way, the pain and fog would clear. I knew that even though my life seemed hopeless, I would be able to make sense out of it and understand it at some time in the future. Whether it was five minutes from now, five hours, five days, weeks, months, or years..... someday..... I would understand it and see the wisdom in my creation or co-creation of that experience.

Time after time, I would reflect back on the information and advice given in this book to get me through some of the emotional storms and the senselessness of what I was presently experiencing. I thought to myself that if the only reason this book was written was to get me through some of the insanity in my own life, and to keep me from "helping myself" leave this plane prematurely.....*(which I candidly confess, was considered many times as an acceptable option)*..... then all the long hours and toil in producing this book would have been well worth it.

It then occurred to me that if the wisdom, encouragement, and energy from this particular modality of information, *via my Higher Self -* ***Soul Suemah*** *and Hal,* could keep ***me*** from throwing in the towel during critical mass times, it would also most likely help other people in their challenging hours as well!

In the beginning, I (silly salamander), went into the writing of this book, with little awareness in respect to the implications of what I was about to present to the masses. I wrote this book because I was asked to write a chapter explaining Kryahgenetics for my ex-husband's book... which made me feel like he was totally patronizing me... like patting me on the head and throwing me a few crumbs. "Here little girl, I will do you a huge favor by allowing you to write a few pages in MY book. You can talk about that thing you call Kriaaagen...whatever it is .....and you'll be forever in my debt. I will allow you to tag along but remember, I'm the big cheese and you're the underling." Part of me resisted this BIG time, but another part of me, the part inspired by Hal, went for the gusto. Several months later, to my surprise, one chapter turned into several chapters, which turned into an entire book! *(The first edition was an author's manuscript with 152 pages, published back in 1999!)* At that time, I had no idea as to the extent of the impact this coded information would have on myself and other people, *particularly the chapters on Money, Adapters, and The Knight's Code.* I was also totally unaware of the variety of challenges that would race to greet me when I started putting the chapters together, ***especially during the final editing of both the first edition, the authors manuscript, and to the EXTREME during this second edition!***

On the other side of the scales, some delightful and amazing reports have come my way in the past years since the conception of this book. One of those is that I seem to be visiting and assisting a lot of people I am consciously unaware of, especially during dreamtime. (No wonder I wake up so many mornings and feel like I just put in a double shift!) One woman related a dream she had of me, in which I gave her some advice that totally transformed her life. In this dream, she was with several of her friends that knew me. Some of them were great advocates and very supportive of me, while the others just thought I was totally "out to lunch" and downright weird! (When she was relating this dream to me, I thought to myself, "That sounds about right. I can relate to this.") Then she said that I walked in the room and was wearing this slinky black spandex outfit... and my hair was orange, green, blue... **and spiked**!!!

In the dream I sat down with her and gave her some council. I told her that with all of the challenges she was having, in order to understand it, and fix it, she needed to ask herself three important questions:

(1) What are you willing to give up?
(2) What are you willing to receive?
(3) What are you afraid of?

The woman told me that if it hadn't been for her focus on the outrageousness of my appearance, she probably wouldn't have remembered the dream at all, and therefore, never would have gotten what she referred to as "the law of her life."

She also told me that she figured Hal had something to do with the outrageous attire part of it... and I totally concurred with her on that one. Hal would certainly use those kind of tactics ...yeah... that one had his fingerprints and signature written all over it!

Other people have told me that I have been there to help them out of scary situations, and gave them comfort when they needed it, whether they were asleep or awake. I have also been told that there are tonal qualities in my voice and laughter that calms people, makes them feel safe, and then they feel like they will be O.K. again. Others tell me that hearing my voice makes them feel lighter and happier. I know that in my heart of hearts, compassion and up-liftment ...especially through humor, is always my intent. There is however, no conscious, willful objective to "tone people into a state of peace and safety" ...I feel it is somehow on "auto pilot."

If this is correct, then I am thrilled to lend such powerful assistance unknowingly! If this tonal healing quality is real... then I accept what Hal told me, that it is one of my Spiritual Contracts here. It may also be a reason why my clients seem to enjoy and be inspired by our telephone consultations without being physically with me, who knows?

NOTE: *It did occur to me today when I was out taking care of my pet chickens and ducks... singing songs to them while I gave them "forced cuddles," and cleaning their pens, that Music is truly an amazing alchemical tool. I reflected back to June of 2013, when I was taking care of one of my chickens who was a rescue from one of* ***the house of horrors*** *called* ***"A Factory Farm."*** *She used to be the ruler of the rescue hen roost, and her name was "Queen B" ...but she was not doing very well. I went out several times a day to encourage her to eat and drink. She was losing weight and her comb was getting pale. She was light as a feather, literally, and when I picked her up, my biggest urge was to cry my eyes out. I took her to see the Vet as she had been egg bound before, and thought it might be a reoccurrence of that. They took X-rays and diagnosed that she was not egg bound, but other tests indicated she had parasites. I gave her worm medicine (...which I hated to do since she had so many drugs at the Factory Farm, but she would not eat the natural remedies I had for her, so I had no choice). She was starting to get better for a while and then took a nosedive. I had been the brunt of nonstop psychic assaults, which seemed to step up the pace a bit at that time, and it was getting very hard to manage. As I held her, I resisted that temptation to break down and weep, but instead, forced myself to tell her jokes and sing her songs with lyrics like, "A-Perka-perk-perk-perk-perk-perk-perk" while bouncing her up and down a little in order to get her to "perk-up" a bit. It worked! So, I did this day after day, each day wanting to cry and fall apart instead of sing.....* ***but did it anyway!*** *Singing did indeed immediately change my state from horrendous grief to happiness, and it helped* *her and all the other animals feel safe and cheerful. I had to go on a three-day trip and told her when I put her to bed that I would be leaving in a few hours, and if she needed to cross over while I was gone, if getting better was not an option, that I totally understood. I got a call the next day with the news that she had "passed peacefully in her sleep."*

As a professional Ghost Buster, I always check and make sure my animals cross over, and did not get shoved into a spirit trap or some such thing. I found that she had indeed crossed, as she had been Egged and was just fine. She told me she was grateful to have spent her last 14 months at our place after being jailed and tortured in a California factory farm with 50 thousand other hens and then nearly starving to death. (See https://www.youtube.com/watch?v=b_FlvuROSWg) She then thanked me for doing what I could to make her last days happy and "Perky" ones! (..... Then I did break down and cry.)

As I reflected back on this experience, I knew that if I did NOT sing, if I did NOT do something drastic to change the foreboding and debilitating energies that were descending upon us, that fear and grief would have indeed set in, and everyone would have suffered because of it. I realized at an even deeper level what powerful magickal Kryahgenetics elements Love, Music, and Laughter are. I could literally feel the alchemy of it all shift the energies from deep fear and grief, to joy and delight... and in seconds! This was a very powerful visual aid and reference point for me as the alchemy was undeniable. I also realized that "singing," (even if you can't sing very well and make up your own silly songs), will indeed make a shift in the energies in and around you, and catapult you into a more empowered, more stable, more in- command position in minutes! I give you the challenge to try it the next time you feel like you're about to fall apart at the seams. Understand this is NOT a ***deny and bury*** *process, but rather a conscious* ***shift & replace*** *process!*

Now that you have a little background on me, and I have spilled some of my guts to you, my reasons were to show you that just because you get some inspiration to write a book, you certainly are not immune to the challenges you write about! (...In fact, to be really honest with you, sometimes it feels like those challenges come in larger packages with the volume turned way up, just because you had the audacity to call attention to it!)

So here you are, nearly at the end of this book. Let's see how my experiences and this information can assist you, and how it relates to ***you, the reader... The Star of Your Show!*** In this giant Hologram we are in, where there are so many directions we could take, and changes we could make in the outcome and ending of this game, I'd like you to take a good look at the title of this chapter ***"Who Do You Think You Are?"*** and contemplate it for a moment.

Since we all have, to a certain extent, the element of Free-Will over our destiny (through our conscious thoughts and actions)... I'd like to ask you what and who you would like to be in this movie/game? Now really think about this for a moment. (Understand, that you can also be several different characters in this movie if you feel up to it!)

Remember in the movie, "Don Juan DeMarco," the power, influence, and downright magick Don Juan had on people? He brought love and romance into the lives of everyone he met... including the psychiatrist... *who was supposed to* "bring him back to reality!"

I was deeply affected by that movie, maybe because I remember existences where romance and passion were at the foundation of grand civilizations! After watching this inspiring and comical drama, the possibilities began to come alive in my mind as I thought of how we could literally create magickal characters in this vivid Holographic reality called "Earth Life."

What would happen if we were to write down, ***in detail,*** a descriptive profile of all the attributes of an inspiring, adventuresome character we would like to become, and every day implement some of those characteristics in our reality?

How much fun would this existence truly be if we were to literally become that character from the creations of our pen?

Is it possible? …**Or is it even probable …**that once created with paper and pen…spending quality time contemplating it every day…bringing uninhibited bliss, fantasy, and playful emotion to this creation, that we could generate mind-blowing outcomes!?

And what if we were truly loving/living by the character description we just created? If we continued to perfect this awesome creation…what might we become? ...Would it be fantasy? …Or perhaps… perhaps maybe, ***just maybe*****…..** we would become precisely **who and what we REALLY are!**

NOTE: *I have to add this little insert here because it is applicable and will resonate to many of you reading this book. Ronnie Foster, my Ghost Buster partner, editor and CCC ally, sent me this little card a few days ago that made me laugh, as it was really funny… but also had some serious implications. This card had an absolutely adorable baby Dragon with big innocent eyes on the front. Ronnie knows about my affinity to Dragons and other so called "mystical creatures," so her sending this was typical of our relationship.*

The caption on the front however, was NOT typical, but extremely profound to me. It said,

"Always Be Yourself… Unless you can be a Dragon...
Then Always be a Dragon…"

Now, I would ask you one more time…..

JUST WHO DO YOU THINK YOU ARE?

To these inspirational messages, I would add only this last thought…

Who E'er Thou Art...

Act Well Thy Part!

LAUGH-AH-GENETICS

It is through Hal's design, that this book's final chapter be something totally off the wall, **AND ALSO**, be something to get you started with some practical application at the same time. (As Swami Beyondananda would say, "It's like feeding 2 birds with one scone.") Therefore, I'm sure it's no surprise to you that the title of this chapter is a *pun* and a *polar opposite* to the title on the cover!

At this time, I need to ask you a ***serious*** question that will probably take a few minutes to answer, because you will first have to flash back to your past, and really ponder, scan, and review what you find there.

How long has it been since you laughed so hard and so long that your sides hurt, or your face hurt from using muscles you rarely use? How long has it been since you cleaned out your tear ducts with tears of laughter? And, how long, *if you can admit it,* has it been since you laughed so intensely that *your bladder let loose too?*

When I posed this question to people from all over the country while I was touring, most of the "adult" people said it has been at least 10 or 15 years! ...And a majority of those polled said it hadn't been since they were a kid or a teenager!!!

WHAT A PATHETIC BUNCH OF STIFF, UPTIGHT, UNRESPONSIVE, BORING ADULTS WE HAVE TURNED OURSELVES INTO!!! (I know...I've been there!)

How did we get this way? When did it happen?

For many of us, it came on gradually, like a frozen pond, and it's hard to really decipher exactly when, where, how, and why... it just happened through a series of events.

The good news is that you have just identified a missing piece to the puzzle of life...*or shall we say, "no life"* ...and now have the opportunity to *"get a life!"*

At this point, I have another very relevant question to ask. When you had your last extended fit of laughter, what were the circumstances around it? What put you into this state of frivolous bliss? Who was there with you, and how long did it last?

Chances are that just thinking and reminiscing about it will make you light up and laugh again...or at the very least, snicker a little... and doesn't it feel great!

One interesting factor that seemed to be a common element as I was taking my uncontrollable laughter poll, was that it never happened while someone was in solitude without outside stimulation. This would lead one to believe these high laughter vibes work best when there's another electromagnetic body to bounce the energy off of, and in doing so, create a buoyant rebound system that is immensely compelling and highly transmissible!

After gathering this laughter data, my creative juices began to flow, and the next thing I knew, it turned into a geyser!

I began to ask myself some provocative questions. What if we had groups of people, young and old, meeting on a regular basis to laugh themselves silly? What would be the results of a major campaign to get this Planet laughing their way out of their troubles and dramas and petty fighting? (I have never yet witnessed someone in blissful laughter that was up-tight or angry!)

Think of the implications here. *You may want to unload your stock in blood pressure and anti-depressant pharmaceuticals... those dang things could be rendered totally useless and obsolete!*

I have decided (*with a little help from my* ***esoteric friends***) to take this humor business seriously… (how's that for an oxy-moron?) …and do whatever it takes to infiltrate and inundate this Planet with "Hal's Hal-arious Healing Humor!"

For those of you who are reading this chapter and feel your *internal tickle bug* activating, and want to get on the *laugh-your-way-to-enlightenment train* with me, I have come up with a few crafty ideas to help you *come aboard!*

Have you ever been shocked out of your reality gourd by an honest to goodness surprise party? Well, if you haven't, you of course, don't know what you're missing; so in the next few pages you will find things to remedy that! You will get the inside scoop on Humor Surprise Party Packages, and also learn about the "**U**nified **F**amily **Of** **S**acred **H**umor **B**eings" (or UFO-SHBs): The only religion of utter nonsense that actually makes sense!

Once we get this humor train moving, there will be more surprise packages to order. They will all come complete with instructions, *and everything you need* to throw a totally **awe-gnar-geous** surprise party! (This word is a **"Hal-ism."** He took parts of ***awesome, gnarly, and outrageous*** and came up with the word **awe-gnar-geous**, which is pronounced… *however the heck you want!*) After you have gotten a few humor parties under your belt and have been seasoned and labeled as a **"*Serious* Humor Party Animal,"** it is then your duty and obligation to write to us and give us your outrageous and gnarly ideas. We need your feedback on how to create new and improved surprise humor parties. Since laughter is highly contagious, let's see if we can create a global epidemic! Together we can send this Planet into the *outer limits,* through humor party-instigated *endorphin highs!*

NOTE: This chapter was written back in 1999. The research and development that went into these 3 Party Package creations raised the endorphin levels of everyone involved. I still think back on these parties with frivolous fondness, as each one was unique and hysterical. When they were tested on my friends and family, we all concluded they were 100% successful in overdosing everyone's laughter quota as our humor meters went off the charts! I had visions of "The Unified Family of Sacred Humor Beings" rising to the top and being exactly what it said: "The only religion of utter nonsense that ACTUALLY MADE SENSE!" It seemed like such a "no brainer" that this *new religion* and *these parties* would sweep the Planet and change the world. I felt that once this was presented, members and party-goers would realize what a powerful, liberating method of healing and transmutation this is and it would spread like dandelions on the lawn!

Just so you can get a glimpse, here are some excerpts from the Laugh-ah-genetics webpage on the Mistyc House Website. https://www.mistychouse.com/welcome

Party Palace Previews!

Since all of our party packages are supposed to be **"Surprise Packages,"**
we can't really divulge any juicy details on what outrageous, absurd,
and sometimes dastardly creative fun we have assembled,
or what exactly is in these packages, because .....
well, that would be called **"Cheating".....**

What we will do however, is give you some hints as to what you as a potential
Sacred Humor Being Party Animal, might encounter
when you receive your

Surprise Party Packages!

Each package is unique.....and has its own "Title."

All of the Surprise Parties are designed to:

*Inspire creativity in the participating Party Animals.

*Cultivate right brain spontaneity in stiff, uptight left brainers.....and teach the right brainers to think straight, ***(or at least with a little more structure!)***

*Give yourself permission to do outlandish things you never would have done before..... ***(without the use of chemicals!)***

*Make you "rethink" your "previous thinks" about yourself, your world, and the Universe!

*Give each Party Animal a sense of adventure (formerly only known by people referred to as "Dare Devils.")

*And most importantly, give all of your Party Animal friends an opportunity to catch up on their "Laughter Quota."

And now, for the first time in Sacred Humor Being History,
we bring you a **"Sneak Peek"**
.....I mean **"Preview"**
into some of the most intimate moments of bodacious pleasures.

You are about to see first-hand, our Party Animals in action!

You will never in 100 lifetimes guess what this "Motley Crew" is doing…
You will just have to order a party and find out.....
(but then again.....you don't know *which party* this is.)

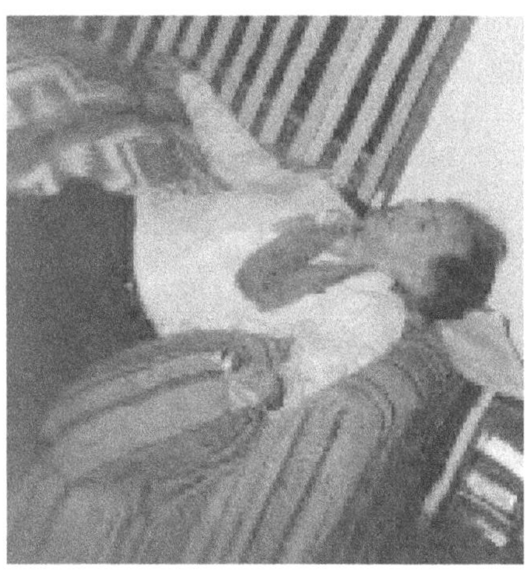

This next picture is "HARD COPY" evidence that taking the "Non-Alco Hal" challenge can create mega endorphins and the paranormal. The beverage that these "Holy Beings" are drinking is nothing more than "Tootie Fruity Herbal Tea" for Heaven's Sakes! It seems that our good Monk acquired the ability to bi-locate, as well as bring in some inter-dimensional energies.....and a lamp on his head!!!

(This is actually the way this photo turned out....
no ***purposeful*** double or triple exposures.)

Who would have guessed that in over 27 years of promoting humor, the total number of people who actually became a member of the UFO-SHBs was ...7... (...and that included me!) And party packages??? ...Would you believe a whopping -1- physical package was sold before I made them digital! After the digital version came out, at the time of this publication in 2026, only 2 more were sold

OK, let's try to make some sense out of the senseless now.

So, what does this tell us? Well, there are several answers to that question. One is that during these years, there had been tremendous opposition to every meaningful task or undertaking I embarked on, and truly it is a miracle I am still alive and kicking! Another answer is that although everyone has heard that "laugher is the best medicine," few people understand the hidden power and magick that it contains. They also don't realize the obvious, **that this is the very reason there is so much willful opposition to this medicine going down our gullets**! (...especially if we honestly really, truly "get it" and internalize this magickal energy!)

To give you a very clear demonstration of exactly how this magick works, and help you accurately understand what a powerful catalyst this is to chemical and energetic alchemy, I have a little tale to tell. It is a true tale that was written specifically for a contribution I did for Brad Steiger's book, "*Real Zombies, The Living Dead, and Creatures of the Apocalypse.*"

Get ready... heeeeere you go!

Curses, Spells and Hexes

"Curses, Spells, and Hexes are all a bunch of hogwash...
until you have had close encounters with these "taboo" dark forces!"

When paranormal investigator **Brad Steiger** was requesting stories for his book: ***Real Zombies, The Living Dead and Creatures of the Apocalypse,*** I replied with the following excerpt, which was chosen and later printed in this book with my picture on page 117:

"About curses, hexes, & voodoo..... I was the target of all of these at once. No one can understand it fully unless they have experienced it. People get sick and/or die every day from this stuff...and the sad fact is, the perpetrators go undetected. No court of law would dare try a case that claimed, "John Doe put a curse on my client and now he/she is dead." Sooo, people are quietly murdered all the time, and no one is ever prosecuted for it. It is much better to do Black Magick or negative radionics and kill someone than to hire a hit man to do it because there are no fingerprints, no guns, no knives, no evidence that our court system would acknowledge."

Brad then invited me to share some of my insights and personal experiences in his book. I hope that it will be of value, and perhaps even inspirational for those unlucky recipients who are trying to get relief from these dark energies.

Just for the record, I have no misgivings about the fact that, among other professions, I am a Solitary Practitioner in Wicca, or in other words, A WITCH! (...Actually I have recently morphed into more of a ***Futuristic Sorceress*** in an effort to help others reverse black magick, spells, curses, and psychic implants.)

I practice "Practical Magick" and have witnessed wonderful Miracles and the unbelievable, through the use of Magick. I have also been witness both personally and vicariously to the diabolical hostility and deliberate devastation of what I call "mean magick" or more commonly referred to as curses, spells and hexes.

As a researcher and practitioner of so called "fringe" sciences for over three decades, I have seen and experienced things that defy logic and the laws of physics. I must admit however, that my biggest education has been through personal experience.

One such personal encounter with "the dark side of magick" was toward the end of 2001. I had become entangled with some of the foulest of the foul on this Planet as I was attempting to free a young man from the clutches of his family...a family that was immersed in what I termed, "The Leather Cult." His father was the leader of this creepy international sect and had been well educated in the ways of Black Magick and Voodoo. My blatant interference in these "Family Affairs" (and I mean that literally too), caused me to be the target of a "class action retaliation" for 5 hellish years! I experienced a myriad of events that caused devastation and extreme personal suffering as well as energetic attempts on my life. (*A more in-depth account of this time in my life can be read in my latest book,* ***"Got Ghosts??? The Bizarre But True Tales of The Ghost Buster Gals"*** *co-authored with my Ghost Buster partner, Ronnie Rennae Foster.*)

At the time of my entanglement with "The Leather Cult," I had previously acquired a diverse education in the "Dark Arts" both through what I had researched and also by personal experiences. I was not naive. As the evil energies prevailing upon me and this young man (who I will refer to as "L.Q.") escalated, I started to show my own teeth and stand up to them. At one point, I was so upset with the manipulation of his family that I aggressively proceeded to psychically shut them down, and take back what was lost and stolen. I also attempted to get into his mother's head and make her go to her bank, draw out the amount of money she had stolen from L.Q. and send it to him. (She was using financial tyranny to make him come back home to the family.) This was "the right thing to do" as far as I was concerned.

Well, I tell my clients "the strongest force wins," and I obviously was not the strongest force at that point in time because what I had just done activated what I call a personal "class action energy assault" that darned near killed me. The next morning, I felt some stinging on the right side of my chest. This persisted and after a few days, I could feel distinct pains of what I can only describe as stab wounds in 5 different places on my chest. (I later realized that it was in the shape of an upside down pentagram!) The pain never let up and continued to get worse. Every movement in my upper torso caused pain. It stung just like a cut and my ribs felt bruised. Sleeping was difficult because it felt like I was constantly getting fresh wounds. I could not even drive alone and had to have my daughter, Ma'Lady, accompany me in my car to help me shift gears and turn the steering wheel! I would periodically check the skin on my chest, fully expecting to see cuts or bruises, but there was NOTHING visible. As the days went on it started to get difficult to breathe and I knew I was in deep trouble. I tried everything physically and metaphysically I could think of to heal this pain. I tried herbs, vitamins, minerals, homeopathics, reflexology, acupressure, energy-work, positive thinking, and even doing the New Age thing of sending Love and forgiveness to the perpetrators. This only seemed to make it worse!

I was at a loss, and I could feel my Life-force depleting. I knew I was in deep trouble but tried to keep my courage up so depression couldn't take over.

At this time, I was staying in my girlfriend Ronnie Foster's basement, because I had also become "homeless." Ronnie and I had been partners in our new venture as professional Ghost Busters for about a year. One evening we were in her basement trying to get a handle on some of the bizarre things we had experienced, and she said something really funny that made me laugh hard. I said, "Ouch, stop it…hahahahaaaa don't make me laugh hahahahaaaaaa it hurts to laugh..." (which only made both of us laugh even more!) I tried to contain myself, but it was difficult to maintain my composure. All of a sudden the light went on inside my head and I thought…..wowww…maybe this is it…maybe this is the hidden answer I have been searching for!

To fully understand what I just said, you need to be introduced to one of my Spirit Guides named "Hal." (How is THAT for an exotic and spiritual-sounding name?) I call him "the cosmic jokester" because he is always telling me jokes and showing me the funny side of life. Hal has helped me out of a lot of pickles, so I have learned to trust him, even though his tactics are a little off the wall and nonsensical at times. He is constantly harping on me to maintain my "laughter quota" so that I won't get stuck in "energetic goo" and get trapped there. After this laughter epiphany, I was hearing Hal in my head tell me funny things and even though it hurt like the dickens, I let myself go and laughed. I repeated these jokes to Ronnie and she laughed too…which caused me to laugh even more, and the cycle began. As we laughed, we started making fun of everything, including the voodoo-kaka or "voodoo-doodoo" as we humorously referred to it, and all the other stuff that had been plaguing me. It all seemed so surreal, and I could really truly see the humor in it all. As I did, I began to feel the pain, suffering and death energy, which had filled my body and magnetic fields, start to rip, split, and crumble. The more we laughed, the more it fell away. Pretty soon we were actually falling to the floor and choking up phlegm as the laughter was clearing out our lungs. This made us laugh even harder as we realized we were experiencing the literal meaning of "rolling on the floor laughing!" We laughed and choked for over an hour, and I barely made it to the bathroom before my bladder let loose. We both knew we were onto something big by laughing hysterically, and when we finally calmed down and Ronnie went to bed, I scanned myself and found that I was nearly 70% better! Each day my pains improved, and within a week I was completely healed! We had literally reversed the death grip of these curses/spells/hexes with intense, sustained laughter!

Remember when I said earlier that "the strongest force wins?" Well, during this intense and extreme "laugh fest," our energy infiltrated the Dark Magick and became the dominant force. It literally neutralized the opposition, as we fearlessly took over its turf and locked into the superior position. The high frequencies of our energy fields and the endorphins we created had overridden the curse and pulled me out of its trap.

One humorous thing that I discovered later is that whoever put this curse on me, did it with some kind of voodoo doll, and I guess they weren't as smart as they thought they were. These "Voodooists" were aiming for my heart but didn't realize when you look at a voodoo doll, it is like a mirror and all the organs are on the opposite side, so they hit my right side instead of my heart on the left! How funny is that!

I would like to say that it all stopped there, but that is not how it happened. I had overcome this particular death assault, but many more were to follow. The good news is, with the aid of numerous spirit/etheric supporters, and also Aulmauracite, the Magickal Stone of Truth & Justice, I now have a grand education on how to address all sorts of Dark Forces.

I had four more years of hell before I developed "The Spiral Curse Reversal Ceremony," which brought it all to an end and removed L.Q. and his family from my life. The Spiral Ceremony was revealed to me in one of my darkest hours of desperation and can be found on my website: https://www.firstwaveindigos.com/post/the-spiral-ceremony. The website www.FirstWaveIndigos.com was created to assist and support all the First Wavers or real life "X-Men & Women" on this Planet, and a large chunk of those are baby boomers.

It is my experience that when dealing with "mean magick" there is no "one-size-fits-all cure." One thing I do know is that you have to do two things: You have to fearlessly face it and stand up to it, and then you have to be persistent in finding the right energetic recipes (some of which have to be done with exact precision) in order to overcome and be victorious. I can attest that Humor and Laughter are key ingredients in managing these energies. Fear is the mind killer. When you are authentically and heartily laughing, fear cannot hold you, bind you, or possess you….. You literally slip through its fingers and set yourself free!

Yes, humor is certainly one of the major keys/elements of Kryahgenetics. The Humor Parties and the "*Unified **F**amily **O**f **S**acred **H**umor **B**eings*" …will hopefully very soon be recognized for the valuable healing mechanisms that they truly are, and be a new cutting-edge healing rage! Can you imagine if groups of people met once a week, or even once a month, for the SOUL purpose of laughing themselves silly, which would TRULY heal them from the inside out?! If people treated this with one-tenth the fervor and commitment they do other religions, it would turn this world right side out!

The following is the "Simple Code of Conduct" for the UFO-SHBs:

THE

UNIFIED FAMILY OF

SACRED HUMOR

BEINGS

THE ONLY RELIGION OF UTTER NON-SENSE .....

THAT ACTUALLY MAKES SENSE!

For A Donation of $105.55, You Can Be A Registered, Bona Fide Member of

"The Unified Family of Sacred Humor Beings."

Upon Acceptance Into This Prominent Community, You Will Receive:

An official valid membership card, to show proof to yourself and others of your admission to this sacred society *(in case of temporary amnesia).

***An authentic looking, convincing wall plaque/certificate validating your membership into this *"truly"* elite organization.**

***An original, one-of-a-kind, bumper sticker available only to members.**

As An Authorized Member Of The Sacred

Humor Beings Religion, I Honor And Uphold My Divine Right

To Live By Our Sacred Code:

"OUR SACRED CODE"

~We laugh when we're inspired to!
~We sleep when we need it!
~We honor ALL Life-Forms, and try to see their viewpoint. We do our best to understand their sense of humor!
~We keep our bodies in the best condition possible, so we can be fully sensitized for enjoying a humorous life!
~We reject any invasive technology from penetrating any sacred body part, or taking anything orally that we know to be detrimental to our body!
~We congregate regularly, whenever and wherever possible, to laugh and hold sacred humor space- - -(space being the operative word here!)
~We recognize that fighting, combat, and war are not humorous; therefore, we reserve our divine right to refuse to participate!

Your donation of $105.55 or more to this Institute will be squandered and wasted on nonsense such as:

- **Books and Publications that enlighten as well as entertain and amuse.**
- **Humor Healing Research.**
- **Extensive Research and Development of new, cutting edge Humor parties.**
- **Anonymous, tasteful "Gag Gifts" sent to selected Beings who are stiff, irritable, uptight, and starving for humor and laughter in their lives.**
- **Comic Relief Audio CDs: WARNING! Each CD is void of cussing, lewdness, and profanity. (We will not be responsible for the paradigm shifts, and reaction of people who previously believed that humor and vulgarity were synonymous, or had to accompany each other.)**
- **Spreading random acts of senseless humor throughout the Planet.**
- **Creating a website for sacred Humor Beings to network and find each other, as well as a place where they can send friends to when they need a good laugh!**
- **Teaching Sacred Humor Beings how to hold Sacred Humor Space for Themselves, the Planet, and Beyond!**

***If you are interested in a Humor Surprise Party, here is the link:**
https://www.mistychouse.com/party-place-humor-packages

***If you would like to be a member of the UFOSHB Click Here:**
https://www.mistychouse.com/unified-family-of-sacred-humor-beings

(In case you didn't know, R.W.S. on our websites stands for **R**eally **W**eird **S**h*t!)

OK. Since you're probably the type of rascal who sneaks a peek and reads ahead in a book, then I'm sure you were amused to find the treasure map on the next page. This map gives you keys and encrypted messages for some of the most ***awegnargeous*** secret ***treasures*** in this life. Now that you have actually *read* this book, it will have a totally different meaning. Study it with your sense of humor, ***and see where it takes you!***

To sum it all up, I can tell you that if you were on the outside looking in, you would see that some of the 5 hidden keys of human alchemy are really quite a cosmic joke, and if you have figured it out, I'm sure you will agree!

Good Journey to you... Laura Lee Mistycah
& of course..... HAL

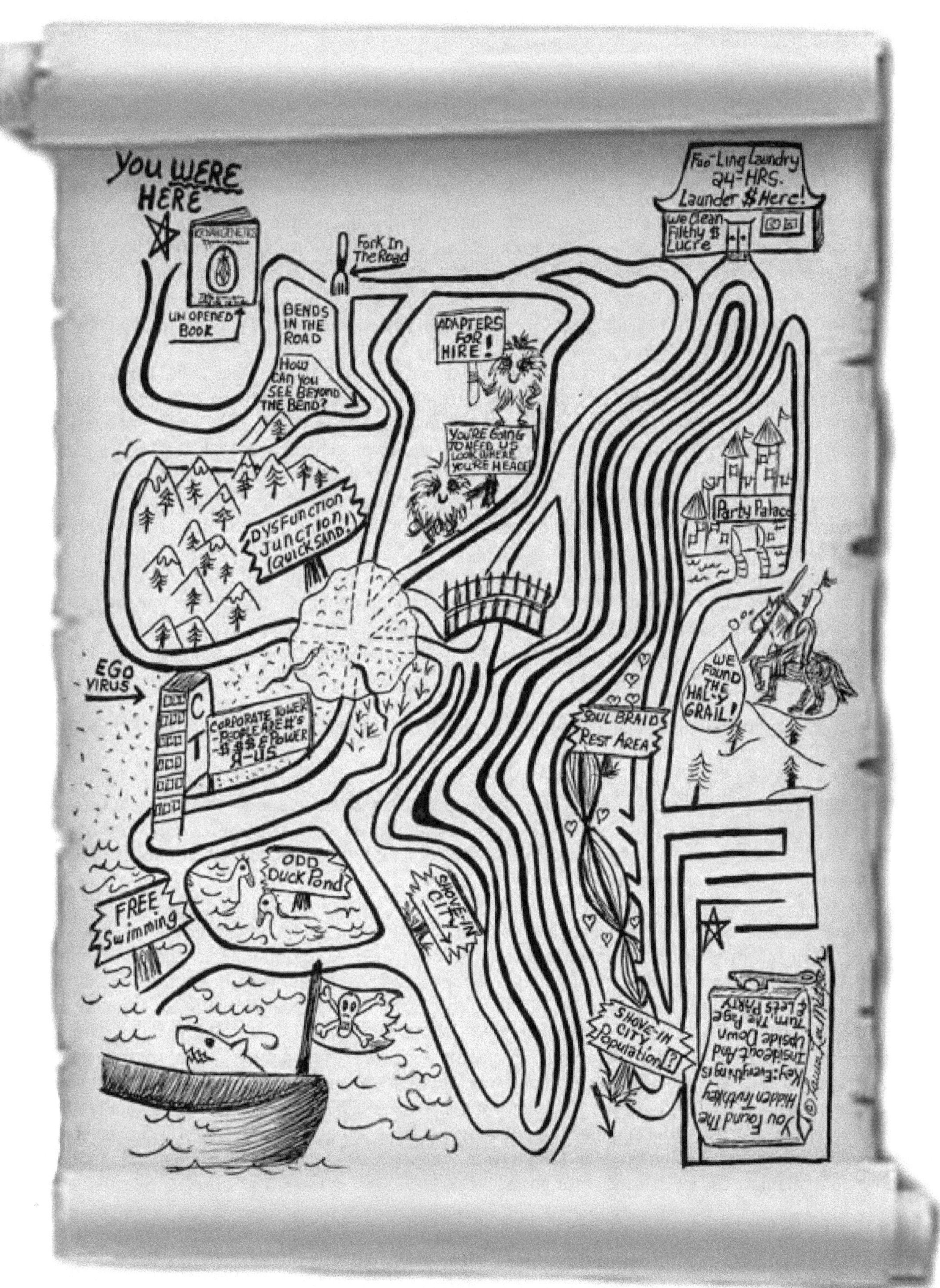
YOU WERE HERE
UN OPENED BOOK
Fork In The Road
BENDS IN THE ROAD
How can you SEE BEYOND THE BEND?
ADAPTERS FOR HIRE!
YOU'RE GOING TO NEED US LOOK WHERE YOU'RE HEADED
Foo-Ling Laundry 24-HRS. Launder $ Here!
We Clean Filthy $ Lucre
Party Palace
DYSFUNCTION JUNCTION (QUICKSAND!)
EGO VIRUS
C T
CORPORATE TOWER
WE FOUND THE HAL-Y GRAIL!
SOUL BRAID Rest Area
ODD Duck Pond
FREE Swimming
SHOVE-IN CITY
SHOVE-IN CITY Population ?
You Found The Hidden Truth Key: Everything is Inside Out And Upside Down Turn The Page & Lets PARTY

POST NOTE

Sometimes when we are attempting to evaluate what positions the people around us are playing in this game, we may find that certain Beings seem to be playing two positions at the same time! There are several reasons for this, which after studying them, will clarify for you what is actually going on.

1. When Betas are on a downslide, they can energetically do a "switch" and play the part of their mirror-image on the opposite team.
2. When any of the Beings are evolving from one position to another, they have one foot on both geometrical spirals at one time. Until all their weight has shifted and they are firmly planted in the new spiral (so to speak), they are *accessing* and *involved* in two positions at once. Sometimes they just put their foot in the door so they can peek in to see, or put a hand in to feel what's going on. This gives them more information and Intel, so they may do their job better in the position they are presently in. They may not be ready to fully commit to that next position, but they will now be better equipped to fulfill their present *mission position*, with new respect for the position they will evolve into.
3. As spirals move into the next level, their geometry begins to metamorph, and take on the shape of that new position. When you figure out what position one of your playmates is in, you may also want to ask, "Did they just arrive, are they in the middle, or are they getting ready to move to the next level?" These questions are imperative in order to get a more clear and accurate perception of where they are in their spiral evolution.

It is also very important to understand that a person may be in any spiral position and still not have had their wake-up call yet.

For instance, a Being in the #4 L.A. Alpha position, born into certain social or dogmatic structures, will most likely play out that dictated role for a while…*even though they almost always show tell-tale signs of rebelling in the future.* They will stay within the confines of that structure until enough of their encoded triggers are tripped and their internal alarm clock goes off.

This wake-up call is the process we all have to go through in order to get our attention and make us wash the sleepers out of our eyes. It gets us cognizant as to exactly what we're doing here, what our Contracts or Sacred Agreements are, and what spiral position we are in. Most of the time, this process takes a while because breaking out of an eggshell or dogma/social box, can be pretty darned painful! In many cases, it means leaving family, friends, jobs, houses, money …people, places, and things that we have loved and felt secure with all our lives! …And now we get this internal urge and drive to totally walk, (or run) away from everything we had always thought was good and true and right! We suddenly feel compelled to trade in our previously perceived Love and security for a new horizon, one we can't even see yet. This is totally uncharted territory. We feel this insatiable longing for something we don't completely understand. There is this strange fire inside us that won't be doused… and as a result, we totally turn our lives inside out and upside down, and we do it all on a "GUT FEELING" for goodness sakes!

It all seems so outrageous and insane, and you can bet your brass buttons that your well-meaning family and friends will all be there in shifts to reinforce the bondage of the past. "You don't know what you're doing!"

..."This is crazy!" ..."You're ruining your life!" ..."Look what you're giving up!" ..."You're going to the dogs (devil) and you don't even realize it!"..... "You are sure to lose your soul!" ....."Please come back to us, we know what's best for you! ...and the list goes on and on and on.....

Yes, it takes a pretty tough turtle to transcend this external and internal pressure, and follow your inner guidance and trust yourself. **You know** deep in your Heart/CoreStar, it's **not** just a phase. These feelings are just as real as anything you can touch and hold, but it seems so blasted abstract from what others are used to, and it's painful to see the ones you love, be so heart-wrenched and upset.

That is why *at this time*, only 40% of the Betas, 90% of the Alphas, and 99% of the Light-Conductors are awakened ***fully, so they can complete their contracts***. It's a hard job, and takes an incredible amount of inner strength and intestinal fortitude. It can be a long, lonely walk until you find some of your "other family members" to bond and collaborate with, and when you do, you wouldn't trade your new life, awareness, freedom, and self-expression for anything!

When you analyze the percentages of who's doing what, **know that it is all subject to change,** and these percentages are what are on the game-board at the time of the second edition in 2014. It is my observation and opinion that although the number and ratio of Beings in each position have stayed relatively the same and balanced, who knows what the future will bring? As I see it, the Light Beings seem to be getting more sovereign and dominant than their distractor counterparts. It is interesting to note that the percentages of Distracter Betas that knew who they really worked for, changed from 10% to 15%. This 5% increase of Distracters waking up happened between January 1998 to June 1998. Draw your own conclusions as to what this means. It is also interesting to note that the Alpha Distracters who have woken up and are consciously aware of who they are and who they represent, have also gone up from 30% to 35% in the same time span. *I personally think it's going to be harder for these Beings to cloak themselves with this information consciously broadcasting from them like a beacon!*

Another little morsel of information... I asked Hal about how long it takes to do a complete spiral cycle, and again the information changed dramatically since 1983 when the frequencies and consciousness grid have been transforming and accelerating so much. This information I think would be best explained in this table.

	AVERAGE (YEARS TO CYCLE) BEFORE 1983	AVERAGE (CYCLES PER YEAR) SINCE 1983 (AND SPEEDING UP)	In 2000	In 2013
EARTH BEINGS	10-18 YEARS	1 CYCLE PER YEAR	2	3
BETAS	5-15 YEARS	2 CYCLES PER YEAR	3	4
ALPHAS	5-15 YEARS	2 CYCLES PER YEAR	4	6
L.C.-L.D.	4-12 YEARS	3 CYCLES PER YEAR	6	8

Why such rapid acceleration after 1983? It may have something to do with the time-space experiments at Montauk, or it may have to do with the Harmonic Convergence in August 1987, or the World Peace Meditation in December of the same year... there are many variables here. This also gives you an idea of why you may be having so many emotional instabilities. Doing several "quantum leaps" per year is practically going warp speed! Does this help you to understand your reality a little better, and why you have been so challenged?

On the subject of constant change, know this: the rules and data can, and probably will, change overnight… and even quicker now that "time is speeding up." **What is true today may be false or obsolete by tomorrow.**

There have been many, many times in my life when my Higher Self - ***Soul Suemah*** & Esoteric Advisors have consistently directed me to continue doing what I'm doing, whether it's how to handle a client or what foods to eat. Then, out of the blue, suddenly they suggest, "Stop what you're doing and try it this way." *Many times, it was the total opposite from what they advised me to do before!*

Leaving my first husband and business partner in our holistic health clinic was one of these overnight changes… *which was quite a challenge, since divorce for me personally, hadn't even been in my vocabulary!* We both knew that separation was inevitable, but every time I would ask my Higher Self - ***Soul Suemah,*** and Advisors, the answer was consistently, "No, No, No!"

Then one day, in 1994 I woke up and my Guides were all there saying, "OK, NOW IT'S TIME, GO GET THE PAPERS AND GET READY TO FILE FOR A DIVORCE."

I went through all the, "What??? …Are you kidding me??? What about the kids?… How will they deal with this?… What's my family going to say?… What about all our clients?... What are they going to think? ...And then wrestling with myself thinking, "Sheeesh… here I am a counselor and now I'm going to have to live out the advice I had been giving for so long"…the advice that said, "When a relationship has completed its cycle/purpose and the contract between the persons is over… **know that you have the internal strength, courage, and trust in your intuition to move on!"**

All I wanted was for everyone involved to understand the bigger picture, and to understand that divorce didn't mean failure, merely that there was another learning program in the works… but it wasn't that easy, and my family, (parents, siblings, etc.)… they didn't understand….. AT ALL!

I cried really hard for about 20 minutes, and then moving on total trust, rolled up my sleeves, took a deep breath and said, "OK, where do I go from here?"

One of the first items of business after the legalities were put into the works, was to help the kids, *who are four of the most incredible little First Wave Indigos / L.A. Alphas I know,* understand that life is full of changes. I tried to impress upon them that you can allow the experience to break and ruin you, or you can say, "What can I learn from this, how does this serve me?"…(And now that they are all young adults, I believe so far, they're doing quite well in that department, as they are all very strong inside and very adaptable!)

It was shortly after I severed matrimonial ties that I met my second husband. When I first met him, I was sitting in an audience listening to one of his lectures, and everyone there was mesmerized, taking in every word he said. I looked around and was thinking to myself, "Sheeesh, you are one of the most arrogant, conceited son-of-a-guns I have ever seen...I can't believe how these people worship you! I have to say though, you're really, really funny!" Then Hal said to me, "He is your next contract, you will soon be hooked up with him!" I almost laughed out loud and had to quiet myself. I then said back to him, "I don't think so! This is NOT one of your better jokes! Get a LIFE Hal! He is NOT my type! By the way ...you don't want me to jump into another relationship right now before I've had some time to adjust here, do you?" And the answer of all things, was...

> ***"You've had time to adjust. Did you think you've had all this practice on adjustment and adaption for our collective amusement?... Now let's giddy-up and get a move on it, it's time for a new Spiral!"***

You can imagine how many times I questioned that one! Well, 4 months later we were an item and got married. What a roller coaster ride THAT relationship was! In reflection, I know it was absolutely necessary for me to get to where I am now. I met some very interesting people through him, and I also learned so much from him. One of those epiphanies was that multiple personalities, (which he exhibited several of), can actually be... ***multiple people in there****! I had some very up-front and personal dealings with what I came to term--****Shove-Ins!***

This is why it's imperative to constantly have your antennas up and your adapters on, and trust your inner guidance...because in a moment's notice, the game-board could change, and you are going to have to acquire and cultivate the ability to adapt **ON EVERY LEVEL** ***...(that is, if you really want to make it to the finish line!)****.*

If you don't, that's OK too... There's a refreshment stand on the sidelines, and you can still root for those staying in the race!

Happy Trails

& Good Journey To You.....

And if you get caught in one of the intersections of Dysfunction-Junction.....

GO BACK AND READ THE RULES.....

They may have been written JUST FOR YOU!

♥ Laura Lee & HAL ☻

BACKWARD

By Ronnie Rennae Foster, Editor – 1999 & 2014 editions

It's only fitting that we finished the 5th and final edit of the first edition of this book at 12:55 A.M., the morning of 5/5. As Laura Lee shut the computer down, I just happened to glance at the time. Amazing, isn't it? That's when (with a little help from Hal, of course) I got the idea of a "backward." It's sort of a retrospect of how deeply this book affected our lives.

The first night I started to proofread, I read for about two hours, and then went to sleep. I was suddenly awakened by *I don't know what*, and I looked at the clock. There it was, in bright red numbers, 5:55. I guess Hal just wanted to get my attention.

The next time I noticed this book seemed to have a profound effect, was right around Christmas time. My Mom was visiting and she had this horrible cold, then my son got it, and usually I would be the next in line. However, I never came down with it. My theory is, that while working with the energy of this book, it kept my vibration so high that nothing could penetrate my auric field. What a great immune system booster!

Then there were the Lexigrams. Once I started getting into them, I couldn't seem to stop. I'd be drifting off to sleep and all of a sudden a good one would come to mind, and I'd have to get up and write it down, (I knew I'd never remember it in the morning). Or, sometimes I would wake up in the morning with another Lexigram playing around in my head. As inconvenient as it sometimes was, I loved the creative process. I always say, "Creativity is food for the soul." With Lexigrams, my soul never went hungry!

It seemed to me this book took on a life of its own. It permeated my thoughts. It took me through my own evolutionary progression. It helped me to see things with a clearer perspective.....and the humor.....sometimes Laura Lee and I would laugh till we cried and our faces hurt. Hal seemed to be everywhere! Even to this day, I still see 5:55 on the clock. Thankfully however, it's usually P.M.

A word of advice, if this is your first time plowing through this book.....don't stop now. Pick it up again and re-read it. It keeps getting better and better. Each time you go through it, you will receive more and more of the encoded information. You will glean a deeper understanding of yourself, your playmates and the Universe. The pieces of the puzzle will start fitting together more easily, and you'll take off on your own evolutionary leap forward. After all, that's why we're here.....isn't it?

UPDATE: I felt it important to share with you, what Laura Lee and I went through during the last few months of this re-edit process. We were under constant psychic assault from; The PTWs, The Cryptos, The AI, and who knows who else. Laura Lee took the brunt of it, and the peripheral KAKA splattered down on me. We were sick, and tired...and sick and tired of being sick and tired. Many times during these assaults we would use the tools presented in this book, and could feel things lightening up. It also gave us the opportunity to clarify and add new information to assist you on your journey. And so, with you in our hearts, we persevered. And guess what? We got the last laugh!!!

BACKWARD PART II

With Nancy Buss, Editor – 2026 edition

In looking back at having read KRYAHGENETICS: THE SIMPLE SECRETS OF HUMAN ALCHEMY several years ago as well as having proofread this edition more recently, I can tell you that whether you purchased this book or someone else bought it for you that, either way, it is a gift: a valuable and perpetual gift that reveals much more every time you reread all or parts of it.

Upon carefully reading KRYAHGENETICS a second time during the editing process, I found that I gleaned so much more than I did during the first reading. Both times, it was as if the book tailored itself for me then revealed how much I had changed in the meantime. An analogy would be having seen a movie a long time ago then watching it again with new eyes, amazed at how different the focus and message was now. Obviously, it was not the movie that changed, but the viewer's perception. That this book remains ever-pertinent in so many ways is its dynamic gift.

The co-author, Laura Lee Mistycah, demonstrates that it's possible to weather hardships, including our Life Contracts, with grace and perseverance, as can you, too. You now know about the power of Aulmauracite & Aurauralite, the protection of the Kryahgenetics Egg, how to handle Psychic Attack, how to Unplug, and perhaps especially about the importance of being a Humor Being, (and more).

Another great specialty of this book (that sets it apart from all others except KRYAHGENETICS-II, THE SEQUEL: COVERT SECRETS & ALCHEMY, THE MANUAL ON HOW TO COVERTLY & OVERTLY REGAIN CONTROL), is the information provided by Laura Lee's Cosmic Informant, Guide, and pal, Hal. Hal is a Fifth Dimension Being from outside this Hologram, and as such, imparts advanced knowledge via the author that you cannot attain anywhere else! Hal's contributions foster and aid in our now accelerating movement towards True Balance in this Hologram. True Balance is the complete absence of evil, not a measured balance of it juxtaposed with Purity and goodness. Can you imagine how we can BE living with Love-based everything!

As Amikah would say, "Onward & Forward" and "Don't let the bastards win!"

As the final finale, we leave you with, "Some Of Hal's Favorite ***Words Of Wisdom***." I hope you have had as much fun gaining knowledge and stretching your perceptual borders with this book as we have, and guess what? .....The best is yet to come..... Now you get to read it again...and again, knowing Hal will show you something new each time!

Some of Hal's Favorite

"WORDS OF WISDOM"

Harboring Anger, Jealousy, Resentment, Hate, and Vengeance…
is like drinking poison….. *and then waiting for the other guy to die!*
(Don't harbor it, FIX IT!)

Living in the past is totally useless…***But going there to visit can be a great education or an awesome vacation.***
The trick is to remember this…
You must examine all your luggage before you come back…
So you don't bring home any cockroaches!

Halitosis (…it's better than no breath at all!)

You know you're a resident of Mastersville when:

- *You perceive driving through a thick cloud of bus fumes as having you and your car smudged in sweet grass!*
- *You pick up doggie doo off the lawn and it reminds you of dolphins!*
- *Instead of cussing & cursing at your computer, you tell it jokes!*
- *Your teenagers stop telling you whoppers about why the odometer reads 95 miles for a 5 mile trip to work... because they know you're psychic!*
- *You talk to your crystals/rocks & plants... and they answer you!*

SUGGESTED READING

GOT GHOSTS???...................... Laura Lee Mistycah & Ronnie Rennae Foster

LIVING IN AN INDIGO HOUSE..Laura Lee Mistycah

KRYAHGENETICS II: THE SEQUEL ....Laura Lee Mistycah

THE ANATOMY OF THE PORN VIBRATION ....Laura Lee Mistycah

PARALLEL UNIVERSES..Martin Gales

YOU CAN HEAL YOUR LIFE..Louise L. Hay

THE BODY ELECTRIC ....Robert O. Becker, M.D. & Gary Selden

NEW CELLS, NEW BODY, NEW LIFE!...................................... Virginia Essene, ed

THE CELESTINE PROPHECY ....James Redfield

BRINGERS OF THE DAWN ....Barbara Marciniak

THE GODS OF EDEN..William Bramley

THE 12th PLANET .... Zecharia Sitchin

THE MONTAUK PROJECT .... Preston Nichols & Peter Moon

BLOODLINE OF THE HOLY GRAIL ....Laurence Gardner

THE HOLOGRAPHIC UNIVERSE..Michael Talbot

ANGELS DON'T PLAY THIS HAARP......................Nick Begich & Jeane Manning

THE END

<u>Hal</u>-Lelujah!

(.....or is it really just the beginning?)

NOTES